The Republic of Reason & *The Poverty of Philosophy*

With best wishes

Fergus Quinlan

The Republic of Reason

&

The Poverty of Philosophy

Published by:
Pylades Publications,
Dooneen, Burrin, Co. Clare.
First published 2015

Designed and set by Pylades Publications,
Printed by Sprint-print in the Republic of Ireland.
A Catalogue record of this book is available from;
Trinity College Library, Dublin.
The British Library, London.

IBSN: 978-0-9932687-0-0

Acknowledgements
I am grateful to: Fergus Brogan for his
assistance and dedication. My wife Katherine
for her copious reading and continuous support,
and the many friends and acquaintances
for their support and advice.

For my wife
Katherine

Contents

AUTOBIOGRAPHICAL NOTE

Born in Cork, my foundation in life was wonderful parents who gave life, love and never said no. Happy breaks, and many magnificent summers amongst fine people on a farm near Mourneabbey sped my way and spread my mind. Periods of canoe construction and exploring the rivers Lee, Blackwater and the great estuary of Cork Harbour, scouting and the Reserve Defence Force contributed further skills. These pursuits lifted me from a generally lifeless first and second-level education. However, even dim schools had sparks of light who contributed to a love of science and literature. Leaving school with average grades, I studied architecture at the Cork School of Art and discovered I was born to think in four dimensions and thrived. Every morning, passing through the hallowed halls of the Crawford Art Gallery, I soaked in the ambiance of paintings and sculptures on the way aloft to the studios and wished all schooling to be of such quality.

Raised a Catholic, I served as an altar boy, became versed in Latin and inhaled the heady mix of ritual and incense. Being of an enquiring mind, I sought answers to big questions but found that none of the complex beliefs of the church could stand up to analysis. Seeking the wisdom of clerics, the more I questioned, the worse it got, and by the age of 17 the whole deck of cards had collapsed. I found myself in a belief void. From thence, I set out to find meaning and construct a moral ethos from the real world, a search that continues.

Working summers in London, I was introduced to the writings of Russell, Engles, Marx, Connolly, Marcus, Orwell, Malatesta and music from Bach and Beethoven to Chopin, Shostakovich and the Irish session. At the same time, there emerged the catalysts of the war in Vietnam, the Civil Rights movement in Northern Ireland and the anti-apartheid struggle in South Africa. These, and a belief that the 'International' could unite the human race, ensured my involvement in left-wing politics. Such events, and their consequent debates became the foundations of my intellectual being.

When children arrived, so did the first philosophical skirmish. It came as social pressure to conform and pass on my inherited beliefs. This was the ultimate chain letter, a blind strategy for religious replication. However, I could see no correlation between the church, a just society, or reason. In fact I found the opposite. In addition, as my first child was a girl, it compounded the issue, for there could be no relationship with a church that was in every facet, misogynist. There were no baptisms, no tattoos as it were, easy to put on at the time but difficult to jettison later. I resolved to encourage these three wonderful new people to develop inquiring minds that could freely decide on religious affiliations, or none.

An intervening 35 years of life's theory and practice passed before I found the time with my wife Katherine to build a 12 meter steel boat *Pylades*. Beginning May 2009 we were privileged to spend three adventurous years sailing around the world. For three hundred days and nights we kept watch, steered our course and worked the sails. On nights, some foul with gale-driven seas, but most fair, we rode down the trade winds under brilliant star-fields, staring out at the far constellation of Andromeda through two and a half million years of time. These were the perfect conditions for dreaming, reading, and writing *The Republic of Reason & The Poverty of Philosophy*, a book which might contribute to a necessary debate. Being an architect helps, as one is competent to be analytical of projects and ensure that foundations are solid. That said, the essence of the book, hopefully, must have some elegance.

Extract from the log of *Pylades* a voyage which commenced on the hundredth and fiftieth anniversary of the publication of Charles Darwin's book: *The Origin of Species.*

Crossing a barrier of fear, we commence our voyage. On the back of a vast, surging ocean, we enter a dream world of boundless horizons. In daylight we scan the sky for those elusive, white, puffy clouds that might indicate the trade winds. At night we are transfixed with the shifting rhythms that play on sea and sail and the billion luminescent swimmers who stream away from our stern in sheets of fading phosphorescence. Time is counted by the waxing and waning of the moon, the distant lantern of an occasional ship and the transit of a giant nuclear furnace, the Sun. Rising astern and falling at our bow, often in a blaze of colour and the odd green flash, the slow spinning sphere creates its measure of day and its shadow of night. Tapping halyards, creaks from the boat's structure and shifting stores are the percussionists of the passage. The taut supporting wires of the mast resonate the wind's tune, from the hum of the trade wind to a pulsating shriek in a gale; these are the rhythm and symphony of our passage, spelling harmony or discord. On black nights of low scudding rack, sheets of rain slash visibility, fear boards as the callous fingers of the gale search for flaws in ship and crew. Squall lines which show their presence by day can now bear down undetected, laying us over in spray furies as we reef.

On easy nights under brilliant star fields we stare out to the constellation of Andromeda, back through two and a half million years of time,. The perception of who we are and the fragile nature of our place on this oceanic planet evolves. We perceive ourselves alone, a small dot on a vast ocean. So too, we see our planet as but a tiny speck spinning in a vast cosmic arena on which our race is completely alone; the infinity of space offers no suggestion of help from any force or being. This planet is the only place we know on which life exists and we humans are the only species cognisant of existence. Alone we stand; there is nowhere else for us to go and it is up to us to face difficulties and enjoy our fragile lives on this beautiful planet.

We have soaked our Earth and oceans in blood so that some king, kaiser or zealot can gain fleeting rule over land or people that he might enrich himself in gold and glory. The squandering of millions of lives in fruitless wars, as one tribe or nation tries to dominate and exploit another, exposes the limits of imagination. Ghastly brutalities of slavery, genocide and inquisitions have been perpetrated to empower temporary political or religious empires. Our species now combines its potential for infinite expansion with perpetual growth, challenging its future in a finite world.

This small planet is cruelly divided by gender, race and religion, squandering loyalty to captains, kings and plots of land. We struggle to conceive how we might more equitably share our planet and its wealth. Many beliefs and divisions have been created by fear and a desire for easy answers; these tear at our reason and fragment the unity of our race. As our voyage rolls on with doubts and elation, ebbing and flowing like a Beethoven symphony, the analogies deepen. We reflect on human existence as with the wind and seas of the world. Our chemistry, born of a thermonuclear explosion, is sustained now by a residual star, the Sun, whose radiant energy lifts warm air and, as its replacement rushes in, ripples form in the giant ponds of the oceans, growing to waves then breaking seas; a storm is born. Chaos reigns, battles rage between wave trains, broken serried ranks of brigades fling themselves on ocean plains as for some great cause. The confidence and fury of the storm is undermined by equilibrium, the gale decays and millions of waves, its angry progeny, dash themselves to death on cliff, rock and beach. Most grow old and die slowly heaving on distant glassy patches of ocean.

Our illusion of some privileged position on our oceanic planet is confronted by our self-image - a tiny speck traversing a vast ocean. Likewise the illusion that our entire species has some privileged position is challenged by the image of all of us on board this tiny sphere we call Earth, spinning through a vast cosmos. It is our responsibility to make what we can of our lives, to deal compassionately with one another and to thread softly on our fragile home.

Introduction:

Reason and knowledge are moving across our world like the dawn chorus; we can listen or not. Many seek ways to structure a more rational caring society, to rebalance wealth through either revolution or reformation. The fragile future of our species on Earth depends on the outcome of a race between two forces: one of blind human replication and the squandering of finite resources; the other, a growing consensus that believes we must change our way of life to allow a worthwhile

continuation of human existence. The latter would require a change of thinking, a change of philosophy. A main premise of this book is that our greatest form of poverty is a *Poverty of Philosophy*. It brings together and connects many ideas which are more deeply pursued by the works and authors referred to in the bibliography.

I will argue for an individual and collective mind, prone to judicial thinking, willing and able to discern plausible evidence, to arrive at defendable conclusions but equally prepared to modify those conclusions in the face of altered evidence. I will argue for an intellect that does not crave solutions and leadership from above, whether political, economic or intellectual, from patriarchs, bankers, sovereigns or saviours, but can with confidence, provide its own rational direction. I will argue for an intellect free of supplication that is not cursed by unexamined traditions or irrational fears. The formation of such an agile and sceptical mind requires curiosity, a love of learning and a schooling based on argument and evidence. A mind so equipped will not be misled by false dawns.

This book can be described as a polemic, a response by the author to half a century of cognitive life. It lays out influences, agenda and the reasons for engaging with these encompassing subjects. It is forged out of a belief that sections of society have achieved substantial material improvements to their lives and that this can continue and be more inclusive. It also springs from anger at rampant injustice and the structure of a society which tolerates poverty and concentrates wealth, for evidence now shows that the construction of an egalitarian society is key to the mitigation of many of the problems that beset society. I believe that the possession of a rational and ethical belief system, by a large enough section of the population, would have negated the economic and moral collapse we have witnessed. Such could also achieve higher levels of individual contentment, responsibility and civil society.

Our knowledge of the cosmos, the myriad fields of science and computers expand exponentially. Science by its application to food production, hygiene and medicine has enabled the world population to double within my short life-time from 3.5 to 7 billion. About 220,000 new humans are added to our planet every day, which is equivalent to a city of over 1.5 million people every week. Add the growing wealth expectations, and take cognisance of all the farmed animals, crops and resources that entails. Also 187,000 private cars and light commercial vehicles are produced every day. Some climatologists argue that we have exceeded the population that may be sustainable, that and distribution disparities allow millions of people to go hungry and over 20,000 children die every day. Humankind expands its occupation of the Earth and the extinction of fellow species accelerates in the last vestiges of habitable wilderness. These difficulties can only be dealt with on the basis of a unified humanity. Thus the importance of science as the mutual language and perhaps the intensity of the common problem may force a collective response.

Our reproductive success and economic growth has been made possible by the expansion of scientific thinking, but a philosophy of science did not expand in parallel. For the majority, philosophy and morality survive in moribund dogmas. Such a division between theory and practice negates our ability to solve problems. The alienation of our morality and philosophy from how we actually live is the basis for our most pervading form of poverty, an intellectual poverty, a poverty of philosophy. Philosophy and morality have been hijacked by a theology that is religion and reduced to a weekly one-way lecture and rituals that bear little relevance to real life. Such belief systems based on revelation are but marginally believed and are embarrassing to an extent that they carry a conversational taboo. Hence we have the contradiction of a science-based society with ethical thinking dating from the fall of the Roman Empire. This is *The Poverty of Philosophy* resulting in the catastrophic collapse of morality that we have witnessed. While surrounded by science, the vast majority of people do not look at the world through rational or scientific eyes. Their image of the world is restricted to a few generations back and with limited projections into the future. Planning is generally executed over government lifetimes and is open for renegotiation at every election. Introduction to formal education is embedded in dogma and thus by nature contra scientific. Mindful also of the threat of a regression into anti-science and medieval theology driven by religious fundamentalism, intellects are required to reverse this trend and defend the gains of the enlightenment.

It is a phenomenon that society which has the skills to meticulously plan complex projects from cities, national rail and highway routes and even war, gives little thought to planning a stable, egalitarian social order or even to conceive of such. Can a perfect society be achieved? Perhaps not, but that is not the point. Society would have a collective mission statement, a unifying goal to strive for. Scientific evidence now shows that as society becomes more equal all of its social problems diminish. However, those that direct the economy, benefit from the way it is and change would be contrary to their interests. Universities should be the brain at the core of the society which supports them. They should be communicating endless ideas on how to restructure economics, politics and philosophy in a more socially beneficial way. Instead, they are but the final stage in the production of well-educated, compliant operatives and consumers. Teachers, toilers and professionals whose ethics have been compartmentalised, individualised and separated from the interests of the planet and the overall human community, have minds conditioned to accept and serve authority. They are mentally gated against seeing when their interests are in conflict with the common good. This conditioning begins in the first day of school.

Our route to sustainability and a future of exciting potential is through rational education. This can be achieved when dogma and rote are replaced by reason, a love of learning and our children are equipped with sceptical but not cynical minds. We face many problems and dilemmas, but possess the resources and the intellectual potential for improvement. While the forums of discussion within the media are limited, new forms are emerging; the internet may be the basis for the international debate that is required. Another positive aspect is that our human morality grows as religion declines. Even the religious who claim that faith and morality are set in stone, drift away from gods of wrath and revenge and now talk in more enlightened, humanist terms. Despite the huge disparities of wealth and tottering economic systems, it is for the moment a good time for some; we are at peace and have choice to engage with our future, one which has many challenging dilemmas, also has many exciting possibilities.

This is not a book of answers. Indeed one is fully cognisant of the fact that there is no end book of answers; all knowledge held by mankind is in perpetual expansion and under persistent critical review. It is an argument that the adoption of a science-based thought process is more important than any single scientific discovery. Also that science is indistinct from the rest of human rationality. A nation, populated by people abiding to the uppermost standards of evidence and reason, will thrive. Our society could become a centre of innovation, advanced social relations, sustainable production in a transparent civil society. Having been thoroughly chastised for our failures and stupidities in the fields of politics, economics and beliefs in the recent past, we are now ideally placed to learn lessons and build this rational society.

A guiding philosophy grounded on reason, linked to the common good and our everyday world, is required to achieve this. It is against the nature of society to stand still. Society and our species shall either progress or regress. We have the potential and intellectual capacity to decide to choose the former, revitalise the spirit of the enlightenment and deal with the tasks in hand. We are particularly well placed for such an endeavour and much in the book shall be devoted to clarifying why this is so and the practical possibilities. Our lives are short and wisely we must use them for there is so much to witness and do in the world, so much to understand, so many adventures to undertake, physical and mental. To deal with the questions confronting our species we need to overcome fear and cast off submissive thinking in favour of a free intellect. This would be akin to walking out of a smoke-filled room and breathing clean, fresh, Atlantic air. We cannot solve our problems with the same type of thinking that created them. **We will never change the way we live if we do not change the way we think.**

Chapter 1   Who are We?

Before running a marathon one prepares the body with exercises. Likewise, prior to constructing a *Republic of Reason* or chasing down philosophical poverty, we need a scientific workout to scratch the surface of a few diverse branches of science and our existence - like a mental scatter gun, to stretch the imagination and remind ourselves of what a fantastic world we live in. Alone we look from our position on our spinning Earth and attempt to comprehend all we see. During our long evolutionary years that vision only extended over the hunting plains, to the Moon and Sun that illuminated them and down to our parasites of nits; we had no reason to deal with any scales beyond that range. Our concepts of time were limited to a few generations back and forward. We mused much, but understood little. This was to change, slowly at first, then at an ever-increasing pace.

With some comprehension from whence we came and why we are here, it dawns on us that in our absence, planet Earth would get on fine. So if we do manage to cause enough self-destruction to bring our species to extinction, given time, the planet will recover and billions of diverse species will reappear. However, there is no guarantee that any cognisant being like ourselves would remerge. At this juncture, we can with some pride, argue that despite our destructive abilities, the cosmos would be a poorer place without us. For while some of our fellow species might run faster, outfly and outswim us, we possess the ultimate advantage of having the ability to comprehend our existence. After billions of years, evolution has brought us to be the first and so far the only species that understands the visionless, unplanned path that formed us. For some uncertain reason one feels it would be a terrible shame if there were no intellectual understanding at all of life, the planet, the cosmos and its wonders.

Our intellectual ability has allowed the seven billion of us to dominate every facet of life on the planet for good or for ill. Unfortunately we are divided by class, nationality, religion, race, and gender. While gender is essential for our reproduction and differing race colour are just evolutionary traits, our relationship with production and the resulting divisions of class can exaggerate these differences and create toxic mix. There are grounds for optimism. We are possessed of intellects which have tried to build economic systems to serve our collective interests, a process, which is on-going. Evidence shows that overall human empathy is steadily increasing, contributing to this optimism. While we are hostages to the present economic phase of capitalism, nevertheless under its dominion there have been steady improvements to living standards. However, to achieve tangible liberation from divisions and secure its future, human society must now venture into the unknown, take risks, and abandon safe servitude. The causes, results and attributes which we require, be they revolutionary or evolutionary, are the motivation of this book.

A released detainee might be nervous and prone to mistakes when stepping out into an uncertain world, like a sailor leaving harbour for the open sea, but, confidence increases as the distance travelled from the jail or harbour increases. Likewise, moving away from familiar comfort as offered by existing economics or religion is a nerve-racking proposition, as a sailor needs a good boat, science must be that good vessel for humankind, with its self-correcting mechanisms it is the only philosophy with the ability to offer intellectual security and unify humanity.

The science of evolution looking back millions of years to our common African ancestry is a unifying proposition. An understanding of the fundamentals of evolution is essential in understanding how to upgrade our existence. Many times in history a class unity was forced under the banner of nationalism, squabbling over boundaries, insisting on the righteousness of beliefs or marching into other countries when the growth imperative of capitalism turned to imperialism. A new common enemy of population growth, diminishing resources and climate change are now gathering. This may force a world-wide unity and be a catalyst for change, there are unfortunately darker options, which shall be considered later.

The Earth is 4,600,000,000 years old, emerging from particles spawned by a cosmic explosion 6,000,000,000 years previously. Our solar system is roughly halfway through its natural life cycle; the sun, a nuclear power plant, has in the normal course of events about five billion years of existence remaining. The end will come when the nuclear fuel of the Sun runs down, as it does the sun will expand into a red giant, consuming all its orbiting planets including our own. With the time scale involved it is hardly something that should worry us, but it is a sobering and a humbling fact to contemplate. The Earth, since its formation, has been in a constant state of change. As it cooled and the crust and oceans formed, the huge land masses broke up and drifted around the globe on their tectonic plates before they formed the continents and islands we now recognise. They are still moving at speeds matching that of fingernail growth. Cold and warm ages came and went. Life emerged from the chemical soup; the first life cells appearing 3,900 to 2,500 million years ago, evolving into millions of species, most of which are now extinct. The various hypotheses on the emergence of life are still under intensive scientific scrutiny. Every day the answer draws closer and the excitement mounts. Who will be first across the line with the unshakable evidence? The emergence of oxygen creating plant life changed the Earth's atmosphere. Then the jump was made to mobile, replicating organisms which continued to evolve into all the diverse species we have on Earth. About six million years ago humankind split from its ape lineages, of the many species of humanoid that emerged at that stage only one, Homo sapiens, thrived and one of that species now reads these words.

Having grasped the time span of our arrival, we can conceive our Irish ancestors, of a mere 5,000 years ago, as being relatively recent. When they built their impressive time clock-temple of the seasons in Knowth they were paying homage to their life source, the Sun. The builders were embarking on the first steps in the measurement and exploration of time and space. They did not perhaps comprehend themselves to be sailing through the cosmos on a spherical spinning planet at 67,000 miles an hour, locked by gravity into a 96,000,000 mile radial orbit around a gigantic nuclear furnace. They certainly did not realise that the entire planetary system was moving at 483,000 mph to complete an orbit around and within our whirling galaxy every 225 million years and that the entire galaxy was escaping from its formative explosion, booting it into deep space at 1.3 million miles an hour. It is difficult to extricate one's mind from such a vision of turmoil when attempting to sit still in contemplation. We, the descendants of these Neolithic builders of passage graves are still on board this great spaceship, planet Earth, and with millions of our fellow species, trapped in this spinning zoo, we continue to be dependent on a nuclear fireball for our energy and existence.

Some of this radiated energy has become trapped on Earth, laid down over millions of years in the form of carbon deposits, such as coal, oil and gas which we are now harvesting at great speed. Energy absorbed by photosynthesis through every leaf of tree and blade of grass converts into sugars and starches, some of which we consume directly or we feed to our domestic animals. These animals in turn, we ingest as meat, a more concentrated form of energy. As every form of life - plant, microbe, fish or animal - is passing through life with a cargo of genes inherited from its parents, so too are all of us mortal humans, each of us part of an evolutionary line linking to a common ancestry with every species on the planet, a procession stretching back four billion years to the origins of life. Such perceptions of unity are crucial in dealing with divisions within society and the dilemmas facing it. However, difficulties arise when the philosophical core belief of the majority is, that life on this Earth is but a minor player in preparation for a far more important, next life.

Each of us is loaded with instinctive and inherited ideas. It should be the essence of our being to enrich this inheritance with vigorous rational reasoning, abandoning those that are negative to our existence and adapting new ideas which might best serve us and to carry these ideas to our children, not as a known, fixed dogma but as the best discussion we can present. We then hope that the next generation shall expand and enrich them further. Any claim which we might make as to not having lived in vain will be judged by that legacy.

The development of industrial production has in a fraction of our history, brought rapid and accelerating change. We have made huge gains in food production, transport, health and general welfare but the advances came with inequality, wars and environmental loss. We have turned the night into day in our cities, towns, and villages. Due to light pollution the majority of the Earth's inhabitants have never seen the Milky Way, the edges to our very own galaxy. We have concreted over vast tracts of land with our habitats and roads. Our agricultural needs have exhausted and eroded large sections of land and we are expanding into the last remaining areas of natural forest. Many civilisations have collapsed because of the unsustainable exploitation of their adjacent resources, only recently we have begun to recognise this and attempts are underway by some to attempt a reversal, but so far the voices are small. Powerful commercial, biological and philosophical forces continue to drive the expansionist path we are on. The wild areas of our planet and their remaining inhabitants are corralled into ever shrinking areas.

The expansion of European power, beginning in the late 15th century, arrived with achievements in higher productivity, agricultural surpluses and wealth concentrations. This, together with knowledge of ship building and sailing, allowed expeditions to all parts of the globe such as the Americas, Africa and Australia. Vastly superior armaments resulted in large-scale genocide and enslavement of indigenous peoples, a colonisation of their land and enrichment for the active colonial powers. Later, new and more efficient forms of exploitation were found through slave transportation, then later still in wage slavery and capitalism, bringing massive increases in production and range and scale of commodities. It brought huge profits to the beneficiaries of capital and productive property. It brought alienation, insecurity and struggle to the dispossessed. The objective ethos of individual and corporate greed brought about gains and disparities, it acts only in its own interest, with no collective responsibility to society or the environment.

Our pollutants and litter have reached the furthest corners of the world. The Inuit indigenous people of the Arctic, are almost solely fish eaters. The toxins, which irresponsible production has dumped in the seas, are carried by a chain of prey and predator fish imparting high concentration of poisons into the bodies of these remote peoples. Plastic which was mass produced in the last 60 years, now litters the land and sea, concentrations build in the centre of the high pressure zones in all oceans. Vast numbers of oceanic birds ingest pieces of plastic that resemble food, their bodies decompose and the plastic floats off to kill again. The insular mind of corporate greed, dispossessed of social or planetary responsibility, is ugly, as are its legacies. The windward side of remote Pacific atolls such as Cocos Keeling, a thousand miles downwind of the tip-head that emanates from the corruption of Indonesia, is piled with plastic litter and flip-flops.

Human activity is altering the chemical composition of our oceans and atmosphere with massive carbon transfers. Only recently is society beginning to tally the results of digging up carbon deposits of oil, gas and coal, squandering them in sometimes futile production and dumping the carbon back into the atmosphere. We are beginning, perhaps, to understand the implications of our ignorance. The caveat of 'perhaps' is added as many still deny any problem exists or if it does, that they have any responsibility and wish the policies of growth to proceed. A salutary lesson from evolution, is that an estimated 98% of all species that have ever existed on Earth are extinct, it has been noted that species that undergo rapid expansion often take a path to extinction. Despite the ominous dark rumblings of doomsayers and climatologists who range from the pessimistic to the slightly optimistic, we still live in a wonderful world. There is still time to stop the insanity and turn humankind down a more rational path, so let us take stock of our wondrous planet and plan for its protection.

The scales by which we now conceive our world and cosmos expand in all directions, ranging between the atom and Andromeda, time and distance measured in billions of light years to picoseconds. Telescopes, microscopes and their electronic derivatives are our tools with which to stare at the wonders and mysteries of the universe and slowly wrest their secrets. Having the tools is not enough, we also require the will to pursue scientific truth, for while that may exist in abundance amongst those possessed of curiosity and within the scientific community, it is a major task to ensure that appetite is extended universally. The simplest first step in this pursuit is on a cold clear winter's night to be in a place far from light pollution and stare deep into space and perceive the wheeling stars. Feel the bitter wind on your face and inhale the heady scents of a land in perpetual decay and rebirth. When spiritual imagination blends with the cold reality of light from the cosmos, that is when our curiosity is most heightened and craves for distant information. Thus we swing from raw inquiry to an ordered scientific approach.

What distance does light traverse in one year? Nothing moves faster. It can ramble along at over 186,000 miles in one second, our sun is 96 million miles away and therefore it is eight minutes in light time. So when we observe the rising Sun, we are looking at something that happened eight minutes previously. Distance and time brings its own illusion! We can no longer believe our own eyes! Light travels 5,878,625,373,183 miles in one year, when multiplied by the $_c$ 2,500,000 light years to the faintly discernible galaxy of Andromeda, the comprehension of such remoteness is a perfect setting for contemplation. Life exists here because we are not too close to the Sun nor too far, everything is just right for life to develop. The most distant planet within our solar system is Pluto, five hours away in light time. The galaxy of which our solar system is but a tiny part, has about 300 billion other stars and is 100,000 light years across, our nearest neighbouring star is 4.2 light years away. These vast dimensions and numbers take one's breath away, but they can also provide an elusive sense of humility and common purpose. Imagine being on board a probe travelling into deep space and looking back at Earth, a tiny point of light fading amongst the myriad of stars and reflecting planets. From that perspective our countless wars and divisions would seem utterly pointless, the self-destruction of our beautiful planet a folly beyond comprehension. It would bring a deep feeling of warmth and empathy for humanity to comprehend ourselves in this manner and accentuate our obligation to share the bountiful treasures of the Earth more equitably and to treasure that little speck, our home, locked into its busy little orbit.

It is interesting to engage in some time speculation. If persons unknown were at this second to look at Earth from the other side of the galaxy they would be looking at us as we were 77,000 years ago, observing traces of the emerging hunter-gatherer society, 57,000 years before the invention of the bow and arrow. A great pity they can't send back a video! In deep space the next galaxy beyond ours is the Andromeda spiral, it's the furthest object we can see with the naked eye, that faint blur left that galaxy 2,500,000 years ago and you see it as it was then. In fact it is possible that it no longer exists. The very act of looking makes the observer a part of this vast time machine. Beyond Andromeda there are 100 billion other galaxies each with their millions of suns and orbiting planets. The most distant galaxy that we know is 10 billion light years out and moving swiftly away. All galaxies are on the move and the distance between them is increasing. Interspersed are the black holes, the remains of very large burned-out stars, packed with matter so infinitely dense and gravitational forces so large that nothing can escape, not even light.

Closer to home, the trials and tribulations of our international space station, mankind's ultimate garden shed speeding around our planet at 27,743 kph, can be followed on www.spaceflight.nasa.gov- a laboratory based in a zero gravity orbit. It is perhaps even more valuable as a symbol of civilisation's potential for international cooperation, with, at the time of writing, American, Russian, European and other scientists sharing the facility. The excitement of these endeavours should be part and parcel of school education and curiosity-building. Forty years ago the Voyager space vehicles blasted off from Earth, they are now at the edge of our solar system and are transmitting information that, to the monitoring scientists, is both unsettling and thrilling. The adventure began in the late 1970s when the probes took advantage of a rare alignment of outer planets for an unprecedented Grand Tour. The arrangement of the planets provided a slingshot type boost to the probes. Voyager 1 visited Jupiter and Saturn, while Voyager 2 flew past Jupiter, Saturn, Uranus and Neptune. A partial list of discoveries includes volcanoes on Jupiter's moon, evidence for an ocean beneath the icy surface of Europa, hints of methane rain on Saturn's moon Titan, the crazily-tipped, magnetic poles of Uranus and Neptune, and icy geysers on Neptune's moon, Triton. In cosmic space itself they discovered planetary winds that blow faster with increasing distance from the Sun. Each discovery altering the way we think of our cosmos and other worlds.

They are now traveling out through the heliosheath, a strange place of magnetic froth never before encountered, echoing with low-frequency radio bursts which only inhabit the outer reaches of the solar system. They have lost sight of Earth. Our Sun is a mere pinprick of light. Voyager 1 cruising at 38,000 mph has now left our planetary system and entered deep interstellar space. Both Voyagers are energized by the radioactive decay of a plutonium 238 heat source which should keep their critical systems running to, at least the year 2025. After that they will become humanities silent ambassadors into deep space. Each probe is equipped with a gold-coated, copper record, containing photographs of Earth, 90 minutes of the world's greatest music, an audio essay entitled Sounds of Earth, burbling mud pots, barking dogs, a roaring Saturn 5 lift off, greetings in 55 human languages and one whale language; the brain waves of a young woman in love and salutations from the Secretary General of the United Nations. A billion years from now, when everything on Earth has changed utterly and our species unimaginably altered or perhaps extinct, the Voyager record may speak for us. However, the chance of a cognisant being finding the Golden Record is fantastically remote. The probes won't come within a few light years of another star for some 40,000 years. What are the odds of making contact under such circumstances? On the other hand, what were the odds of us evolving to have the intelligence and the ability to develop spaceflight that sends such probes into the cosmos? http://www.nasa.gov/voyager

An interesting aside to communications with 'other civilizations' was drawn by J. Diamond (see bibliography) when he pointed out that if a superior civilization was to find us with the help of these probes, there is every likelihood that they would behave as we did and still do when we find a civilization or species slightly less armed and more vulnerable than ourselves, we generally engage immediately in genocide, grab their land and brainwash the survivors into believing that it was all for their good. Western Europeans with a military advantage did precisely that with just about every indigenous race encountered. Perhaps we should be cautious sending such directions!

The big bang theory emerges from a series of observations that the galaxies are moving out and away from each other at a very fast pace with their historical track lines converging back to a point in time. It was speculated that at the specific time of origin, all the matter of the universe was compacted into an infinitely small size of infinite density. Such a situation would only be sustainable for an infinitely short length of time. The resulting explosion would have put the entire nuclear arsenal of mankind exploding simultaneously as but the flare of a damp match in the Sun's heart. Particle research can now see that such a cataclysmic big bang might have been essential to forge many of the elements required to form matter. Furthermore, it now appears that all the stars and planets belong to the same family, sharing a common cosmic and chemical ancestry. At the CERN project using the large Hadron Collider, science is attempting to replicate those milliseconds of particle and element formation. There are many things that humankind cannot yet explain or predict, such as that most fascinating question: will the cosmos stop expanding and revert to an accelerating convergence to engender another big bang, thus explaining the cosmos as a reciprocating cycle or will it cool to a lifeless entropy? In which case; what existed before the big bang? Physicists have developed more speculative theories of the cosmos through mathematical modelling, multi-universe, time curves and a block universe in which there is no past, present or future. A recent book, *The Singular Universe and the Reality of Time*, by Unger and Smolin has dragged these theories back to the realm of more rational arguments. One way or another such questions should keep us busy for a while. Our quest for knowledge of space, matter and our beginnings are as exciting now as was the quest to discover the unknown world by sea and land in the 17th century.

Humanity is constantly improving and building new tools of curiosity. The Hubble telescope, mankind's orbiting intergalactic eye, constantly peers into deep space. It can lock on to a distant target with an accuracy that could shine a steady laser light on a coin 200 miles away. Thousands of scientific papers have been published as a result of its findings. It continues to provide ongoing information and amazing photographs. Like most space research, its achievements are shared and can be followed on www.hubblesite.org. A new, larger infrared telescope, the James Webb, is due to go into space about 2018. The plan is to place it in a stable position 930,000 miles out from Earth. Its main function is to push the boundaries of cosmic knowledge back to its beginnings. We should always temper our knowledge of space and indeed many other things with a sense of humility. As Albert Einstein muttered; "only two things are infinite, the universe and human stupidity - and I'm not sure about the former".

As previously referred to, on the Swiss-German border is the gigantic CERN project which has hundreds of Europe's top scientists beavering away into the mysteries of particle physics. The benefit of these very costly explorations to mankind are enormous. Such research contributes to not just general scientific knowledge but also to a spiritual unity, the search itself becomes a common purpose for humankind. These explorations are an extension of the first questions asked by our ancestors. Perhaps there is in the psych of our species an innate loneliness, an insatiable desire to find causes and perhaps a fellow creature out there in the cosmos. We can satiate or need for answers by creating gods or proceed to find them through chemistry or particle physics. Will our curiosity ever be satiated? Hardly, for with every discovery, more wonders beckon to be explored. Our inquisitiveness is enhanced rather than diminished with every step forward. Consider the dullness and shame that would be our lot if we were to abandon such pursuits and seek but the accumulation of sticky buns and the illusions of revelation. Unfortunately there are forces that would wish for just that.

Knowledge, like tools can be a two-edged sword, the splitting of the atom could have been regarded as a disaster - as it was for the residents of two cities in Japan and their descendants - but in an unexpected way it brought an extended era of peace to the world with the realisation that any fracas between the superpowers would result in mutual assured destruction. The world has grown complacent about the presence of nuclear weaponry but new radical cultures, which place little value on this life, pose a new threat. A motivation which has brought suicidal killing by bomb, gun or the hijacking of commercial aircraft could be extended to nuclear weaponry. On the other side, nuclear-powered production of electricity is mainly carbon-free and despite recent disasters that have befallen nuclear power plants, it might well provide the only carbon free possibility of mankind maintaining its energy consumption rate.

We are fast gaining knowledge of the wonder-world of cells, parasites and viruses, their plans and specifications as well as our own gene codes. Such an understanding of our own bodies and minds allows enhancement of our benign instincts and negation of malevolent ones. As part of that understanding, it is essential that we have a grasp of the evolutionary path that brought us to where we are. Our DNA structures are, to the discomfort of some, remarkably close to the primates of our common ancestry. We share 98.4% of our DNA with the chimpanzee, the 1.6% difference covers such things as hair, posture, brain and penis size. Although, we are not descended from any living species of ape, they are our closest cousins and we, both the ape and humankind, have descended from a common ancestor that lived about seven million years ago. Going back further in time, we shared an ancestry with all living organisms, plants and bacteria as they emerged 4.6 billion years ago.

What an amazing machine we have become - a heart, pumping blood through 50 miles of plumbing, a body with 100 million cells and thousands of complex production lines, running in precise sequences, driven by chemical cogwheels spinning 100 revolutions per second inside a maze of 200 acres of folded membranes. The cogwheels are housed inside mitochondria, bacteria-like bodies with a separate ancestral heritage. About a billion years ago they formed a symbiotic relationship with our distant precursors. Each of our bodies is a vast city of cells and each cell, a thriving town of bacteria, we have far more bacterial than human cells. Then, there is the vast complexity of mind and nerve structures, vision, hearing and voice. This vast amount of information is passed by the gene from one generation to the next using a single male sperm and female egg. Each new human is constructed in a fantastic female biological chemical plant in nine months, we are worth the caring.

The gene is the molecular unit of heredity of a living organism, possessing an almost immortal nature as it passes through the generations. All life forms, including ourselves, are but the temporary survival machines of such genes, they build a temporary home, our mortal bodies, a mechanism for their survival and replication. The best description of gene DNA is as information-like bar codes, sets of detailed plans and specifications instructing new cells how to build hearts, noses, skin and the millions of parts with which we are assembled. The remarkable distinguishing shift that has taken place specifically in humans, is the development of a cognisant brain, a machine that allows us to leapfrog the blind purposelessness of our genes and make conscious decisions regarding our lives and future. The forces that determine those decisions are the recurring themes of this book.

Staring into the universe of space, time, matter and energy, back through evolution to the beginnings of life one observes nothing but blind pitiless indifference. The emergence of life itself and its evolution into the fantastic array of forms, including ourselves, was dependent on many critical elements coming together - the right chemistry, temperatures, the size of our planet and its gravitational intensity. These conditions, ions of time and chance were central to our evolution. Our species, humanity, achieving cognisance introduced the concepts of cause and effect, good, evil, gods and the afterlife. To some this can be a frightening prospect, to others it gives a sense of heady freedom. The question arises, where shall I be after my death? Most likely, the same place you were for billions of years before your birth. Life-everlasting might appear to be desirable, but after the first billion years, stuck with all your siblings and in-laws praising the gods and singing hymns, it could well be the ultimate 'Midas Touch'. Midas a greedy man wishes that everything he touches turns to gold. His wish is granted and the only person in the world he loves rushes into the room - his beautiful daughter. He hugs her and she turns to solid gold. Be careful what you wish for.

Life itself is a process, rather than an entity, it is a formation of molecules capable of signalling and also of absorbing energy to combat the natural slide to entropy and can replicate. Pre-Darwinian thinking proposed that all design and species came from a higher mind. Science now understands all life as bubbling up from mindless, motiveless mechanisms, struggling for survival and replication, an observable reality that is the mainspring for evolution by natural selection. An understanding essential for the resolution of conflict and our survival as a species.

A portion of the understanding we have gained of our origins comes from fossils. Generally this is a slow and methodical endeavour, like most work in science, but with the occasional stunning breakthrough. Fossil evidence of our very distant ancestors is rare. It can only happen if the ancestor dies in very specific circumstances, such as in a flood and buried quickly in mud of a preserving nature. It must lie in a stable geology undisturbed for millions of years. The remains then require to be slowly uncovered by the elements and discovered by chance just at the point of exposure. Such happened at Hadar in Ethiopia when 'Lucy' was discovered, so called because the Beatles *Lucy in the Sky* was playing in the fossil hunter's camp that night. The find was dated 3.2 million years old and identified as a possible, rather than a definite human ancestor, for we now know there were many hominid species in Africa at the that time. All branches, bar one, have become extinct and the construction of the definitive jigsaw puzzle goes on.

The perception of evolution, has in the past two hundred years, turned human philosophy on its head. One cannot overstate how essential it is that we understand its implications, it shapes our attributes and contributes to an understanding of what we as a species, might and might not be able to achieve. An understanding of just who 'we' are is essential to the sustainability or otherwise of our species.

CHAPTER 2   Roads to Knowledge

Information comes from revelation, testimony, intuition and scientific research. It is communicated by parents, schools, universities and media. We also determine and store knowledge by direct experience, experiment or even accident. The key point is how the recipient can determine what is true, or when that truth is relative. 'Smoking is bad for you', is true if you are a smoker, but not true if you are a non-smoking cigarette salesman. Rational thinking 'is good', from the viewpoint of the majority if used to build an egalitarian society. It can also be used by an elite to maximise exploitation and misery, for the majority, it is then not good. The source and the beneficiary of any proposition concerning something being, good or bad, usually ensures that it is relative. While academic deconstructions of good and bad are useful for discussion purposes, the relevant point is the result of such positions. From an ethical human perspective the question is what contributes to the greatest well-being in society. What contributes most to the unity of humanity?

Arguments concerning the primacy of religion or rationalism will, on occasion, be reduced by a claim that both sides are similar. The rationalist, believing science books to be true and the religious, believing the holy books to be true, hence the claim that both are the same as it's just a question of different beliefs. Not so, the key difference is that the conclusions in any scientific proposition are under constant review and test, they can also be checked from many different perspectives. The believer of the Bible, Koran or Torah, has no such options as those books are fixed; they stand as they were written, with all their good words, their vengeful gods and contradictions. There are no revisions, no proofs; they plainly indicate they were written by the hand and through the eyes of a man of the period, containing the images one would expect of an advanced tribal and slave society, highly misogynist and with a limited understanding of the world.

While it has always been impossible to prove the non-existence of gods through science, a reading of the Bible itself would go a long way. The book of god's word, the Old Testament, is limited to a confined geographical area of the planet, and to sad tribal squabbles with appalling retribution being meted out to non-chosen tribes. A particularly horrible story is the mass drowning organised by god in the great flood [Genesis 6.7.8]. God becomes disenchanted with his creation and asks 600-year-old Noah to build a boat, to house his family and a pair of every species on Earth together with all food for 311 days. The size of the ship at 450x75x45 feet, was some amazing shipbuilding project for its day, but Noah's troubles had only just begun. For now he had to gather a pair of every animal, bird and scurrying creature from the Earth. One can have sympathetic visions of poor Noah herding cats, kangaroos and leading polar bears. Then gathering every insect species from the Amazon where in just one tree there can be over a thousand, perhaps up to 30 million little boxes. Then all the birds and animals from all parts then unknown. To determine, catalogue and collect a pair of each would take hundreds of specialists hundreds of years, for Noah with just seven days it was a very tall order.

Then came the promised 40 days of rain and the image of a loving god looking down from above as tens of thousands of men, women and children who, on realising the inevitable and screaming in terror, fight for the diminishing high ground before slowly choking to death in the rising waters. Likewise he watched the millions of animals crowding on the same dwindling sections of ground, before they too, swimming in panic through the chaos of communal panic were finally overcome with exhaustion and succumbed to a horrible death by drowning. He witnessed the huge flocks of birds rise into the air as the last of the tree tops became inundated and one by one in exhaustion they fall from the sky and they too in their millions perish in the ever rising water. Such scenes of deliberate, planned, mass slaughter are comparable only to what we have seen in Auschwitz and the many death camps of fascism, but at least we are not asked to base our morality or swear on Mein Kampf.

The truth or otherwise of the Bible is not the issue here but the repellent moral character of the god that is portrayed. Horrific Bible stories, could well be ignored except for the fact that the Bible is the foundation stone of Christianity and thus the foundation of almost our entire educational, moral and philosophical system. Such a document, packed with illegal statements and incitements to hatred should have no part in the judicial system or any other swearing ceremonies within a republic. Churches which are based on the Bible, but now moving towards a more humanist outlook, could be asked to rewrite it in keeping with their evolving human empathy. This would quicken the transformation of the churches in a more progressive and caring direction. The morality of people who still follow these dysfunctional texts, including the priests, bishops and popes, would now, in most circumstances, be of a much higher level than that of god portrayed, as would any person selected at random on the street.

Like the first learnings of a child, the first assimilated writings of humanity have taken on an exaggerated significance, but a story is still a story, regardless of how often it is repeated or how old it is. However when they became imbedded as inherited beliefs they assumed such credence that if rational evidence contradicts these books, it is more often the evidence and reason that is rejected, not the book. For example, despite all the evidence, evolution is rejected by millions of faith believers because it contradicts creation as indicated in the Bible. If science looks like it might win the day, amazing contortions of logic are proposed such as 'intelligent design' in an attempt to hold the literal, biblical line. In the United States there are now intelligent design museums, in addition it would appear that the most devout believers or the wilfully ignorant run the schools. When Darwin, at 26 years of age, landed on the islands of the Galapagos in 1831 he made copious observations that led to the publication of the ground-breaking book 'On the Origin of Species by Means of Natural Selection'. On the Galapagos today there are magnificent museums dedicated to Darwin and evolution. Tens of thousands of visitors visit the museums and observe the wildlife to enhance their understanding of evolution. However, as of 2010 the children of the islands were still being taught creationism.

As aircraft design progressed from the early Wright Brothers model to our present jet liners, designers redesigned each new model from scratch; they had no compulsion to carry forward any unnecessary traits or faults from one generation of aircraft to the next. At present this does not apply to animals nor indeed us humans, genetic engineering might alter this situation in the future. Because our species passed through so many stages in its evolutionary path, the human body has inherent defects which would not have been the case if our bodies had been the product of an 'intelligent designer'. Our eyes are wired backwards and the urinary tract passes through the prostate gland, which develops into a pressing urination problem in later life for men. Each and every one of these can be explained when looked at through the eyes of evolution, for at some stage in our long path from a primitive bacteria to our present form they made perfect sense.

When a body becomes infected by a virus, the virus then stimulates the body to spread it by inducing sneezing and coughing to project itself out of the contaminated body to others. Likewise belief adopts the character of a replicating virus and compulsively wants everyone on the planet to share that belief. All faiths except Judaism, send out missionaries across the globe to spread their particular 'correct' viewpoint. This expansion contributes to holy war as each religious viewpoint- with god on their side -feels justified to kill those who do not. Hardly a day goes by without an example of inter-religious slaughter of some kind.

However, religion is not the primary problem; it is but the mask and mentor of the ruling elite and serves the interests of the prevailing power structure. If the bulk of society can be persuaded by early inculcation to kneel in supplication and be conditioned to beg favours and consolation from a higher power, it makes it easier for any elite or rulers to maintain their position, particularly if the ruled can be persuaded that the political power of the rulers come from a god. These are the principles which make it vital that church and state contrive to control education and from the very beginning block the curiosity and free thinking of the young. The structures by which religion serves these interests are not so much the consequence of some vast conspiracy, although that exists as well, but more an objective result of economic and political power. The conspiratorial or repressive side only becomes apparent when one attempts to unravel the collusion or challenge the power structure.

Authority comes in a multitude of forms - parents, schooling and the state - all of which express knowledge in the various ways outlined. A child has to trust that the information given by parents and guardians is for their protection, even if it is not all true. To enable us to function normally in our day to day existence, we have to determine what sources we can believe or not. One cannot be expected to scientifically investigate and ratify every piece of information. It is not possible to have the ability or time to acquire evidence on all subjects. We cannot, in our short lives, but scratch the surface of knowledge. The essence is to distinguish just who to believe and the key to that is a symbiosis of trust and science. One accepts the vast majority of information because it first passes a common sense test and because it comes from an authority such as verified scientific sources. For example, one may never have been to, or seen Tasmania, but it is illustrated in an atlas and because we have seen and been to many places which are in the same atlas and they are correct, we accept that Tasmania exists and is, as shown. The detective in us might corroborate that conclusion by asking; would anyone benefit from providing false information on the existence or location of Tasmania? Hence in an atlas, and maps in general, we can determine that we have a trusted source. There are thousands of such examples which we can safely accept at face value. Three protectors combine to ensure truth - a sense of reasoning which might alert us to a breakdown of logic, the status of the information source and questioning who might be the beneficiary if false information were to be accepted.

To testify, is a form of personal revelation, often spoken at a time of great loss or stress in the life of the speaker, thus making it difficult to confront or question. It will usually take the form of personal evidence, 'when my mother was dying I saw angels lift her hands to heaven', 'I saw the statue shed tears and move' etc. The rationalist is generally far too polite to question the 'testifier' or shed a negative light on their story in such situations. So one usually stares, and says nought; it is a form of social and cultural blackmail. Similarly it is a favourite form of collective brainwashing indulged in by revivalist-type preachers. Individuals are called forth to testify to more and more outlandish claims, with the hysterical congregation chanting, clapping, speaking in tongues and driving themselves into a fury of blind belief. It was not long ago that thousands gathered at various venues in Ireland and swore they saw plaster statues moving. This is a collective testimony that spreads from a devout individual to a group and becomes viral as a collective hysteria. As an aside to testifying, moving statues and visions, I tell a personal story. Some time ago, waking in the night I observed in the faint light a hunched figure breaking into our house. Gripped with fear I sprang from the bed and rushed to get a torch, phone and a weapon of sorts. However, as my viewpoint changed, the figure melted away and became a bush gently moving in the breeze. Feeling a bit of an idiot I slipped back into bed where, as I looked again my imaginary burglar reappeared. But now with my instinctive, pattern-forming imagination overcome by evidence, I returned to sleep. We are geared to accepting patterns or belief systems that appear to provide answers and explain things regardless of evidence. As the system is emotional, it is a powerful form of story-telling, it exploits empathy, disarming confrontation or question.

Divination is the obtainment of knowledge by implying mystic interpretations on material patterns. This was particularly prevalent in primitive peoples but is now, gaining momentum again. These forms of revelation can be as diverse as hieromancy, which is reading the scattered entrails of dead animals, capnomancy which is reading smoke from sacrificial altars, palmistry, crystal dowsing, astrology, divination by planets and stars, to name but a few. A significant indicator of the level of superstition still about is the widespread belief in astrology. The belief that the position of the planets at one's birth can determine or influence the character and career of a person and that the daily positions of planets and stars determine the daily events of every human on Earth. Every down-beat newspaper and magazine has some 'Mystic Meg' churning out such nonsense. In most bookshops, the books on astrology take more shelf space than those on astronomy. All this, one might argue, is harmless fun and that may well be the case. But it is still another prop to lazy, irrational thinking and to children immersed in such a culture by their parents and peers it must surely have a negative effect on their development as rational thinkers. However, it can also be seen as a cry in the wilderness of an alienated human spirit looking to some outside force for direction and purpose. For the practitioners of astrology it is a search for a living; for clients it is a search for a pattern, meaning and indicators of the future in every observed material manifestation. One should ascribe no blame, condemnation or ridicule to participants, only perhaps a compassionate introduction to more rational ways of looking at the world.

Intuition has many faces, it can emerge from mystic spiritualism. It can be a form of revelation from the inner self without any scrutiny from reasoning. At best it is an informed opinion or guess which may prove to be correct but would always require more measured verification. While any of the foregoing in philosophical terms would be unsound for arriving at conclusions, elements of intuition combined with imagination can be used in the formulation of hypotheses, prior to being subjected to the rigours of science. Rational thinking is constantly confronted by propositions which cannot be disproved, such as the existence of a god or life after death, Bertrand Russell's teapot proposition is usually invoked in such situations. His contention was that a teapot is orbiting Earth out of sight of our most powerful telescopes, it therefore cannot be proved or disproved but common-sense might intervene. Thousands of similar inane propositions are contained in the holy books and are accepted as fact. Like most propositions in religion they can neither be proved nor disproved by science, but intuition or common sense, tuned by engagement with rational thinking would cause them to be rejected. The first and best course of action is to invite the proposer of any such notions to instigate the proofs. Once the answer of faith arises, then all is lost, for the proposition is then placed outside the reach of query, question or science.

The word science comes from Latin, 'scire' to know. Over the last few hundred years this has become the universal method of attaining knowledge and has been responsible for a massive growth in our technology and our material well-being but, like every tool, it can be just as easily used for war and destruction. It might be assumed that science and scientific thinking are common sense, but this is not necessarily so. In fact many scientific facts would be counter intuitive, take one of the earliest observations; in the mid latitudes the Sun rises every morning in the east, passes overhead and sets in the west, at night the stars wheel about in the same direction. It would be a fairly obvious and a common sense conclusion that the Earth is the centre of the universe and the Sun and stars circle the Earth. The fact that the Earth was assumed to be flat would have only reinforced this outlook long before the concept of gravity was understood. It took Nicolaus Copernicus 20 years of observations and calculations before he published in 1543 *On the Revolution of Heavenly Spheres* in which he proved it was the Earth that rotated on its axis and circled the Sun, explaining the days and seasons. As this was in contradiction to the Biblical description of the cosmos it provoked a consummate subjugation of science by the religious elite and the book remained on the Vatican's index of forbidden books for more than 250 years. The term 'the revolutionaries' was used to describe Copernicus and his supporters and has been used as a term describing radicals since.

Science is the best way of attaining knowledge of our universe or a specific phenomenon within it. All the most advanced assumptions about the origins, composition or nature of whatever piece of knowledge one is trying to get a conclusion on are assembled and structured into a hypothesis. Predictions are then made about how the proposition might behave under certain conditions and it is tested with experiments and trials, if these continue to support the hypothesis, confidence grows that the initial assumption was correct. The opposite being that, of course, if they do not, then all assumptions were incorrect and the whole approach must be rethought. The most secure results are achieved when the scientist or inventor initially assumes that the hypothesis is incorrect until proved and tested. Some science fields are initially purely mathematical or theoretical, such as deep searches in particle physics, clarifying the nature of quarks, the Higgs Boson mass-giving particle and beyond to more nebulous ground of supersymmetry. To bring some of these propositions to the test table required the construction of the gigantic CERN project, an underground laboratory housing the Large Hadron Collider on the Swiss French border. Other endeavours such as motor cars, aircraft and machinery for the manufacture of various goods are more amenable to a process of fabricating and refabricating models. This is a chain route to achieving perfection, but even in that situation, science occasionally needs to revert to the beginning of the process looking for alternative approaches.

In the search for the origins of life on Earth we have the layered evidence of fossils, the observations and conclusions of a biologist such as Darwin and evidence from geology, zoology and DNA. In these incidences, layers of evidential proof consistent with ongoing observation converge to form an unshakable conclusion. Each scientific idea is reliant on hard evidence and the more it is buttressed from different directions and by different people the more conventional it becomes, but is at all times open to challenge. If one has an opposing theory on any subject, all one has to do is gather sufficient, well-tested evidence and present it to the science community. There it will be either accepted or rejected, not on grounds of faith, gender, nationality, class or age but on the evidence presented. That open approach would include, the Lough Ness monster, big foot, gods, UFOs or spiritual healing, they will all be believed on the strength of sound scientific evidence.

Scientists can be wrong, sometimes, very wrong. The history of science is replete with serious errors of judgment, bad research, faked results, and simple mistakes. The word 'Thalidomide' drives fear into every medical research laboratory. Legalised in Germany in 1956 this drug led to the death of over 2,000 children and the maiming of over 10,000 worldwide - a gross example of where market pressure overrode research. It was detected as harmful and banned in the GDR from the very beginning, but was not taken off the Western commercial market until 1961. However, to put such an error in context, the success of pharmaceutical research outweighs its failings by thousands to one. The beauty of science is that in the longer term it corrects itself by its own structure, for each piece of scientific knowledge is used as a building block to formulate new hypotheses and as they are assessed and proven it ensures that the underlying knowledge is constantly under review. By this means, science provides us with increasingly clearer views of how the world works. The acid test of any scientific truth is that each tested claim is written up as a paper in the various scientific journals for critical assessment by the peers in that particular science field. Like a lone violinist playing before a professional orchestra, there is no hiding place; the truth will out.

Consider all the wonder and enhancements that science has brought to our lives - medicine, abundant food, electric power, clean water, the various means of transport, TV, radio and the internet. It has also brought us poison gas, machine-guns, bombs and bombers, missiles, the nuclear bomb and the potential for a self-inflicted Armageddon. While science has potential to unify people and serve their interests, it can also subjugate and terrorise. It has allowed powerful imperial nations to kill millions of our species. Science is like the blind, motiveless mechanisms of evolution and nature itself - beautiful but indifferent. It requires an empathic philosophical mind to ensure it serves the interests of humanity and its fragile existence. Only a collective economic and political approach integrating with science and scientists will suffice and presently there is no great evidence of that. For science too is affected by a Poverty of Philosophy.

Once knowledge is attained, the family, school, social interaction and media are the day to day vehicles by which it is transferred. The family is seldom an independent source of information, usually the parents have inherited ideas from their parents with a collection of unexamined traditions and belief systems which they see as their duty to pass on to their children. Traditions are passed on in the field of economics; the farmer's children would see the land as the primary source of survival, the judge's child might see law as the option and have the resources to study it. The labourer's children would be thus formed by their experience. This is not to say that mutations and exceptions intervene and distort these patterns. The main legacy that one inherits is thus the whole social economic structure and one's place within it together with unexamined economic, political and belief loyalties. These allegiances are often loudly proclaimed; 'this family has always voted Fine Gael (or whatever) and always will'. It is akin to standing aloft and proclaiming, 'I do not think, I am a sheep, I have been trained to follow and I do'. The same applies to religious beliefs. The highest form of invective is reserved for one who changed religion. In some countries one might be labelled an apostate which could mean death. In Ireland at one stage changing to

Protestantism, one would be labelled a souper and ostracised. Generally it would be more acceptable to stop practicing ones religion than to change it.

The formative years of a child are its most vital, thus whatever information is absorbed at that stage is the most likely to be embedded and in later years passed on, therefore similar unexamined traditions repeat at every cycle of replication and nurturing. The main information streams acting on the family are these beliefs and traditions and it is the degree to which this cycle can be broken and subject to critical analysis or otherwise that matter. It is said that science advances by a succession of burials, as one can seldom change an idea that has been embedded at an early age, but as one generation dies off the next generation is more likely to bear the new idea. The media is the other force streaming into the family environment and influencing its information flow. The bulk of media - television, radio and print - is owned and controlled by private interests and ensures they represent the systems and interests that maintain that ownership and control. The state media is likewise controlled by the ethos of its advertisers and forays into controversy generally serves the interests of the kleptocracy. On a shallow analysis it might appear that the media question and comment with fairness and impartiality; this is not the case. The fundamental questions are never asked; the fundamental nature of society is never questioned; the fundamental poverty of philosophy is never discussed. When the recent catastrophic collapse of morality and the economy is discussed, it is in a constant search for individual scapegoats such as corrupt bankers and investors. Exposés of dysfunctional, exploiting priests and nuns have been done well, but again it is against individuals not the core philosophy, the cracked foundations from which these poor disordered clergy emerged. But the church is not a main advertiser and is now seen as a declining power and so can be more open to pillory. It might be even perceived as a menace as its old, fragile 'gods of wrath' systems crumble and it swings towards a more threatening humanism. Likewise from a standpoint of a traditional old-money capitalism, the new neoliberal deregulated corporate agenda might also be seen as fair game, but not its foundations or roots.

The birthplaces, the foundations of these crumbling edifices of corruption and sexual and exploitative scandal remain untouched. Take a thick Sunday newspaper and measure the column inches of shallow political reporting, tame columnists and commentators, sport, interviews with players and managers, fashion, travel, celebrity gossip, recipes, stock market and financial reports, religion, reviews of motor cars and a thousand other consumer goodies, vast amounts of advertising for goods and services which we do not need, but are persuaded we do. When all those column inches have been measured, now search out and measure the space given to the radical voice calling for the extension of democracy over economics, calling for a society rather than an economy, a voice asking if wealth is being transferred up to an elite or down to the majority, just how many column inches might be measured? This is reflected in all the other media strands. The agenda of neoliberal corporate ideology is well served to the detriment of any radical or fundamental change in the nature of the economy or society. Of course the odd - very odd - radical opinion appears, but seldom if ever in any substantial, developed fashion.

To test the openness of a society to ideas, one might apply a measurement or percentage question to any stream of thinking being propagated. Approximately 90 hours per year are dedicated to the teaching of a specific religion to each child in faith schools. Why not, for example, put forward an alternative viewpoint such as humanism for just one hour a year, just 1% of the time. Such contrary interventions would mitigate the charge of brain-washing and encourage a far more enlightened debate on the whole issue of belief, faith and morals. The fact that such a simple idea might seem preposterous to school patrons and parent bodies tells its own story. Many parents are now moving to a more rational appraisal of the world and do not raise their children as Catholic, Protestant, Muslim, Jew, or atheist, but as a child. A child given due access to the various religious and non-religious views that exist and on reaching the age of reason, allowing the child decide its own affiliations. Where there is reason, there is reason to hope.

In the media, similar percentages of time or print are required to contradict the agenda of the Washington Consensus within corporate Ireland. There is a thirst for alternative ideas or methods for running a society; not alone are these not actually tried, alternatives are seldom if ever even discussed, a situation that is not accidental. A charge that the media are infected with a 'Poverty of Philosophy' might not be applicable, as their philosophy is formed by revenue and the interests of the elite, it is, to maintain the agenda of corporate economics, sport, politics, charity, and church, all justified with a thin veneer of debate. Media is a constant background to our daily lives in all its forms, while some strive to be independent, they cannot be anything but partisan, representing the interests of those who advertise in and own them. But many people listen to a new voice and have fled to the internet and social media.

The construction of a sensible economic system serving society will not commence until a sufficient percentage of citizens have the information and the critical ability to determine what serves their collective interests. That will require higher levels of social morality. It will require collective action with the confidence to reject the traditions of supplication. The alternative is servility for the majority in a post-democratic, dystopian corporate world.

"We can never trust what the old books tell.
We cannot trust our senses, only reason
gives us knowledge" Rene Descartes; 1596.

CHAPTER 3   Cold Science, Warm Humans.

Comprehending ourselves as a machine for the survival and replication of a gene that came about by purposless chance, can be a shock to the ego. Some revel in its stark simplicity; others might feel gloomy at its coldness. Regardless of feelings, one cannot fiddle the equations to alter the answers. However, upon reflection, other horizons emerge. When it becomes clear that we are responsible for the quality of our own intellectual and physical existence, then our life's potential becomes more apparent. Involvement with lovers, children, society, nature and creativity becomes our essence. Our legacy can be worthwhile goals achieved, the enrichment of our own lives and those of our fellow humans. Thus out of the impersonal mechanisms of reality we can grow, for it is our responsibility and to our benefit that we cultivate human warmth, empathy and love.

Survival is our essential instinct; the fear of pain is our first line of defence. As we grow; a fire burn, fall, dog bite, nettle sting, or shouting adult are our first experiences of pain and fear. The fear of suffering and pain protects us from worse. Life becomes a balance between fear and survival. We are willing to take risks for our own survival and for that of our children. Risk-taking, enduring pain, or making sacrifices for others diminishes with their genetic distance. When thousands die by earthquake in a far-off country, we express sorrow and maybe contribute to a collection, but little else. We have to self-limit our empathy to enable a reasonably happy existence, nevertheless evidence would suggest that as a species our empathy is growing.

The universe with its evolutionary path of supreme indifference, contrasts with what we now perceive in human society. We alone can rebel against the tyranny of the selfish replicators and that is what makes us unique - our ability to challenge governance by gene. The simple example is our knowledge of contraception; from the first moment we engaged in sex for pleasure, without the chance of reproduction, the power of the gene was defied. Defied the gene might be, but fully controlled, it is not. We shall explore this in another chapter. Over time the organisms from which we evolved reached awareness and the first traces of co-operation emerged. As we became a cognisant and social species, a delicate web of cooperation and trust arose for the purely utilitarian principle of survival.

This co-operative spirit did not emerge because of ideas from individuals or groups. It came to the fore because the groups who by chance practiced co-operation survived better and thus came to dominate. Hunting was a precarious occupation. It made sense for any successful hunter to share a catch as the next time he or she might not be so lucky. In gathering fruits, nuts, berries and fungi it made sense for an individual or group to specialise in one skill and share the bounty with other gatherers. Elements of cooperation and care would have extended by evolutionary pressure into every facet of the groups' relationships, increasing its survival rate. We humans share the basic values of caring passionately for a partner with whom we are replicating and for children of that union. The biological imperative of the gene for intimate love and the care of its offspring has been the cornerstone for inter-human compassion.

We feel empathy, sadness and anger if anyone of our family suffers or is under threat, sentiments that weaken as the person under threat is further away from our immediate gene responsibility. Such indicators would suggest that our empathy extends only to where the survival of our gene might be at risk. But how does that explain people risking their lives in the protection or rescue of complete strangers? Perhaps our most productive approach would be to accept the gene foundation of empathy as intrinsic but that its influence has grown to protect our expanding social organisations. We have to discover how best to harness these forces for the benefit of our species.

An organised cooperative fighting formation is far more effective in defence or attack against predators or hostile groups. In almost any category for survival, co-operation would score over individualism. However, within every group, individuals vary, some being less or more selfish than others. Statistically it is inevitable that individuals would seek to benefit by exploiting the goodwill of the majority. Strictures were required to curtail such aberrations which gave birth to taboos and laws to establish parameters of behaviour. These responsibilities combined with the spiritual beliefs of the group forming its culture and morality.

With the development of agriculture and production of food surplus came a slave society. As the foundation of human empathy was based on compact groups it did nothing to prevent such a social development. In fact the way empathy was formed and operated could be construed as a trap made for the development of class society. The food surplus required specialist military protection, the leaders morphed into being the owners of that surplus and in turn, owners of the people that produced it. Now sharing empathy and common cause they formed a descendant 'royal family' supported by their military. These upper echelons of power, the pharaoh, caesar, or king would be of a tight ruling family, casting themselves as 'royal' blood, and if not claiming to be god then at least claiming to rule by the authority of one. Likewise each underlying level of the hierarchy has its own loyalties which would not have extended down to the vast toiling hordes at the bottom.

Each level looked down on their subordinate social strata, radiating control, suppression and terror. The subservient social strata in turn looked up with supplication and fear. The only unifying care of the upper echelon was to ensure that the serving masses were kept alive, controlled and in fear. Fear, was and still is the common characteristic of any exploitative society. Within society at any level comes an identity and common bond that engenders its own internal empathy and perhaps poses a threat to another level. For no society remains static and power flows and shifts at all levels, when suppression intensifies, the common bond of a lower social order can strengthen and if fear should lose its grip, dynasties can and do, crack and crumble.

Rulers objectively do everything to ensure that the unity or interests of their vast supporting army of slaves, serfs or in more recent times, a mass of working people are never expressed. They endeavour to divide their subjects into competing fragments. The divisions are reinforced with titles, dress codes, accommodation, accents and indeed any scrap of status or slight privilege that would separate one group from another. Likewise when an imperial power invades another country it benefits to have the occupied country riven by religious or tribal antagonisms and it will do everything to maintain that situation. Apart from ensuring the weakness of the occupied country such internal conflicts give the interloper the excuse for keeping peace and order. Witness recent divisions intensified by the interventions of global corporate capital across North Africa through its proxy, the United States army. The legacies of such power struggles dominate history. However, accounts of history, like their authors, are servile to the same forces as any media. Conflicts born of exploitation and class are eviscerated of their content and rendered as a benign list of battles, divorced from the taciturn reality of exploitive greed.

Throughout history where conflict occurs between nations, captured gentlemen of the 'officer class' were generally treated well and released at the end of hostilities. This speaks volumes for ruling class solidarity which can override most national, linguistic, religious or economic rivalry. In contrast, slaves, tenants or workers of failed rebellions were dealt with savagely and in particular their leaders. Tales of retribution against lower classes that might deign to assert democracy over economics or challenge the power of the ruling class, litter the pages of history. After the Jamaican slave revolt of 1831 it was reported that up to 500 were executed 36 were flogged, many dying from a sentence of 500 lashes.

The crushing of the Paris Commune in 1871 by the French army resulted in the killing of 30,000 Communards, more were imprisoned and 7,000 deported. Such a threat from the lower orders was something to be particularly feared and was capable of engendering remarkable international solidarity amongst the nobility of Europe. Despite having recently been at war, the Prussian and French generals collaborated to ensure the Commune's defeat. Following eight days fighting the last defenders of the Commune were overwhelmed and the massacre of defenceless men, women, and children, which had been raging all through that week, reached its zenith. The breech-loaders could no longer kill fast enough; the vanquished workers were shot down in hundreds by mitrailleuse fire. About 38,000 were then arrested, many were arbitrarily selected from the prisoners' ranks and shot while the remainder were incarcerated for trial by courts-martial. It was an exercise in terror to ensure that the workers would know their place and never try to control their own lives again. But within the communards had grown a legendary comradeship and a vision which was to have lasting echoes.

In war, where millions of soldiers of mixed religion, race and even nationality are facing a deadly foe, a unique common bond is formed. Extraordinary tales of selfless sharing and care emerge from the trenches. It extends even to the officers, despite the fact that part of their mission is to execute anyone fleeing the battle lines. The point being made is that the pain and fear, responsible for individual survival, came to be harnessed for the protection of a specific communal structure or state. The empathy bond formed can be made to extend through each separate layer of a fractured society. The objective of rulers is to drive that bond to unify all segments of society and mask its fractures. The driver of such calls is usually for protection against a common enemy, real or perceived.

Empathy and love can, and sometimes does, cross social divisions. The fact that such widespread common bonding can be achieved by any means, even if somewhat idealist or for defence, gives hope for higher levels of social relationships.

The ruling elite have always favoured the idea that morality or rules of conduct have sprung from an external force, a set of divine instructions, with heavenly rewards for compliance or hellish punishments for infringement. Such a diversion of morals into a celestial direction away from the real suffering of people, serves their interests. Sam Harris, in his book *The Moral Landscape* proposed an interesting way of measuring morality. First establish a base level, a scenario of the most horrible level of despair and pain for most people; once it is envisaged that nothing could be worse, then every small step that improves the situation is a step in the right direction. These steps can be determined as an improvement and are measureable. Once we can envisage well-being as a measureable entity it can enter the realm of science and reason. As morality is how we envisage rules of conduct to achieve well-being for others then the ethos of society shifts away from the gods onto the shoulders and responsibility of us individuals and humankind.

At present we have myriads of graphs and indices covering stocks and shares, currencies, economic growth, centres of education, political personalities and football teams. If we can scientifically measure the gains and losses within various economic and social spheres, then similarly we can measure the gains and losses in human well-being. If the results of such were transparently available, surely the imperative to improve the lot of humankind would combine with democracy and seamlessly move to a higher order. Such idealistic thinking is worth pursuing but must take into account that the social strata which controls research and media will do everything to maintain inertia on such proposals. However, the structure of the whole social elite is not a monolith; cracks and crevices will always be found to enable the skilled to climb the barriers.

Understanding the foundation of morality is fundamental to its improvement. The idealist proposition is that humanity was manufactured by an external force, a god, who laid down morals as a set of instructions for the people he created to get a good place in the next life. Life is seen as an exam and if one had good marks at the time of death heaven was the award. However, if one happened to be in the bad books at the time of death then they were granted an eternity of suffering. In contrast the materialist sees morals evolving as part of human survival instincts and the ordered interaction between individuals and society. Good or beneficial service to society could see praise or material reward, gross abuse of others could bring punishment, but all in this life. Another theoretical concept of morality stresses that there are no standards by which we can measure 'good and evil,' they generally emanate from abstract academia. Sam Harris has a charming reference to such in his book *The Moral Landscape*, where he says, "I don't think one has fully enjoyed the life of the mind until one has seen a celebrated scholar defend the 'contextual' legitimacy of the burqa, of female genital mutilation, a mere thirty seconds after announcing that moral relativism does nothing to diminish a person's commitment to making the world a better place".

Most people have a natural aspiration to 'better' themselves and the world, which is laudable; the importance is in adopting an approach which actually makes a difference. If the foundations on which this desire is based are flawed then all the paths along the road of improvement will lead into a cul-de-sac. The good intentions of religious people, who wish to better the world are subverted by the divisive character of their religion. For the objective interest of a religion is like any business, to serve the interests of its own structures at the expense of other persuasions or broader humanity. In the universities, even if reason could be rescued from the confused waters of academia, there would remain the overlying problem as to the function of the universities. For there is no indication to suppose academia serves any interest but its own perpetuation and that of the existing social system. The conclusion is we need to exclusively connect morality, ethics and the pursuit of happiness to some definite objective such as, the well-being of humanity and its environs.

There are thousands of charities in Ireland, many operating for a single cause. Each has its management structures, advertising budgets and collection strategies. The grounds for establishing a charity as defined for tax exempt status are: relief of poverty, advancement of education, advancement of religion and other such purposes the state deems as beneficial to the community. The main strategy for the operation of a charity is to circulate images of misery and deprivation to harness and exploit the natural altruism of the giver. The majority of donors who are moral and compassionate get a little poorer but derive some mental satisfaction from sharing. The widespread acceptance of religious nihilism on social progress - 'the poor will always be with us' - explains in part why the ritual of charity is so prevalent and acceptable. There are further negative aspects. Donations can and are used to enhance personal status and reinforce divisions by competitive giving. Corporate donations augment a company's prestige and become an accountancy balance between image gain and tax savings.

People who are obliged to benefit from charity are already in a situation of some humiliation, feelings that are reinforced and dignity further degraded by being its recipients. Anger against the dysfunctional nature of society is subverted and the guilt and shame that should rest with the structure of society are transferred to the most vulnerable via charity, a privatised, social-welfare painkiller. Exorbitant remuneration for top management in some charities plus bonuses have shown their true colours; they are a business and a big and lucrative business at that. The state provides tax-exempt status and in some cases contributes a majority of funding. Charities have become the Band-Aid of dysfunctional governance and for that they are adequately rewarded, they develop an imperative of their own and become self-perpetuating. As Christopher Hitchens said, referring to the charity of Mother Teresa 'She was not a friend of the poor. She was a friend of poverty. She said that suffering was a gift from God and spent her life opposing a known cure for poverty, which is the empowerment of women and their emancipation from a livestock version of compulsory reproduction'.

Unfortunately there is a need for many of these charities. This is an indictment of society and not of the organisations, which in the majority of cases are staffed by people with high levels of compassion for other less fortunate human beings. It is interesting that in the legislative rules applying to charities it states, that they must not engage in political lobbying, which is as good as saying that whatever problem the charity is engaged with, we do not wish it solved, just patch away! The positive harnessing of all the goodwill, warmth and empathy in this sector would be that they work for the elimination of the need for such in society. The very concept and the dreadful reality that any of our fellow humans require charity should be, and will be, an abhorrence in a future correctly functioning society.

While human empathy emerges from an evolutionary trait, it can be impeded by another one, for as empathy grew within the group or tribe, hostility and traditions of raiding were maintained against adjacent tribes. This was understandable as groups expanded and battled for their survival over hunting and gathering lands. In the few areas of the globe where hunter-gathering groups still exist, this practice continues. A dichotomy develops; while plundering the hunting lands or grain stocks of an adjacent tribe can immediately benefit the attacking tribe's survival, it is a gamble, as the causalities sustained could negate any benefits. But the development of an enemy produces a secondary benefit, that of a greater internal unity. This secondary benefit has often been exploited to force a coherence across social divisions; calls are constant to serve your country in both peace and war. With the emergence of centralised societies, such as kingdoms, came semi-stable borders determined by military strength. This strength was determined by the states level of surplus which was in turn determined by the efficiency of exploitation of those whom it controlled. The more surplus produced by the least numbers, the more were free to serve in the military. Thus the most efficient could push back the borders of neighbouring kingdoms sometimes eliminating or incorporating them. A balance of forces ensured the stabilisation of borders and emergence of peace agreements. While this gave hope that inter-state war could be controlled in the right political circumstances it did not necessarily translate into a reduction of internal exploitation and oppression. Nevertheless within the various strata of a state, human empathy spreads as conditions permit. But a surfeit of human empathy could lead to a dangerous bonding or class solidarity across the lower orders, a situation that might force an insecure leadership to opt for an external rather than an internal rebellion. A slight change in circumstances and an opportunity is seized by one side or another to take advantage, to grab power, expand, to let loose the dogs of war.

Once the dogs of war are howling, all the worst instincts of group advantage come to the fore and humanity's gains are lost. To wage war efficiently we deliberately desensitise our humanity and dehumanise the enemy. They and their society must be branded as Redskins, Nips, Commies, Gooks, Paddies, Brits, infidel, terrorists or whatever. We must remove their identity as fellow humans. It makes the killing, gassing and torture easier. The fact that we require to do that, to distance ourselves, says something intrinsically positive about us. However, we have begun to discover how difficult it is to achieve intellectual segregation while killing our fellows. Recent wars have given us a greater understanding of the psychological damage done to the killer. In the Vietnam War three million of its population were killed, many still die from unexploded ordinance and the residues of chemical warfare. As many as 58,000 troops of the United States army were killed. Thousands of the individual soldiers on returning to the USA were found to have been traumatised by their experiences, their natural empathy shattered. The attempts to isolate human empathy, the mental subversion required to machinegun fellow humans and witness their butchery without repercussions failed; the mind of the killer was also butchered. This is not the format to analyse the specifics of this inner mental destruction, but we can conclude that humans at war or otherwise, whether winning or losing, derive deep unhappiness from observed killing.

Killing becomes easier for humans and with less psychological cost as it becomes remote with technology. High-level bombing allows ordnance to be dropped at some remote waypoint and the crew returns home without any witness of the mangled, screaming agony on the ground. It allowed the dropping of an atomic device over Hiroshima in August 1945 where tens of thousands disappeared in a blinding flash and tens of thousands more died slowly of radiation. The placers of countless landmines in a million fields do not bear witness to the legless, shattered children. The drone with its cameras and rockets can now be directed to kill by an operative thousands of miles away. The awesome power of technology is harnessed to impose the will of corporate interests worldwide and targets can be rendered by a surgical strike. Instant death is brought by the equivalent of a PlayStation and maybe collateral damage for the family and neighbours too, but what matter! The operative has gone to lunch.

Research on human interaction indicates that helping and sharing with our fellow humans contributes more to our personal well-being than exploiting them. Well-being is found to be further reinforced within societies where widespread equality prevails. We can claim with some confidence that nationally and internationally humans are becoming increasingly aware of suffering and generally have become more caring and inclusive. It is just a matter of developing the economics and social system to allow such instincts to flourish. Think of the misery that recently poured from pulpits, the blackening of names, the reality of ill-educated girls being separated from their babies and incarcerated in slave laundries. This was done with the connivance of parents, peers and community. Could it happen again? Perhaps, but is less likely. The out-pouring of collective shame, the crash of church morality and confidence, the rise of human morality and confidence have stabilised into a more moral situation.

While it is now fashionable for a young woman to deny being a feminist, if one was to suggest removing the vote, access to contraceptives, pints in a pub and her participation in a hundred differing sports, one would find out how perceptions and confidence have improved. People with a disability who were previously placed in institutions are now integrated. Those with an intellectual problem, who were once rendered powerless and incarcerated in bedlams are similarly being included in the mainstream of society. Ireland is just beginning to adapt to people of differing ethnic origin and there is a potential that racism could get worse before it gets better, for fear of the foreigner and the unknown still exists. Racism was rampant in the United States over a long period of time but diminished, even though there are signs of its revival with growing inequality. The overall point being that in the realm of human empathy there is hope for optimism.

While the visual media of television and film are mainly regarded as entertainment, they play a large part in attitude development. A negative aspect might be seen as the sheer volume of violence, murder and rape portrayed, however a more positive view might be that its portrayal is to seek the viewers' involvement through empathy. Does such exposure breed indifference to suffering or have humans been telling such tales of murder and hero's since first sitting around the campfire? The positive aspect of visual media goes back to our relationship with the known, close group, for when we see their suffering, we empathise and act to alleviate it. The screen, big and small, has brought world-wide visions of deprivation and suffering which have stimulated reaction and some alleviation. But media is only a tool and can manipulate the viewer at will. It can stimulate laughter and human empathy as well as a triumphant view of death and destruction; it can engender hate against a race, religion, or nation. As a child watching 'western' films we screamed when the painted 'redskins' galloped whooping around in a frenzied circle and empathised with the ragged band of brave pioneers in the wagons. We cheered our hearts out when the glorious cavalry came charging over the hill to kill and banish the savages. A few years were to pass, when in silence we watched portrayals of what really happened when the cavalry and armed settlers reached the men, women and children of the indigenous 'Indian' villages.

So again, it is depends on who is telling the story and who gains from the telling.

Up to recent times, the term 'gay' had a very different meaning. While homophobic jokes and attitudes still push many young men to despair and even suicide, the situation has greatly improved. The hate against homosexuals was driven by fear and a biblical morality, for absolute autocratic rule required control over mind and body including sexuality which was tolerated but degraded by laws, taboos and guilt. Sex for love, affection or fun was discouraged with prohibitions in the majority of cultures. The rise of tolerance could be traced by the corresponding rise of freedom in the upper echelons of Greek and Roman civilisations only to fall before the onslaught of the dark ages of Christian power. However, from the renaissance on came the slow return of human-based morality. Recently as oppression ebbed, dramatically the gay community lost its fear, came out, formed clubs and paraded. The media brought the stories of the lesbian and gay individuals and their all-too-human stories of fear, hate and love into the living rooms of the nation and the people accepted what they had known all along. They had all known friends, relations and people in the community who were different. They had known that sons and daughters could be gay and if they were it would be more love and support they would need, not less. The morality of care and well-being now supersedes that of prohibition. Most people would now accept that sex by consenting adults, is solely the concern of the consenting adults, a consensus underlined by the acceptance of marriage equality by referendum.

It is important we see the mangled bodies of the war dead and the misery of survivors. It is important we hear the tragic stories of the girls torn from their babies by religious morality. When humiliated men cry their childhood stories of a forced penis at night and a holy communion by the same man in the morning, we squirm in shame. When we see the homosexual being battered and kicked on the street because he looked for affection or the injured faces of women telling of mental and physical violence perpetrated against them, we want to comfort. The vacant stare of a beautiful girl, betrayed by parents and family telling of being held screaming to have her genitalia cut away for some foul, religious - cultural reason, makes us cry out with her pain. Deep down, we relate to our own childhood and the enormous love we bear for our own or any children. That empathy can jump over prejudice to people of any race or creed. This is the importance of a media providing visual connections with what we perceive to be morally unjust. This is the force that can and does make us angry, boil with rage and at times, brings millions onto the street to protest and help change the course of a war, a social policy, a madness of immorality.

How much more difficult might it now be to screen a blatantly racist, homophobic or sectarian film? Vestiges of these attributes still appear in a condescending fashion, woven into silly counter-terror, pro-corporate, car-smash and explosion films. Seldom will one find portrayals of the empathic nature of man being harnessed to promote the well-being of the collective people. It is a perspective that has been deliberately removed from the fashionable consensus of media. Was it John Lennon who said? "Imagine all the people living for to-day..." the people of the world uniting, co-operating and sharing. What a catastrophe this might lead to, at least for a few, as power and privilege tumbled down onto Earth's common playground, but that is another issue.

The objective interest of those who possess economic, church and state power is to usurp morality away from economics. The objective interest of those who do not possess economic, philosophical and political power is to ensure that economics is based on morality. The interest of those who possess economic, church and state power is to usurp democracy away from economics. The interest of those who do not possess economic, philosophical and political power is to ensure democracy extends over economics. Heady and worthwhile gains are made on these issues through political and ideological reforms pushing steadily in a progressive direction. The starfish opens and devours the oyster by slow, relentless pressure. A similar strategy would appear to be the best option at present for social progress, the application of relentless pressure by an informed social democracy working for its interests rather than a revolutionary process; such a direction is achievable and necessary.

Phil Zuckerman in his book *Society without God* demonstrates that as societies democratically drift into higher levels of collective care and further away from religion they become more moral. Mainly referring to Denmark and Sweden, pointing out that millions of men and women live loving, satisfying and prosperous lives without religion. They might well be the first countries ever to live without such. As an aside, he also observes that the people there appear to have less fear of death. It is acknowledged that these countries have the highest levels of social well-being and if that is the criteria for judging the success of a state, then they are the most advanced societies in the world. Equality within society has a direct bearing on all social problems, this is well documented in *The Spirit Level*, a book by Richard Wilkinson and Kate Pickett and they further explain how equality within society has more relevance than how wealthy that society is compared to others. As both of these studies show an apparent correlation between religiosity and inequality, the question arises, did religion diminish within a society because it became an advanced, more equal and socially caring society, or did such a society arise because religion had faded? While both to an extent are interdependent, the former is most likely, for as an educated democracy and equality advances, discontent and the need for supplication weakens.

While the Czech Republic has the lowest level of religious practice, similar declines are being recorded in Scandinavia, the UK and throughout Europe. Countries which had a de facto state religion and no opposing churches of consequence have seen the most dramatic falls. Whereas in the United States which has thousands of rival churches, religion has only recently started to decline and at a slower pace. This appears due to two influencing factors, large disparities of wealth, imply large groups in relative poverty a situation associated with belief. Secondly many of the churches are a multimillion dollar business, competing for cash flow, working the people over with bellicose preachers and managers. Further statistics which comfortably align with political progress and reaction, show that while 40% of the people who expressed no church affiliation in the US were liberal only 9% were conservative. The growth of people in Ireland and worldwide who declare no church affiliation or atheist, offers ripe ground for further social research.

While there are negative aspects to the corporate globalisation of sport, there are positive sides. Hostility to racial discrimination is enhanced by sport and its media coverage, for now all shades and races are represented. The racist cries of racist fans have withered over the years, until eventually they are delighted to get an autograph from a former figure of hate. More players are 'coming out' announcing their homosexuality and often weathering a storm of abuse in the process. However it is usually just that; 'weathering a storm', for once they can stand firm for a while and people can see that the sky hasn't fallen, their own fears diminish and so does their particular phobia.

In most cases it is down to an individual with courage and a group of loyal friends to enable the broad base of human empathy to kick in. Various sporting associations are then obliged to take a strong line against discrimination and another little victory along the road of human progress is notched up. The Olympic Games have been a positive force in international human relations, with diverse races and nations celebrating the fitness and beauty of their youth. It makes it harder to dehumanise another's race or nationality, thus war, is made that little bit more problematic. The games have facilitated female emancipation, the sight of such freedom, power and grace can do nothing but challenge concepts of misogyny and the burka. Likewise, when the vast army of watching males realise that the female athletes could out-run, out-jump and out-play them, it does little to enhance any lingering chauvinism.

The point made previously regarding European state religions and how quickly belief can fall, is applicable in the Irish context. In theory we do not have a state religion, in reality we do. Schools are the repository of religion with over 90% of them under the control of Catholic patrons, but the bulk of their funding is provided by the state. Religion also permeates many sections of hospitals, health care and the mechanisms of state. There are no competing religions of any significance so the implication, based on European model, is that, as the decline is coming, it will be catastrophic. According to a recent poll 50% of peopled in Ireland now describe themselves as religious. The question is no longer, if the collapse will happen, it is happening as we watch. It is vital now to develop an alternative moral ethos, a morality based on relevant life and sustainable economic, social and spiritual needs to fill that void. This quest will have allies from thinking and disillusioned religious seeking to serve society against the onslaught of corporate consumerism. The encouragement of empathy in humans to pursue objectives beyond material success is within our control. Our social organisations have the ability to achieve higher levels of consensus and indeed happiness. Since our cold purposeless beginnings, we have come a long way building caring societies. It is worth pursuing such dreams, for the pursuit itself is essential to what we are, warm humans.

Chapter 4   An Instinct to Believe

Humans over the ages have been striving to make sense of life and death and all questions raised by existence. They were the first and so far only living organism to develop a complex language, make implements and evolve their main tool for survival and replication, a cognisant brain. Once cognisance arrived so did the questions. Where did we come from, where are we going? What is that big hot thing in the sky? Can we do anything to ensure it comes back after the dark of the night? Lightning and thunder, now that is terrifying, sickness, how can we deal with it? There were and still are thousands of situations and other species that threaten our existence, from large predators to an unseen virus. Some of these problems had practical solutions: from the rain, wind and lightning they could barricade themselves into a cave; fire and tools like pointed sticks helped keep off wilder animals. The caves developed into built dwellings, the pointed sticks became spears and eventually a bow and arrow. Killed animals were put on the fire and were easier and safer to eat. A million little improvements to existence and all the time the brains and questions grew.

Where no answers were obvious, a supernatural explanation was offered. Genes involved in directing brain function favour a belief over a void, any belief, for all things must have a cause. If it can be rationally explained, real progress can be made. Inability to find explanations leads to mental discomfort and an imperative arises to conjure up an answer using imagination. Lightning and thunder must have been a real dilemma, as it would be many thousands of years before there was a scientific explanation. Unseen forces or gods were imagined as the cause. But gods and power structures go hand in hand, for once the beliefs develop and take hold, the manipulation of belief is quickly realised and can be exploited by those who claim to hold this knowledge, the priests, the captains and the kings.

Since the emergence of Homo sapiens, there has been evidence of god worship and with hindsight we can trace the emergence of highly complex belief systems which now abound. The gods became responsible for all things and if offered sacrifice and worship, they might respond to human requests with anything from prolonging life, curing sickness or winning the lottery.

But first, a note of reconciliation. The majority of people, even in a cultural way, look for answers to the big questions through revelation in sacred texts, by way of their inherited faith. Mindful of their sensibilities, this chapter will attempt discussion in a fashion to avoid animosity or insult to individuals who hold firm on such beliefs. For many who profess a faith have a progressive view of the world and also put the well-being of humans and our planetary existence at centre stage. Such a conciliatory approach may prove difficult, for while in a free society it is perfectly normal to persuade or argue with people on any action or idea, but when it comes to religion it is seen as invasive or rude. It is not regarded as a 'polite' topic of conversation. All one can offer in mitigation is to point out that it is the ideas of belief that are under discussion and there is no attack or slight intended on any individual. Part of the problem may well be the fragile nature of the belief itself, as it attempts to exist in a world of science. As many of the beliefs are patently absurd, they are generally only marginally believed or believed as analogies and are embarrassing to discuss. If a rationalist were to explain to a neighbour's child, the exact nature and religious rationale for baptism, communion and confirmation, it would be regarded as a hostile intervention.

The contradictions between contemporary science based existence and a two thousand year old theology has seen doubt growing amongst the majority of those professing a faith. The extent of that doubt is demonstrated as the main churches drift towards a more secular and humanist outlook. Seldom now, is there talk of the devil or the dammed burning in hell for eternity. Limbo, where the unbaptised baby souls went, never to experience the joys of heaven, has been abolished.

St.Agustine had originally concluded that unbaptised children who died would spend eternity in hell. Even the church fathers of the time thought that this was a bit rough, so by the time of St. Aquinas a new state of 'Limbo' was postulated, it had no basis in scripture, but illustrates the sort of trouble theologians get into when attempting to apply empathy to the illogical, this was endorsed by Pope Pius in 1905. But in time even the state of Limbo was perceived as dodgy and had to be side stepped on some sound theological basis. Picture the scene around 2004, the setting is a beautifully designed and magnificently adorned room in the Vatican, thirty leading theologians gather in gilded gowns to re-evaluate the question of Limbo. Can any mind conceive of a project more intellectually forlorn than these male theologians from many parts of the world debating the fate of the souls of unbaptised children? It is however an indicator of how the church is being carried by the rising tide of humanism and grows evermore doubtful of its own spiritual foundations. The revelations that were soon to follow of the endemic sexual molestation of real living children, brands the entire enterprise as a theatre of the diabolical and the macabre.

The church which had run its flock on a diet of terror began to change to a god of love. With Limbo eliminated, purgatory, a place of temporary torture, is in doubt and the perpetual fires of hell are moving off the agenda for interesting theological anti-hell arguments have emerged from expanding human empathy. The question was posed, how would those in heaven enjoy perfect eternal happiness, knowing that billions of their fellows who by chance had never heard of the saviour were screaming in torture for eternity? Contrast such modern humanist thinking with a saintly maxim from the past, 'one of the great pleasures of heaven will be to witness the tortures of those in hell', reiterated in chilling formats by Augustine, Tertullian and Aquinas. The Christian churches are now almost solely concerned with the welfare of humanity. The vanguard of this modern Christian dilemma will provide allies in many of the social actions required for progress. It will become more apparent when those within the church who strive for the elimination of poverty supersede those who require a poverty to support.

As the fear factor within the church diminishes, so too does its power, society becomes more humane and caring and where previously the religious led, now they simply wish to keep relevant. The churches themselves are finding it difficult to recruit and replace their ageing administrators. Religion and its rituals are becoming much more a cultural artefact. If the churches are naturally evolving to a better philosophical place, why then is there a problem, there is, for they still control the majority of schools and remain in a position to make respectable their unfounded anti-scientific and anti-intellectual premise. This maintains a negative effect on society as church theology displaces a philosophy which would allow the formation of morals and ethics on a rational basis.

The story of a god creating Adam and Eve in the Garden of Eden with enough curiosity to get them into trouble is an interesting lesson in power retention. For he, and it is almost always a he, created a paradise with a trap - seeking the tree of knowledge, of sex, of life, of perhaps, just about anything. The original creators of these legends were the powerbrokers of the day and found them to be an excellent way to control the minds and lives of their subjects. The first and most powerful lesson of the Bible, Torah and Koran, the core documents of the three main monotheist religions, is obedient submission and a prohibition against seeking rational explanations! Sin is the search for knowledge.

As our species progressed our minds grew more active and observed more characteristics of the world. For many questions, solutions or answers were found, many stayed beyond comprehension, but answers were still required, the cycles of night and day, the seasons, weather. At the same time assistance was sought to overcome fears of darkness, diseases, hunger and death. Countless gods and demons were imagined that gave explanation and comfort. Multifarious belief systems arose within the tribes and kingdoms, many of the beliefs themselves fracturing to dwell in hostile camps, each claiming to have the one true path to the gods. The gods are prayed to and adored that they might provide protection and favours; sacrifices of all types are offered to placate and plead favour, the more precious the sacrifice, the greater the perceived return. Thus humans through the millennia have been sacrificing time, objects, animals or even fellow humans. The gods evolved into monotheist belief systems and various 'Holy Books' were written; these and their offspring are now the dominant belief form. Just as a child's first influences are readily adopted to its formation, so too did humanity adapt the first written instruction books as its most enduring and influential. Homo sapiens, the great survival machine of our gene, had become a belief machine, and belief had in turn become a component of its survival before it became a threat to it.

The adaption of Christianity by the Roman Emperor Constantine was critical for its rapid triumph. For the Roman Empire was a vast conduit for those beliefs to spread everywhere it controlled or had influence. Despite its fractures, Christianity was the dominant belief at the time of Europe's great expansion. That occurred when Spain, Portugal, Holland, England and France raced into the 'new worlds' of the Americas, Africa and Australia. Their conquests and colonisation ensured the spread of Christianity, thus from the power of great ships and guns were the belief systems of so many formed. Once adapted the beliefs are passed down through the generations as a tradition and whatever shade of religion each child in turn inherits, it is most likely to be by that geographic accident of birth. In most areas of the world at various stages these beliefs become strong; they can hold science at bay and become forces that are divisive and dangerous. Sectarianism linked with nationalism has become a divisive plague internationally. In every conflict on every side from the imperial elite of the United States to Isis, they all persuade that they have god on their side.

"Give me the child and I will show you the man", so went the catch phrase of the Jesuits, for they understood well the essential natural gullibility of the child and knew how to take advantage. The power of a triumphant church in the middle ages was fully integrated with that of the state and dominated every facet of life in Europe. Inquiry was silenced, the clergy were in full control and dissent was dealt with by the inquisition. Intellectual darkness descended on Europe, it became an arid desert of culture, hope and learning for over a thousand years. The Renaissance was a time of rebirth when the vision of the depraved human drenched in original sin began to be challenged. The sculptures of Jesus being nailed to crosses and saints being tortured to satiate his father were now challenged by the confident, naked David of Michelangelo. Born without original sin, without shame, David was proclaiming a human to be the centre of the universe and the creator of gods. The final phase of that emergence from the darkness is still being played out. As an aside, the church has managed to turn around perceptions of the 'dark ages' and now purports to be the bearer of wisdom and truth that brought learning and light to dispel the very dark ages for which it was responsible. A bit like Hitler arguing that the death camps were built for the benefit of their inmates and were liberated by the Nazis.

This Dark Age survived in Ireland well into the 1960s and beyond, with almost every politician bending knees to bishops whose rings were copiously kissed. Most semblances of a republic and what it might mean were swamped, even today a remarkable number of people still believe the colour of the national flag to be green, white and gold. Perhaps this was the real symbol, a unity of nationalist Ireland and the Vatican; they are surprised to discover that the last colour of the flag is orange representing the protestant and dissenter tradition.   While the church reigned unchallenged, its view and ethos, spread over the land like a wet blanket. Its confused ethos allowed every physical, sexual and psychological savagery to be perpetrated against so many under its control. Many of these were institutions of the state, but the state and the church were one. The prison schools, the Magdalene laundries, the violence, abuse and rape that took place within has been well documented in reports that defy belief. Ingrained misogyny perpetrated by the church led to the churching of women. This humiliating practice was akin to a public confession that as they had given birth, they then must have engaged in sex, thus exposing the failings of their sinful nature, they had to be blessed by the male priest to become pure again.

The attempt to build a theocratic state led to the crushing of diversity, control of the schools was seen as the main way to achieve this. Under English jurisdiction an act was introduced in 1831 to unite children of different creeds within one school with separate religious instruction and up to 1862 most schools were in this situation. However, this was seen by the more sectarian as a danger to faith and the Catholic bishops asked parents to remove their sons from these schools, it was not until 1965 and 1971 the national school rules and the curriculum were changed in a way that legally converted 90 per cent of our national schools from formally non-denominational schools into Catholic institutions. Up to that point religious instruction had been confined to one half hour class per day but that was altered on grounds that "the separation of religious and secular instruction into differentiated subject compartments served to throw the whole educational function out of focus". Now indeed was education thrown to the wolves, the intellectual maiming of children was more consistent.

The schools record of education in the obvious subjects of maths, writing and language is not being challenged. What is being confronted are the explanations that deal with the big questions of existence, the anti-scientific answers and the destruction of critical thinking. The world of science, the challenges facing our distorted economic and social system and the very survival of our species, require rational, sceptical minds. As soon as a child enters a faith school an unconscious progression commences which militates against this. Of course a fraction of pupils will have the curiosity and the will-power to resist the oppression and emerge unscathed. Preparing a child for Holy Communion, the teacher has to instruct the child to believe in a series of events which are wholly irrational and without a shred of evidence. The unquestioning acceptance of this instruction is a key factor in what they are told will be one of the most important days in their life. They will be rewarded for this acceptance by being dressed in the finest of clothes, have a day of celebration, a party at which all their extended family will attend and they will receive money and gifts. A few years later they will be checked again to 'confirm' that they have not deviated from the belief path and the celebrations will be repeated. All of which will reinforce the importance and establish the permanence of the data they have received.

The children will have been introduced to anti-scientific concepts of a god, turned man, changing bread into his body and wine into his blood. That on their special, Holy Communion day, a male, and only a male priest can now re-enact this magical miracle. This is not a symbolic act, but a dogma of faith. They must accept this to be actually true despite the fact, that the bread tastes, feels and smells like bread, not raw flesh; the wine, smells, tastes and feels like wine, not blood. They become part of a tradition that stretches back thousands of years, long before Christianity, where man after victory in battle, cannibalised the best warriors to gain their spirit, their strength. Here again, this ritual is played out, the children gain complete communion with god by eating him. Such ceremonies, with its adult and community support, enacted at a most vulnerable age, injure the curiosity and potential rational abilities of a child. The child is now programmed to accept authority without question; this will be reinforced throughout its schooling by constant repetition of further contra-rational information, but mixed up with perfectly good areas of education. The ability to discern the difference between myth and math, legend and logic is thus eroded. This erosion of curiosity and confidence will in the future stay the adult from questioning the status quo in politics and economics.

The objective interest of the existing beneficiaries of the economic and political system is for the church to maintain control on the majority of schools. The church might have its most important goal as the preservation and the propagation of faith, in other words, the production of more Catholics. The real beneficiaries, the controllers of capital, just require the production of polite, compliant, operatives. This control has been supported up to now, 'lock, stock and barrel' by the state and church. But internal pressure builds and cracks are appearing in all organs of the economic system and the church and the state has shown itself to be plainly, incompetent. One of these pressures is the disappearance of priests. There are now almost no recruits to that way of life. The most likely reason for this situation is; a weakening of faith, the reluctance of more liberated men to emasculate their sexuality, and the declining relevance of the church. It is growing more difficult for an idealistic young person to dedicate his or her celibate life to being an administrator in a declining church? The hope that flourished briefly for a transformative Christianity with a theology of liberation has been set aside in favour of a systematic theology, running schools, the administration of sacraments, all becoming increasingly alienated from reality.

There is an argument that the ethos of the church is necessary to generate a moral and loving society, but the evidence is scarce. The two great wars resulting in the slaughter of millions and untold suffering emerged in a Europe that was packed with churches and schools of theology, almost all Christian. Racism, social inequality, anti-Semitism, gender discrimination and for a time slavery, all thrived under thousands of years of church influence. Every slave ship jammed with its wretched cargo, carried the 'word of god' for none sailed without a Bible. When these ships arrived in the new world and sold their chained humanity to enrich the few by their 'free' labour, it did not bother the deeply religious Christians of the new world of North America, neither did the fact that they had ethnically cleansed the stolen land of its indigenous people in their millions by genocide, a disputed figure ranging from 1.5 to 36 million. The former colonies of Latin America have never known social justice and they have been almost exclusively under the moral guardianship of the Catholic Church. Their enslavement provided gold for the enrichment of the Spanish and Portuguese state and church. The statues of saints cast in bloodied gold adorn the magnificent cathedral of Compostela, Spain and in churches all over the Iberian Peninsula, an insult to the millions of enslaved or dead indigenous peoples of the Americas, 500 years after which the area is still struggling to recover from this economic, military and philosophical rape.

It is claimed that great music, such as Bach's or Beethoven's masses and Mozart's requiem, and great architecture such as the medieval Cathedrals were inspired by faith in God. That well may be the case, but like the gods themselves, all was created by humankind; every note in these great orchestral works was written, played and sung by men and women; every cathedral was designed and built by man. Likewise we must accept that while torture and death of tens of thousands and indeed millions took place while religion was in effective moral control, none of the murder and mayhem was carried out by gods. The gods are innocent; it was all by the hand of humans, serving the interests of an ideology. The key point is that all religions are but the mask and mentor of a social order which serves the interests of the economic elite of the period. It is vital that a correct analysis is made on any situation in history or now, by constantly asking the question 'cui bono', for if you find the beneficiary of a crime and you are well on the way to solving it. But for real solutions it is never enough to seek out the perpetrator, it is necessary to find the source. When the dysfunctional cleric is caught abusing and raping those in care, blame not just him or her, look for the source of the ignorance. When that stagnant steel tank of ignorance is uncovered, it can be drained, little pinholes of reason will suffice and one may also find that it is already rotting away on the inside.

The fact that schools, hospitals and other social works were provided by church organisations is quoted in their favour. That was the case, but during the period in which these institutions were established, the church, state and ruling elite were one and no alternative structure existed under which they could have been set up. In addition these institutions facilitated the agenda of the church to expand and intensify their core mission of indoctrination and control. The foundation money for all these institutions ultimately came from the populace at large either through taxation or tithe. The first purpose of the schools was religious formation and the provision of compliant workers. The hospitals equated the care of the body to that of the soul, with treatment influenced as much by theology as the interest of the patient. These institutions would not be divisive, if provided under a purely secular structure.

Negative aspects of religious thinking spring from an ideology based on salvation, a pass into the next life achieved by an individual obeying the rules of a cantankerous god - a god who has little regard for the quality of the environment or the common good. The importance was to be in the pleasing of the god or, more to the point, the pleasing of the church and state authority. Service and adoration was proportional to the levels of fear of damnation in the afterlife. The wrathful, jealous god is getting harder to sell as reason and empathy advance, the power to be gained from manipulating that fear is ebbing away. However, concepts of individual and private salvation still permeate the social order giving little cognisance to the common good, an ethos matched by that of commerce. The commercial and theological positions are to some extent a mirror image of one another. The individual's relationship with capital can be likened to a relationship to a god, it is purported to be the only one true system that can thrive and if we reject that path, then we shall have to bear the wrath of capital. But like the diminution of the wrathful god, reason can do likewise with capital and seek new paths to earthly material salvation. The fabric of the church, state and capital still cling together for their mutual support. It was and still is an economic and class issue; the entire huff and puff of sanctimony comes down to supporting a rich minority in maintaining control over the toiling mass of people.

No one in their right mind would put tattoos on children, big colourful ones with proclamations of love or faith imprinted across their bodies, easy for the parents to put on, but very hard for the children to remove or change in later life. No one in their right mind would now introduce children to smoking, "hi kids have your first fag it's a tradition in the family going back generations!" This book is a persuasion against doing the equivalent to childrens' minds with any fixed belief system, easy to implant hard to amend. It is an argument that all our children be positively equipped with the intellectual tools for rational decision making, that children be given access to all information and be tutored to form their own outlook on life with its ethical codes and moral structures. It is a plea to parents and educators to move to an education based on rational thought and to universally replace compliance with curiosity.

Credulity in a child is a virtue; in an adult it is a vice. A child of our species has only basic instincts for survival, but as part of its evolutionary structure, a huge capacity and need for learning. In comparison to its parents it knows nothing and they are the source of its knowledge and its protection. For our species to survive and thrive over the millennia, the passing of vast quantities of information through all the senses of smell, touch, hearing and vision, to a child was and is paramount. The child is primed to absorb information, language and the ability to communicate in a myriad of other ways. It learns to detect happiness, anger and danger from the pitch of voice or the facial expression of its parents at a very early age. The child believes everything it is told. Its credulity is easily exploited for the parents' enjoyment - tooth fairies, never-never land, Santa Clause and for the benefit of the status quo.

At what point can a parent safely challenge the credulity of a child and encourage its natural curiosity? When is it expedient not to answer a child's question with straight information, but with an encouragement to the child to weigh alternatives or engage in experiment? Too early and the child is sticking needles in the electric socket "just testing this thing about electricity mammy", too late and credulity is carried into adult life, where they can be duped by peddlers of the occult, dodgy politicians and financial advisors of all kinds. The child turned adult will have accepted authority as the norm and will vote for the same political parties and follow the same belief system as its parents. This reality is often expressed with statements such as "we always vote for that party as the family have always been loyal to that tradition". Likewise religious beliefs are inherited by the geographical location or inherited tradition. If born in the south of Ireland there is a ninety per cent chance one will be a catholic, if born in the north of Ireland, but a forty per cent chance. If born in India there would be very little chance of either faith, one would almost certainly be either a Hindu or Muslim, and each and every one thus born would profess and defend their faith. Awareness of such simple realities would go a way to developing a questioning mind.

Supplication, an unfortunate predisposition of humans to adoration and obedience leads us seeking not just gods and spiritual leaders, but also temporal ones, from great Pharaohs, Caesars, Kings, Emperors, to Hitler and Stalin. The realisation that faith in strong leaders, power from the top down and worship from the bottom up is very misplaced, a fact that should be obvious to anyone who glances at history. This thinking, or lack of it, is what brought mankind to tramp along the egotistical blood trails of Napoleon, die in their tens of thousands in the trenches of the first world war, wave in adulation of Hitler and jackboot their way into every country in Europe, die in their millions for the Emperor of Japan, or die in their thousands killing Vietnamese. On first glance it usually appears that the power of the idea, nationalism and religion are what drives war, but analysis will demonstrate economics and its beneficiaries are always the culprits. Nationalism, racism and religion are valuable tools to a status quo; they can usually swamp any coherent humanist philosophy.

Humans often accept mystic answers over scientific enquiry, whilst this unfortunate tendency is diminishing, it still exists; we tend to believe in the unbelievable. Modern scientific assessment strives against the mysticism within our collective physic; however, such thinking is only a few hundred years old and has a lot of catching up to do. Natural selection would have favoured those who read all patterns as having meaning or message. During our very long predator verses prey period, it might have been an error to conclude danger from a movement in the bushes; if it was only the wind, it would have been an error of judgement, but one would survive. If one decided that the movement in the bushes was unreal 'just the wind' when in fact it was a predator, it would have again been an error of judgement, but now could be fatal. Survival would depend on constantly reading more into patterns than justified, assuming much to be true even if they were not. Those that did would be more likely to survive and therefore pass on that trait. Thus our race becomes conditioned by evolution to look for and read patterns. We are much more likely to mistake a shadow for a burglar than a burglar for a shadow.

Around the campfires our species invent tales as answers to troubling questions; these evolve to a belief system specific to a tribe. The explanations and imagined deities for all religions have remarkably similar features. Early imaginings led to all the diverse religions we are now familiar with, but we still go there. One of the remarkable unifying features of religion is the amount of awe that is sought by breaking the laws of nature. Gravity is constantly defied, virgin births abound, winged horses and angles flutter about and substances change their nature. In a similar fashion humankind's inherent loneliness on the blue planet in the vast darkness of space drives a search for signs in the cosmos; we reach out seeking direction from the alignment of the stars, to the gods, to contacts from UFOs. These are the inheritances shaping the foundation for our irrational beliefs in every area of the mind. They form the basis for shamanism, paganism, animism, polytheism, monotheism, intelligent designers, angels, aliens, leprechauns, trolls and fairies. These are the concepts that align with the great puppeteers who created humankind and the existence we are conscious of, hence beliefs that all life and power comes from the top down and these creators demand our adoration and whimsical obedience.

Returning to the analogy of fear, the 'rustle in the bushes', courageous humanity can now arm itself with weapons and organise to march forth into the bushes to investigate, if it is but the wind, so what!, if it is the predator too bad for the predator, for we are now taking command. Faced with sickness we have less recourse to chanting, prayers and lighting candles, our first call now is the doctor, the hospital where the miracles of science prevail, even if we sometimes slip around the corner and light a candle in the church. As spectres of the gods and goblins that make threatening shapes in the night melt before our lights, most fears can be made to melt with our reason. There is a prayer 'The Hail Holy Queen' with a line at the end which called out like some banshee, 'mourning and weeping in this valley of tears'. To me as a child, it summed up the darkness and despair of religion calling hopelessly across voids of time. A call to some imagined being, to solve one's problems instead of facing up and dealing with them as an individual with the support of our fellow humans.

The scientific mind seeks and finds the basis for a preponderance of mysticism within the body of mankind. The initial purpose of the brain is the control of body movement. Plants do not move; they have no muscle so no brain. The brain that provides all our imagination, music, arts, is but an extension of these original control circuits, outside our bodies we can have no experience of ourselves. The mind seeks reason and logical connections between cause and effect. While we can understand that pain follows a simple accident, we often seek a mystical explanation as to why it happened. We strangely defend a god by reacting to a disaster where thousands have been killed by a tsunami and express a miracle and thank god as a few survive.

A de facto humanist, science based society is evolving, but it has no structured format or coherent philosophy The decaying religious theology still confuses and occupies the philosophical space available, forming an obstacle to a creditable alternative. Protective barriers such as 'polite society' and embarrassment exist which prevent the critical discussion of existing theology, thereby militating against the emergence of new ways of thinking. Out of this belief void emerges a confused pursuit of spiritualist answers, ranging from esoteric contemplation to the paranormal. Rationalists will have to live with this regardless of the irritation and maintain stoic evidential thinking. There is a determining test for all clairvoyants, shamans, spoon benders and predictors. If they had a fraction of truth, if only one person in a million had these powers, the laws of science would be thrown into disarray. These practitioners of the occult would be the richest people on earth, all betting shops, horse racing, gaming machines and lotteries of all descriptions would close down and disappear overnight. For these soothsayers and remote viewers, would be able to pick tomorrow's winner of the 3.30 with impunity, stop gaming machines by mind power on winning combinations, and constantly have the lottery winning numbers. The laws of random chance would be overthrown; we would be living in a different universe.

James Randi is an American magician. He and his organisation keep a watching brief for any magician who claims tricks to be paranormal, his foundation takes delight in exposing them. His foundation offers a million dollar reward to anyone who can perform anything remotely paranormal.

After many years it remains unclaimed. The potential harm of delusional belief is real, such obvious flummeries as astrology or fortune-telling can appear -quite incorrectly - to give confirmatory results, and that can lead to the victim pursuing more dangerous, expensive, and often health-related scams. Blind belief can be comforting, but it easily cripples reason. Efforts could be made to engage with the paranormal and superstition, particularly to get young people thinking critically and bravely about these subjects. Those who have not completely surrendered to careless acceptance can be encouraged to think about their delusions.

We teach and pay lip service to a religious, and in Ireland's case, a specifically Catholic ethos. These highly structured ideas, or as Richard Dawkins might call them 'Memes', are inserted into the heads of the host over a long period, overcoming rational resistance by encouraging a receptivity in the child and who better to do that than the parents themselves and the teachers. The full extent of this surrender of reason is manifest in the religion of Islam which literally means submission. The person or people who become infected by such ideas become their slaves. When Islam took hold in the Middle East and the priests achieved ascendancy over maths and science, the societies stagnated and have hardly moved on since then as they said that all one needs to know is contained in the Koran. Once science and reason lose their sway, every mutating religion and ghastly pyramidal dictatorship combining fundamentalism with fascism can ride into town.

CHAPTER 5   The Poverty of Philosophy

Philosophy is the fundamental nature of knowledge, reality and existence, its essential nature is asking big questions. Where did we come from, why are we here, where are we going? Looking back at people who have dealt with such questions, the first characteristic was that they were human the only cognisant species capable of perceiving cause and result. The next attribute required was curiosity and time to assemble thoughts, subject them to reason and offer answers. Over the millennia of philosophical discourse, it has become apparent that there are two diametrically opposed ways of looking at the world. That fundamental split is between the idealists and the materialists.

> The 'Poverty of Philosophy' was also a booklet title published in 1847 by Karl Marx as a critique on The 'Philosophy of Poverty 'by Proudhon, a French socialist.

Idealists argue that the idea or the spiritual aspect comes first, the idea determines everything. This is the oldest stream of philosophy, and is the basis of religion. It contends that the gods always existed, a concept of spirit, and it was they who created matter and energy and all things, including mankind. Some, including the Catholic Church, now accept that evolution is the likely explanation for the emergence of all life forms and mankind. It just insists that god started the whole chain of events, then intervened at a certain stage and inserted a spiritual entity, a soul, into humans. Others branches of Christianity maintain literal biblical interpretations and insist that all was made in a week. Earlier idealism asserted that nothing existed outside the mind; the essence of all things was the spirit and that real things like a cow were but manifestations of that essence, that all we perceived was the idea of a cow, we humans, were all manifestations of an idea, the essence of god or soul and made in his image, eternal and immutable. They concluded that if living things such as humans were of two separate parts, an essence or soul and its material part the body, then as the body was obviously going to die, the soul lived on forever. The readers of such idealist tracts are required to endure a great deal of rational discomfort.

Early hints of the opposite or materialist viewpoint emerged from Democritus, a Greek philosopher about 2,400 years ago. He arrived at conclusions from pure reason, that all things were built from very small parts called atoms, that nothing can come from nothing, that matter is constant and only its form changes. He still believed in souls but concluded that they were not immortal; at death their atoms flew loose and built new souls. Much of his philosophy was to prove accurate, with the revelations of atomic structures and particle physics. As time progressed, investigations began to rely more on observation, experience and experiment. This is referred to as scientific reasoning; answers came in frightening and exciting rapidity. Where did we come from? The big bang. Why are we here? By random chance and evolution on the 'Goldilocks' planet. Where are we going? Nowhere. Materialist philosophy states that matter and energy have always existed and are ultimately indestructible insomuch as only the form changes. The philosophy contends that material is primary from which evolves the body, in turn the brain and that all ideas, imagination, and gods spring from matter in that order.

Idealists believe that the mechanism for asking questions and offering answers arises from an ethereal spirit or soul that accompanies our bodies. Materialists hold that the mechanism is material, the brain; our main tool for survival is a biological machine at the hub of our nervous system. Taking information, from eyes, ears, nose and touch senses, it analyses and responds, issuing commands to limbs, fingers, and every facet of our amazing bodies. Much remains to be discovered about the detail functioning of the brain, but every day understanding grows. We perceive the brain, as a biological computer, similar to electronic, but far more powerful, driving a robotic body through muscle-motored limbs. We see the body as feeding back millions of bits of information to its core computer for analysis and reaction - a fast interactive organism of information and analysis.

When the body encounters food it scans it with visual sensors, analysing it for colour and texture; it then instructs its extend-and-grab limb to pick it up. Sensitive pads test for temperature, texture and moisture content, other sensors check odour and taste and it is then pulverised and sent to the stomach for final separation into energy and waste. If it fails any of these tests, the food is rejected. The location of our hard disk, the brain, adjacent to the fuel intake system and the primary sense recorders, of eyes, nose, mouth and ears is the same basic configuration in every vertebrate animal on earth, all of whom, like ourselves, have been a few hundred million years in the evolutionary making.

The brain is the physical structure that generates our contemplations, ideas and viewpoints. From that organic hard disk - an astonishing thinking and reacting machine - emanates all our joys and sorrows, discussions and philosophy, into which we feed thousands of folders, with sets of ideas and beliefs on political, religious and moral issues. Some are subject to rational contemplation; most are taken at face value or lightly scanned. When parents give us repetitive traditional food it is seldom questioned, its repetition gives familiarity, sustenance and comfort. Strangers giving strange food in a strange country would be a different matter, the touching smelling and tasting would be much more circumspect.

However, applying analysis to all food intakes might discover that the bacon, sausages, burgers and chips, milk and butter, that one had grown to love and be comfortable with, leads to obesity and early demise. Whereas the 'strange' alternative diet of fruit, bran, water and hardship might keep one fit and healthy in old age. This is not diet recommendation, but how a science-based analysis applied to food intake could improve the long-term health of the body. That analogy applied to intellectual intake, could likewise dramatically improve the long-term health of the mind. We have become obsessed with the quality of the food we consume, we should give more thought to the quality of the information we absorb, for as food streams in from birth until death so also does information. As fatty foods block arteries and heart valves, reducing agility and quality of life, so too, poor-quality, unanalysed information entering the mind causes blockages and deterioration reducing mental agility and quality of life. Information from traditional sources is the least likely to be checked and the most likely to carry a virus programmed to block any form of thinking which might pose a threat to its stored information or beliefs. To remove an embedded virus or irrational idea is more difficult than blocking its entry in the first instance. Thus, if the parents and educators wish a child to develop an agile critical mind, it is vital that the child be encouraged to construct a firewall of reason.

The child has been conditioned by evolution to believe what they hear from their parents and those they see as trusted by their parents. This knowledge is absorbed quickly and runs parallel to the survival instinct. Much of this information is vital for safety: "the road is dangerous, keep away from the water, that plant is poisonous, do not touch and don't talk to strangers". All this is perhaps essential for initial survival but stitched in amongst advice is a whole range of misinformation. "That snake is dangerous, it's an agent of the devil", "that plant is poisonous because of a witch". The child has enough curiosity to ask questions and will absorb good and bad information, unable to distinguish the difference and not yet possessing the confidence to challenge it. The child can be shown how the information received from certain sources is based on evidence. He or she can be thought how to check that information when competent to do so. The child can be introduced to danger and how to deal with it. To fall into water might be to drown; to do the same when one is a competent swimmer is fun. It is every parent's instinct after passing on their gene that their child should survive, but under conditions that may not allow their child to thrive. The worst definition of which would demand obedience and submission, the negation of query, the acceptance of traditional beliefs and all its burdens of sexual sin together with enough guilt heaped on the child to force it to mind its parents in old age, leading to a life of quiet desperation and the nightmare scenario of a hundred, dark, Irish novels.

A surrender of the mind to authority favours the ideas of the parent, the teacher and the preacher. It is the stamping ground of tradition, that bogeyman with the unctuous smile where conventions of nationalism, politics and revelation are transmitted. The quote *'give me the child and I will show you the man'*, has all the charm of tattooing children, easy to apply, hard to remove. This is a programme for closing down the child's critical facilities for an adulthood of polite compliance, of non-judicial thinking, of alienation and of service to a controlling elite. Such adults will pass on the same stultified information to the next generation without critical examination. Whether the parents are Protestant, Humanist, Catholic, Muslim or Jew, most wish to imprint their beliefs on the formative mind. The inclusion of humanism might seem surprising, but for any child a belief system that is self-formed from enquiry, debate and critical analysis is likely to be a far sturdier foundation.

At the positive liberating end of the parenting spectrum is a child, reassured with love and confidence-building with its questions encouraged and wisely answered. A child who has been brought to the edge of fear and given the skills to deal with it, provided with skills to scale a cliff, sail an ocean or stand against a social wrong. A child enmeshed in the joys of creativity, engaging with music, the arts and intellectual fulfilment. A child, curious of the world, with an ability to join its complex dots and with the ability to accept constructive criticism. Hope prospers, for such children are slowly appearing, the blocking of rational thinking is not a united conspiracy to which all parents and teachers are in league.

Arguments against indoctrination have no quarrel with imagination, the majority of books, films, TV etc. while relating to real life are as such, structures of the imagination. Thousands of books ranging from *Alice Through the Looking Glass* to the *Lord of the Rings*, and *Harry Potter*, play a part in enriching a child's imagination, as well as their reading abilities. Imagination matters a great deal; it might be a mental liberation from a closed cycle of dull schooling. Imagination is a necessary part of scientific thinking. Albert Einstein said, "It is the preview of life's coming attractions": a vital ingredient in the first stage in a scientific search, for one has to imagine a hypothesis, before proceeding to prove it. For an architect, imagination is the fourth dimension when working on a project. Likewise, society has to envisage an ideal structure for itself, one with a pervading sense of purpose and beauty serving the well-being of the majority, an egalitarian utopia, before providing the political imperative to achieve it.

A distinction needs to be drawn between works exploring imagination or encouraging human empathy and those such as the holy books of the desert, the Tanakh, Bible and Koran. For while these books are of the imagination, they claim to be far more than that. They purport to be an explanation and guide to this life and a gate to the next. They provide simplistic, blocking answers to complex questions doing a great injustice to a child's mind and humanity in general. They turn morality away from what it should be, an interaction of responsibilities between humanity and our world, into a set of obligations to celestial masters, adding strange taboos on sexuality and foods. Over the generations and the progress of scientific knowledge, these 'holy books' with their religious and moral law grew further apart from reality. But these books still have a purpose; invocations to obedience, to worship and the promise of a better life in the hereafter provide a vital function in exploitative societies.

The philosophical clash between idealism and materialism comes to the surface when society proclaims in constitutions, swears on Bibles and practices rituals in which few actually believe. The belief systems of faith are so uncomfortable that they are never discussed in any normal social context. In services, such as christenings, weddings or funerals, the religious rituals are muttered by the participants generally with a pervading air of embarrassment. Where beliefs are discussed in the media, the majority express a vague acceptance of an afterlife or spiritualism but seldom express any attachment to a specific religion. Morality is perceived as being connected to the religious side of life, not with the real material side. Such a disconnection between the inherited, but only partially believed theological foundations and real life, are the manifestation of - the *Poverty of Philosophy*.

This general philosophical fog obscures the contradiction between economic and social goals; it contrives that examination of society by the media take place within limited agendas. As an example; the simple question of whether society exists to serve the economy or the economy exists to serve society should be a primer for any discussion on society and the economy, but is seldom asked. These questions will be explored under a chapter on 'the social order'.

A collective morality will not emerge without sufficient intellectual minds having the courage for action. It will not emerge until the poverty of philosophy is overcome by a sufficient number of citizens who can forge a tipping point. Mechanisms leading to philosophical fogs are either an accident or a conspiracy. While both play a part, it more likely evolves to serve the objective interests of the systems beneficiaries. Whether such controlling strategies emerge within a doctrinaire, Stalinist society, a fascist oligarchy or the more enduring capitalist social-democratic system, it serves the interests of such societies to have a confused philosophy with trained and compliant operatives. This situation is consolidated by the inherent inertia of any natural or social structures, for nothing moves or changes unless there is no choice. However, dialectics conspire against such lethargy, thousands of tiny changes made by time, contradictions and thousands of focused people can, with a common social purpose, change the world.

Supplication is defined as 'a humble and sincere appeal to somebody who has the power to grant a request'. Supplication begins with conditioning to worship. Theologians have described worship as 'a feeling of absolute dependence' or an 'essence of authority and obedience'. Training starts young with demonstrations of kneeling and begging before images of a celestial royalty. This behaviour is reinforced and assumes an air of normality when the child observes his or her entire social network behaving in a similar fashion. In the middle of rituals with flickering candles, incense, solemn music and words, it would take a brave child to step forward and proclaim, 'The emperor has no clothes'. The questioning child would be quickly coerced into seeing what fine clothes the emperor wore. For such behaviour would be dangerous inside a china shop of fragile beliefs. With such a nullification of self-confidence, the metaphorical and real cap is tipped to landlord, banker and bond holder, international corporations and the lure of consumerism. Supplication to all powerful gods to whom we grant gifts and worship, is perfect conditioning for the acceptance of the most powerful heads of corporate governance. With awe and respect for their vast wealth and power the conditioned will kneel and beg that they may be granted leave to enrich and admire them. The trained supplicant, will for life be looking up to the 'they' who might give a blessing, protection or work, *the poverty of philosophy* deepens.

The transmission of belief is aided by sexual selection. Studies show that the choice of sexual mates is strongly influenced by religious and cultural compatibility. In replication, the instinct to pass one's genes into a safe future is paramount. For a devout believer, while fiscal security might be important, more so, would be the child's religion and place in heaven. It is likely to be a more significant selection criterion than appearances or money and highlights a philosophical phenomenon which manifests itself in different ways. Imagine a situation where the poorer Catholic girl was to marry the Protestant man of means. A droll contradiction between fiscal advantage and religious threat was solved by a pragmatic church issuing a decree ensuring that all offspring were brought up as Catholics. In such situations it is more common for the less dogmatic person to change religion, to gain the favours of the more dogmatic. Likewise it is more common for a person of no religion to marry in a religious service. In all instances the least devout or the most rational will give way to the most devout. For the devout will be utterly convinced of their position within the world. One who is less convinced of a religious position is likely to be more open and tolerant and likewise with the non-theist, the real comforts of the sexual relationship will far outweigh vague worries of the next life and the spirit world.

It is feasible that the belief engine could, in each subsequent replication, become more exaggerated. Irrational belief systems in humans could be seen as militating against survival. But like the brilliant burdens of some birds they might have some other explanation – fashion. The female, African long-tailed widowbird males' tails are 20" long. Biologist, Malte Anderson cut the tails of nine males to 6" long and glued the parts to another nine male birds so their tails were now 30" long. The males with the lengthened tail attracted four times more mates. Many traits that enhance sexual selection are quite arbitrary and a species can get away with them if they do not endanger its survival. The sexual selection model might explain some religions success. A strong religious ethic in society can stimulate a stampede towards it. But there is a point when the magnificence of a peacock's tail becomes an encumbrance, a bar to survival. Likewise when belief systems are an encumbrance to social progress, the balance tips, it now seems to be swinging in the other direction. This is indicated by the gathering momentum of non-religious, life ceremonies. That impetus may accelerate as sexual selection might wish to see the future of one's genes in a more socially normal and advantageous science-based environment. The intellectual challenge is perhaps no longer confrontations with a declining religion, but to lay the foundations for a more stable moral society without it.

When science and religion confront each other, the religious will argue with biblical and theoretical certainty, the degree of passion proportional to the depth of belief. Such conviction develops an impulse to impose that religious vision on the population at large, be it a Catholic state or sharia law. The scientific thinker will never be so certain, understanding that offered evidence is true in varying levels of probability. Science is anti-dogmatic, its nature is scepticism and doubt and all branches of science are under constant research, review and knowledge upgrade. This often gives the impression that the rational community is weaker, less sure and capitulates to the certainty of religion, a perception that is neither good for science or society. If science does not defend rational argument against dogma there are risks to the quality of education and even to political freedom. Hopefully, the confidence of the scientific and rational community will mature into a greater involvement with philosophy and the economic and social order.

Apart from the 'selfish' instinct for survival pertaining to an individual, society needs a guiding philosophy for its collective survival and welfare.

The laws and power structures of any social group are determined by its relationship with production, which in turn determines its ethos and philosophy. If it were an egalitarian society, its ethos would reflect that social reality and be structured to maintain it. Likewise in an exploitative society the social ethos reflects and objectively organises society and its power to maintain the gained wealth. The materialist reality determines the ideas, not the other way around.

In history petite, the male could hunt faster than the pregnant female. The better-armed hunter became the most effective protector, even if not necessarily the better provider. The effective protector became the leader, whose importance grew with the advent of farming and stored surplus, two developments crucial to the emergence of exploitation. An adjacent tribe might consider it easier to steal the surplus of another group, rather than gather its own. The proverb of "political power comes from the barrel of a gun" or perhaps in this case the point of a spear, came of age, for who now within the tribe could oppose the armed protector, who became the owner - the first protection racket. When power consolidated and concepts of private property emerged, leaders for the first time had wealth to transfer to their progeny. The leader wanted to guarantee that he was the father of a particular child; this ensured that the sexual life of the female had to be controlled. Thus emerged the sequence of social structures we are now familiar with; private property, the family and the state. Stitched into these pyramidal power structures of the tribe and state were the justifying belief systems, with similar pyramidal power structures - one a perfect mirror of the other. The materialist reality merged and created a reinforcing spirit world, generating rituals, symbols and pageantry which flourished like a peacock's tail. This became the philosophy and culture of the group, tribe or kingdom to be handed on as tradition, consolidated and moulded by each historical period, the precursor of all our present ethics and philosophy.

Rapidly changing science-based society has outpaced the static nature of its theologically based ethics, an ethos that is now dysfunctional, this disconnection from the reality of life, has resulted in a moral freefall. The state has been racked by scandals. Politics, religion, the civil service, banks, regulators and finance houses have provided thousands of examples of corruption, theft and pure stupidity. This has been more than adequately highlighted on a daily basis over the past years. The religious ethos, apart from its own internal scandals, purported to be the guiding light in Ireland for over a century had been the moral educator to all of the perpetrators of corruption and collapse. By any criteria it can clearly be seen to have failed. While the dysfunctional situation enriched a few, pressures are building for change. In philosophical terms the momentum of progress now clashes with the inertia of the status quo.

As a science-centred existence penetrates the collective consciousness, the church retreats from its god-centred morality. To regain ground, the church inters Old Testament gods and emphasises a more human-based morality. Some sections of the church are sliding towards humanism and are looking for allies. In the conflict between science and religion, a few scientists, who may see more at stake than belief, spring forth as apologists? They propose a non-overlapping magisteria, contending that science and religion occupy completely separate spheres. The implication being that one can be a fully grounded scientist, accepting all the methodologies and conclusions that entails and at the same time be religious and accept its conclusions. This raises preposterous contradictions. The foundation document of Christianity, the Bible, both new and old Testament, is packed with unverifiable statements that contradict the laws of science, resurrections, ascensions, miracles, hierarchies of angels and a world made in six days. If such were to be accepted by science, then any basis for morality and the grounding of a society on human well-being would be challenged. For these allow that moral precepts can emanate from the gods, it allows philosophies which misrepresent the origins of the cosmos, earth and man. It allows the branding and division of children from birth, into Protestant, Catholic, Muslim, and Jew. Rational thinkers such as scientists should be the bastion against such viewpoints and provide the basis for the liberation of children's minds and humanity. Such confusion and ignorance serve the interests of the status quo, but then perhaps some scientists do not oppose the status quo and are in fact beneficiaries. But enough do and like the palaeontologists hammer chipping away, uncovering fossil evidence, so too shall the radar of reason penetrate these obscuring fogs. Science and religion are incompatible and to argue otherwise is to misrepresent the foundations of science and ultimately defend the existing order. However the battle between science and religion, while it might provide stimulating intellectual jousting, is a side issue. The focus of philosophy and action must remain on the well-being of our species.

Consumerism, mindless non-stop entertainment and encouragement of instant gratification increase to fill the vacuums created by collapsing beliefs. The brand icons of the shopping mall overtake the plaster icons of the church and the worship of terrestrial celebrity supersedes the celestial. Pressure to consume and the provision of credit coupled with the get rich quick Lotto mentality, all are supported and encouraged by media and state. The whole display is ugly, alienating and damaging to the human spirit. Consumerism linked to status enhancement and a corruption of the replication instinct grows, it dazzles and impoverishes. The Lotto is encouraged by the state and media as a lure to the mathematically challenged to spend hundreds of euro's, saying 'It could be you'. It is not just the low odds, about one in five million, but the poverty of values it engenders. For the state, selling the spell of instant riches is an easier and more diversionary task than building a decent society.

A great deal of happiness and well–being comes from the perception and degree of control we have over our lives. The implication is that in production it is only the owner of enterprise, the entrepreneur, who can have that degree of fulfilment. As a business expands, so does the number of employees who become more alienated as they move further from any sense of control. A savvy owner will pack the company with inspirational speakers and management consultants whose job is to make every employee feel ownership and involvement even to the day of their firing. The challenge for the reduction of alienation in enterprises is to enhance perceived ownership with real responsibility while maintaining remuneration and rewards in proportion to responsibility and innovation.

Professional philosophy as spoken in universities appears as an abstract concept, broken into fragments such as metaphysics, logic, ethics and mainly studied for its own sake with little evidence of application. The musings of academics appear to guide a disconnected philosophy around in circles, engaging in the production of internal papers and lectures almost for their own sake. They have become so unconnected that they could accept a school of theology in their midst without notice or objection. Many engagements with professional philosophers are trying affairs of nihilism leaving one gasping for air while drowning in a sea of cynicism. As presently constituted, they are divorced from any goal of social well-being, for that is not a discernible role of the university. It is understandable why so many bright young lecturers become disillusioned. Many, perhaps as an intellectual defence mechanism, appear to favour fields of philosophy, questioning whether they exist at all. This negation of existence as contained in the saying "all is imagination" can be of course settled by tossing a brick at the proposer [metaphorically of course]. The laws of mass, force and gravity immediately come into play and the proposer has no choice but to sue for material injury, thus rather spoiling the original case, or perhaps sticking to their guns, stating that the pain and blood are but figments of imagination. This disconnection has a negative effect on building a national philosophy, for as soon as it is mentioned, people reach for the off button. For philosophy to regain relevance it must transparently deal with matters pertaining to everyday life. But again like some scientists, perhaps some philosophers have no objective interest in social progress as it may be in their interests to keep this vital discourse irrelevant.

Other manifestations of philosophy such as cultural relativism can set one coughing on philosophical smoke. Here again, it is not a harmless enterprise. The wizards of smoke and mirrors can throw doubt on definitions, the relevance of human well-being and turn rational opinions into a fog. The argument goes that if you impose your narrow view of what is right and wrong within another's culture, it is but a western cultural judgement and is an act of arrogant imperialism. But a philosophy based on the human well-being, asks how fares the individual experiencing the genital mutilation, the forced marriage and the honour killing. How fares the well-being of the society in which these practices pertain? Over 3,000 girls have been subject to the illegal and foul practice of genital mutilation in Ireland, without a single prosecution. Some women who have been subjected to these practices condone them, but such a response can do nothing except prove the power of social conditioning. Would society accept the consent of the victims in slavery or underage sex? One can, with sadness, accept such statements of compliance, if it can be demonstrated that no sanctions had been placed on the participants. The answer must be to break the cycle of inherited beliefs and practices and through the actions of international human empathy. A unified compulsory secular education system subjecting inherited beliefs to transparent critical examination would ameliorate this problem.

A social philosophy not grounded in the well-being of the majority or based on scientific thinking profoundly affects every aspect of society. However, a characteristic of nature and its resulting ideas are that they are subject to dialectics, laws of change both quantitative and qualitative.

Over human history, many ideas and practices which appeared to be written in stone such as slavery, feudalism and the death penalty have changed, for the better. If the church which claimed to be immutable has been changing dramatically, then all the aspects of commerce and governance are capable of being changed in an equally dramatic fashion.

Morality has been hijacked and corrupted by the church through celestial definitions of good and evil. Imagine a father allowing his children play in the garden with all sorts of tempting toys, then instructing that one of the toys not be touched but, being bright, curious children, they do. For punishment they are banished into the wilderness of hardship by the father who places a curse on them, their children and grandchildren and on down the generations in perpetuity, that they live in shame and sin. The father reappears with a list of commandments on, amongst other things, how he is to be adored. If his children err, he will banish them to a hideous fire pit where they will be tortured for countless billions of years. But then god changed his mind and as the bible says, 'sent his only begotten Son into the world that we might live through him'. Thus by using a surrogate angle to place his sperm in a virgin, he had a son. This son Jesus has to endure ghastly torture and a death by crucifixion, so that the father will gain enough satisfaction for the wrongs done by his other children playing in that garden hundreds of generations before. Whoever of the world's people hear of the crucified son and carry out his wishes might be allowed into his heaven when they die, there they can sing his praises forever. This story is the foundation of current philosophy and morality; it is therefore not surprising that both are dysfunctional. These stories became the holy books, they reflected the moral ethos of the time, a slave society where human empathy was at a very low level. However a story, purporting to be the truth repeated often enough for long enough becomes to many, a truth. If the imaginary words of an imaginary god, were now to be drafted in a contemporary holy book, it would be a happier affair. For any normal, sane woman or man picked at random on the street now possess a higher human empathy and moral code, one which would be reflected by such a manuscript.

Without conscious humans there is no morality; for morality, does not exist without its perception by us sentient beings, it is only from a relative viewpoint can we understand good and evil, happiness and pain. Can one conceive of a situation where good and evil are not linked to happiness and pain and happiness and pain linked to well-being of a cognisant human. If on the other hand, good and evil are linked to a spiritual, moral law, say a law of a god or that of some holy book, they can then be construed to mean anything. What possible harm could arise by taking a god's name in vain? None to god, for, even if he did exist, surely such an amazing creator of the cosmos would exist on a level well above what it takes to be so easily insulted. But one could do harm by taking the 'lord's' name in vain deliberately in front of a devout believer, one would not have hurt a god but a conscious human who can be wounded related to the depth of their belief. In such a situation morality can be judged by the depth of the pain given. Defining evil as pain and misery, can give a clear spectrum for judging morality. Let us envisage the very worst situation, a starving family, cold and wet without shelter, in a war, watching their children dying. If such were to happen on Earth, and it unfortunately does, then it would be an immoral act of humanity. Any mitigation of that misery would be a measurable improvement and a moral act of humanity. First if they were taken to a place of safety, then made warm and dry, then medically treated, housed, given work, education, hope and a secure future. Every step towards the improved well-being of that family by an individual or society is a morally quantifiable act.

> 'You must acknowledge no god but me, - But they worshiped Baal, they will be killed....their little ones dashed to death against the ground, their pregnant women ripped open by swords' [Hosea 13:4:16]

Where there is no understanding of why gods emerged, total belief in the instructions of that god is the morality. The strength of these beliefs can become hysteria and overcome natural human empathy. Morality then becomes the twisted apparatus of that belief. When Christianity was dominant, the tortures devised by the brothers of the inquisition the Dominicans and Franciscans, to extract confessions of heresy, and the witch burning phenomenon, demonstrated the distance between faith-based morality and human empathy. Currently, driven by similar demons, the Shia sect of Islam, suicide bombs a mosque of the Sunni sect killing dozens, maiming hundreds. The next day the reverse happens. Isis are so morally confident in the instructions of the Koran to kill infidels, they behead them on video. In societies where the honour of the family is perceived as vested in women, it is moral that the subjugation of woman is enforced with mutilation, flogging and stoning. When the Hindu, Buddhist, Muslim and Jew, Catholic and Protestant are convinced of the righteousness of their belief, other gods and ways are perceived blasphemous. When such beliefs, which more often than not spring from oppression, reach a certain level of intensity, they overcome the natural empathy to fellow man and the killings themselves become a moral duty.

In every court house in Ireland, those giving evidence are asked to swear on the Bible. The alternative is to affirm, however, an implication emerges that somehow the evidence might contain a lesser truth. At present, there is no alternative for either judges or the President taking office, but to swear religious oaths. A statistical average, based on the number of non-religious people, would imply that a similar percentage of judges, swearing the religious oath, must be lying which is a poor start for an office supposedly based on truth. If judges were given a choice of a religious or secular affirmation, it could be held as prejudicial in some cases. The simple solution is a singular, secular oath, more in line with the concept of a republic. The Bible is not studied by Irish Catholics comprehensively; the church felt it would be better if the clergy would interpret it on their behalf, one can understand why. Nevertheless it is the core foundation document of the Christian churches; it is their Achilles heel which will fester as human empathy grows.

As the theologies of religion divide mankind into fractious bundles, so too can nationalism. Over the last century, economic and social reformers repeatedly dreamed that international solidarity amongst workers could overcome the divisions of nationalism and religion. They saw in a general way how Catholicism was linked with feudalism and Protestantism with capitalism, both providing a necessary supplication within the nation state, while socialism was perceived to be international and secular. But time and time again kings and kaisers, captains of industry - in particular the arms industry- priests and pastors called on young men to perform their patriotic duty. With all participants claiming that god was on their side, the years of careful training in supplication, of kneeling to kings of heaven and earth paid dividends. Dreams of international working class solidarity were shattered as the tricked and the trained, poured out of the trenches and slaughtered each other in their millions. They did so in the cause of greed and the expansion of capital. The green shoots of empathy had been wrenched from their simple roots in the welfare of human kind into the illusionary morality of service to king, country and god. In our own fair land the shadow of such fractious hatred lies barely buried.

References to how a country thinks or acts must never be taken at face value, but be analysed in the light of who benefits? The interests of a country or state as expressed are but an illusion, there are no unified interests of a state. It is in the subjective interest of the ruling elite and the objective interest of capital, assisted by media, church and education to sway the majority to dreams of a false national unity, to work hard for the good of the country, or fight for its expansion and glory. So often, mankind has seen how remote from glory the endless white crosses and the anguish of the maimed are. Even in victory how miserable have been the gains to the sacrificing civilians and soldiers, but whether in victory or defeat how little affected has been the situation of the ruling class. While we live, we have empathy, understanding, sympathy, compassion, responsiveness, all expressions of the same word, all slightly different ways of saying morality. Without us there is no morality, our existence as humans insists that we consciously live it, encourage and apply it. Only sentient beings like us can turn 'the poverty of philosophy' into riches.

CHAPTER 6   You Believe in Nothing!

On our voyage through life, subject to circumstance, we have an option to make the best or otherwise of our time alive, there are no obligations either way. Responsibility and care for our children, partners, parents and humankind is our greatest possibility of happiness. Involvement in the sciences, arts, literature, and the intellect grant our greatest satisfaction. Engagement with the countless challenges of the great outdoors, the sea and mountain, active participation in sport, rather than observation, contribute to our joy. Surviving as a tiny cog in the huge productive and consuming wheel of humanity is how we will spend most of our lives. It is this engagement and how we respond to it that more than anything else establishes the contribution we make to humanity and to ourselves. Our inherited belief systems, which we shall accept intact or modify, will determine how we view and live that life. In my own case, many of my inherited beliefs shattered after a short engagement with real life. I was left drifting in a void, like some bewildered player wandering the pitch after scoring an own-goal; the side-lines and stands were occupied by confident religious spectators chanting 'you believe in nothing'.

At St. Marx cemetery in Vienna, on December 5th 1791 a corpse was buried in an unmarked grave. A gravedigger may have commented "another wasted life" and wondered who that 35-year-old man was? It was Amadeus Mozart and hundreds of years later our lives are consistently enhanced by his legacy. The riches of such human endeavours have plied us high with art in a thousand galleries, magnificent symphonic works and architecture of such exquisiteness as to chill the spine and stir the senses. Some might claim that these works were inspired by belief in gods but, like the gods themselves, all are the product of human genius in mind and hand. The belief that I am part of that human claim is richness itself.

As a teenager, I was fascinated by big questions, such as: Where did we come from? Why are we here? Where are we going? It troubled me that children were born with original sin and needed to be redeemed and if they died without baptism would suffer. Inherited guilt, connected with ridiculous explanations of a god's prohibitions on apples - an analogy for knowledge – was confusing. When concepts of everlasting hellfire were shouted by demented preachers at retreats, I retreated. The ideas, all of them, were intellectually dismal and morally repugnant. The confusion of inherited belief became untenable when I realised that almost any human had a far higher level of morality than the gods. It took many more years to figure out that religion was but a mask and mentor for another force.

At that time of separation from Catholicism, I perceived inherited religion as somehow akin to processing a sacred scroll with detachable sheets, each one representing an article of faith, a sacrifice or sacrament, a heaven or hell, a part of the complex story of creation. As each sheet was examined and failed to withstand the simplest reasoning, it was reluctantly discarded. Soon the core was reached and found to be empty, the whole moral and belief edifice which had been carefully built in and around me collapsed. Like an ocean sailor without compass or chart, one had to look for guidance elsewhere, to logic, reason and the stars. With a profound sense of betrayal at having received such a fragile set of beliefs, I started out on what was initially a lonely search for new and more substantial structures of morality.

In my late teens, I worked my summers in London and as a student of architecture spent many days roaming buildings of note, learning, musing and sketching. One morning, wandering the great city alone, I entered one of the many churches designed by Christopher Wren. With cognisance of when it was built, I marvelled at the simplicity and beauty of the structure, detailing and space. It appeared deserted; I sat in contemplation, on the overhead balcony was the sound of someone shuffling papers. Suddenly, like a tidal wave breaking on a shore, the space overflowed with magnificent sound. The 'somebody' on the balcony was playing a most powerful organ and playing it wonderfully. It was Bach's Toccata and Fugue in D minor that reverberated through the space. I was transfixed and rendered deeply emotional at the beauty and wonder of it all. Was this some great celestial sign?

Indeed it was a revelation and a comprehension which has lived with me since. The church had been designed by a great architect and had been built by dozens of highly skilled craftsmen; so had the organ. The music had been written by a genius and played by a brilliant musician. The stone materials had been quarried and cut, the timbers felled, milled and all delivered by countless hands. Every participant who contributed to that moment of euphoric experience from the material manifestation of the building to the unseen musician, represented the remarkable skills of our species. The design of the magnificent church, the writing of the sublime music and the creation of the underlying motivational god represented the imagination of humankind in its quest for answers. Drifting out of the building deeply enriched, instilled with an ownership of everything seen, heard and experienced, I was at one with the world. A base had been established from which to cast about and search for more intellectual secure positions. This quest would be protracted and whatever position was adopted it would require to be strongly based. As an atheist about to return to a profoundly Catholic society, the walls of my citadel would need to withstand a long-time battering.

The question or charge from the- 'you believe in nothing' point of view - was and is still made. Initially, my answers were weak for the first response on leaving a religion is not one of belief, but disbelief. The process is akin to moving house, cleaning out shelves and attics of belief files, inherited and accumulated over a lifetime, examining and keeping interesting sections, discarding the rest. The beliefs one is sending to the trash-can are based on texts and traditions built up over thousands of years and are not disposed of lightly or without emotion. Another problem was family, relations and community who were solidly Catholic. One had no ambition to cause hurt to parents, siblings or friends. The dilemma was that one could go on pretending to believe and live life as a lie or 'to one's own self be true' and face the consequences. But hurt there was, for an idea such as a specific religion which has the tenacity of a viral infection is very difficult to dislodge and is immune to reason, for what has been accumulated without reason cannot be dislodged with reason. Religious belief occupies a unique place in society where an attack on the idea of it is perceived as an attack on the person holding that idea. So, while threading as softly as possible on others' dreams, there was no choice but to abandon delusion and seek a more substantial world of beliefs elsewhere. Bertrand Russell's *Education and the Social Order* 1932, was the first book I read to suggest foundations, followed by Engels's *The Origins of Private Property the Family and the State* 1884, Errica Malatesta, collected works, the difficult Karl Marx and so on infinitem. Reading novels of Joyce, Behan, Orwell and Lawrence continued the awakening as did encounters with the liberated girls of London. Life was indeed beginning to show promise.

As a student in dull, sometimes violent, oppressive mills that were primary and secondary schools of the '50s and '60s, I hovered around the B league, with truncated ambition and similar test scores. Outside school was a different and far more creative life of building things and exploring. For five summers, I was tolerated by wonderful relations to live on their farm at Mournabbey, a time packed with real, hands-on education. Studying architecture in the Cork School of Art changed my perceptions and standing in education, I discovered that I could think in many dimensions and construction was my forte. I thrived. For the first time in 14 years, formal learning was a joy. The physical atmosphere of the school played a large part in this new-found euphoria. The studios were on the third floor and accessed through galleries packed with art and sculpture. My memories are of sunlight flooding the sweeping stairway and halls, with hundreds of enchanting works enriching my every day, their essence etched into my core.

The lecturers were young and brimmed with passion. If only all formal education could be such. I spent summers in London working to earn money for fees and lighten the burden on my parents, it was an exciting time. London provided copious intellectual stimulation and liberation. This was intensified by action as theory and practice mixed with participation in protests against the apartheid regime in South Africa, the Vietnam War and civil rights issues in Northern Ireland. Involvement with people ranging from the London anarchists, the Anti-Apartheid and Northern Ireland civil rights movement - which unfortunately on the brink of success, was subverted by a divisive militant, nationalism. Overall, the period added up to an intellectually liberating mix. Conversations seldom strayed from politics, economics, religion, sex or the next demonstration to liberate the world.

Out of this burbling amalgam of ideas and action surfaced the bones of a new way of looking at politics, economics religion and the world. The important proviso was to maintain and indeed intensify critical analysis on all the ideas and propositions now knocking on my mind. Never again would some unexamined inheritance or virus penetrate and lodge behind my firewall of reason. A critical discovery at that time was my assumption that religion was the central enemy of reason and the main culprit in man's inhumanity to man; it was not. The main problem lay in economic relations, religion was only its mask and mentor, its first line of defence with a role to ambush reason and promulgate supplication. The vast majority of people do not have ownership or access to the means of production except by selling time and effort. This arrangement is at the core of gross inequalities in wealth, health and the well-being of the world's people. The concentration of power by corporate capitalism becomes the fuel of war and terror. It is at the core of the 'tragedy of the commons' [see chapter 12] now magnified to threaten the future of humankind. It is at the heart of the theft of humanity's natural morality, it is the sponsor of religion which provides its ideological justification.

In a community where religion, believers and theists were the majority, the simplest definition of someone who stepped away from the unanimity was a non-believer, an atheist. However being defined by a negative has a negative connotation. The term humanist is a more positive classification; it's interesting antonym being a godist with a belief in godism. A humanist is a materialist who believes, matter and energy came first; humans evolved and are central, they created ideas, values, and form morality. Catholics are required to simply believe in a list of articles of faith. It is on this point that humanists often appear less sure in argument than their religious opposites, for religious people, at least in the past, came across as one hundred percent certain, whereas wise atheists will say they are atheists only insofar as they are awaiting evidence to the contrary.

There is an implication that spirituality is not perceived within an atheist perspective. Whilst difficult to define in scientific terms, spirituality should be repossessed by the rational, as the concept expresses fine values of sublime thought, music and art in its many forms. Can spirituality be used to describe the feelings which emerge at night 1,000 miles from land, running under full sail before a warm trade wind, the sea is easy, a pod of dolphins streaking sheets of phosphorescence leap with exuberance around the boat. Inter-galactic debris flashes burning green across a wondrous southern cross. While these moments of sublime and extravagant beauty occur all the time without being seen, it is only when observed by conscious human eyes that the wonder and beauty can be comprehended, stored and transferred. Such conscious wonder, moments of spirituality based on the magic of reality, cannot be outside the narrative of the rationalist.

A combination analogous to merging spirituality and the hypothesis of communism is an orchestral symphony. Conditions had to be right to have a composer with sufficient talent and resources to write a full symphony. Blending separate scores for each instrument requires a genius with vision, themes and passion. A typical orchestra would consist of stringed, wind, woodwind and percussion - a total of 23 different instruments and enough top-class musicians to play them. Artisans would be required skilled in the production of each specific instrument, backed up by hundreds of others workers from those logging and milling the timbers to miners, metallurgists and haulers, sailors and port workers. The concert hall requires an architect, a builder and hundreds of skilled trades to construct from foundations to roof. Each musician must be accomplished in reading music and working in unison. Finally the conductor tips the baton, and the perfection of Beethoven's 7th Symphony reverberates through the hall. The moment is sublime - a spirituality based on human cooperation at its highest levels. I believe all such moments and achievements of mankind should be looked at in a similar light.

When a magnificent, jet-powered aircraft thunders down a runway and becomes airborne, taking its passengers to some dream destination, it embodies the millions of international workers that cooperated - from each according to their ability - to make that moment happen. It is important to remember that every action we engage with and every product we acquire emanates from the minds and the work of that collective human community. When people feel they are an active part of this vast network, this worldwide web of co-operation, they engage with the self-esteem of being human. That self-esteem would be greatly enhanced with a transparent knowledge of real ownership and responsibility.

I believe, living without a sense of ownership and involvement economically or philosophically conveys a lack of meaning to the individual. It is the root of alienation leading to frustration and despair. A disconnection from day to day production and responsibility diminishes self-respect; it separates the person from history, evolutionary time and the cosmos. The alienation of the wage earner arises where the only involvement with production is selling the actions of his or her mind, body and time in return for money. That alienation deepens even further for the many that never get to sell their labour or time and have to sit on the sideline of society surviving on welfare.

Previously, religion gave solace in the idea that the next life will be of bliss and the poor will achieve equality with the rich. That solace is now for sale as a pervading consumerism. The brand which used to be a specific religion is now as likely to be a fashion house or a football team. The idol which used to be a saint is now as likely to be a celebrity, a star of sport, fashion or screen. The dispossessed who were previously awed by the display of garish garments, smoke, bells and chanting at cathedrals are now enthralled by displays of garish goods at the shopping malls which have become the temples of worship. They are organised to be stagnant spectators of TV, films and sport, a participant only in production and consumption. The holy books are now the celebrity and fashion magazines, read and followed as ferociously as the Koran or Bible. While the level of production and consumption has improved the material well-being and lifespan of most people, the majority are not players in the main economic field; they are but passive and alienated operatives or consumers.

I believe that all people through education and a participatory social order can be the writers of scripts, players of sport, designers and producers. Individuals' involvement at many levels in both theory and practice, is an essential part of our social-animal existence, the opposite, is a mind packed with absorbed dysfunctional philosophies. When these philosophies come with a discouragement of enquiry it diminishes the possibilities of ever achieving reason, for what is not used, ceases to function. Such intellectual lethargy allows the dominance of beliefs, as diverse as astrology to Mormonism, and the rape of the social order by bondsmen, bankers and financial instruments. The weakened intellect is easy prey to the predator.

On February 22, 1943, a 21-year-old, German student was brought to the guillotine in Munich and beheaded. Her name was Sophie Scholl. She had been part of the 'White Rose' non-violent, resistance group in Nazi Germany and was convicted of high treason for distributing anti-war leaflets at the University of Munich with her brother. Her legacy and that of her group - five of whom were executed, - is a demonstration of exemplary courage and of social dissent at a time of violent repression, censorship, and conformist pressure. While the courage and death of Sophie Scholl and her compatriots did not change anything in Germany at the time, it highlights the fact that thousands of people opposed the regime, many paying with their lives. These acts of resistance in the most hopeless of situations give a desperately needed moral boost and pride, not just to the people of Germany who had lost so much by a wretched mistake in politics and philosophy, but to all of humankind.

On December 1, 1955 Rosa Parks a 42-year-old African-American woman boarded the Montgomery City bus. She sat behind the seats reserved for whites, when all of these were occupied, a white man entered the bus. The driver insisted that Rosa Parks give up her seat, her decision to quietly refuse initiated a new era in a quest for freedom and equality. She was arrested and protests and boycotts spread across the states. Bus segregation was soon abolished and Black pride flourished; all human pride advanced. Thousands of courageous acts were sparked by a single one. Courage is required by an individual when social values or a conformist consensus is apparent and an objection becomes necessary.

We can be in possession of all the correct, philosophical, economic and moral arguments but if we do not have the courage to live or at least express them, then our social contribution diminishes. Our lives expand or contract relative to the amount of courage we possess. Courage does not signify an absence of fear, it is our ability to overcome that fear which is essential to living a full life. For a person to move even marginally outside a social consensus requires courage. In company of friends and acquaintances who are using derogatory terms against fellow humans such as, niggers, queers, knackers, one takes a social risk to launch an intervention and introduce a polite and then perhaps a not so polite objection. The reaction will depend on the proportion of backers to the objection within the group, a majority may retain prejudice and the objector risks being isolated and perhaps humiliated. If however, even a small degree of support is offered, then the point is usually won as the majority who have never thought about the issue will now more likely concur with the intervention and the problem will not arise again in that company. The most prejudiced loser may then require being 'face saved' to maintain group harmony and avoid developing an enemy. Good humour and empathic testimony such as: the charming helpful man who turned out to be gay but became a close friend of the homophobic neighbour, the travellers who gave a lift when hitching and were great fun, the black man who welcomed you to Africa when you were the only white in town, will usually win the day. If that fails, simple questions to the prejudiced on why they are so fearful or what formed their opinions can often yield positive results.

Fear of ridicule or loss of status particularly amongst one's peers is widespread and can be paralysing, becoming a barrier to innovative actions or radical ideas. The only guarantee against such failure or ridicule is a mental and physical paralysis - see nothing, hear nothing, do nothing. To stand up for one's beliefs, be they based on reason or not, or to build any entity outside the norm is to take a risk and carries the possibility of failure. One should learn by harnessing the example of entrepreneurs, who argue that if an enterprise should fail, analyse why, learn the lessons and start over again. This approach is applicable to all ideas, activities and enterprises. Fear needs to be looked at objectively to understand its sources for once they are understood, it is easier overcome and easier to encourage children to grapple with it. When little fears are overcome then bigger and bigger fears can be challenged. It is essential that during their formative years children are allowed to engage with danger-not life threatening, but challenging, such as climbing walls, swimming and overcoming all sorts of obstacles. Likewise on a more emotional front performing, singing, reciting poetry, all carry the risk of embarrassment, but are an essential contributor to confidence and having the courage to fail.

Ocean sailing and heavy weather often prompt questions on fear and how best it is overcome. The answer is building confidence; one ensures that the boat and its crew are operational and survival actions are well tested and rehearsed. When conditions deteriorate and one is either hove-to or running off under bare poles, fear and confidence is in balance. The revelation that one has fear but still proceeds is a liberation to others who wish to sail offshore and to know that fear grips and not just in the midst of a gale a thousand miles from land. Fear can kick in leaving harbour, but once the sight of land dims and the journey is underway, confidence builds and fear fades. Actors will often admit to debilitating stage fright before entrance but having rehearsed and polished their performance over and over, once they commence they are at home on stage. Knowing that fear is part of our human make-up, our defensive mechanism and none of us are unique in suffering from it, is reassuring. Fear must be analysed and faced down to achieve worthwhile goals in life, be they physical challenges at the limit of our courage or philosophical ones which lie outside the social consensus.

Cognisant creatures like us also have a pervading fear of mortality. As we become aware of existence, we also become aware of our aging and death. While we have witnessed it, we have never experienced it, it is the unknown and we fear the unknown. This is exploited by oppressive systems and their ideological apologists. It is exaggerated by some who find that death itself is not enough of a threat; images of everlasting tortures by fire are added to compound the misery, all of which may be avoided if you obey the demands of the god-appointed leaders. Science has to some extent pushed back the fear and time of death; it has managed to reduce and almost eliminate pain. Combined with rational thinking these advances can reduce the power of the fear mongers. Surveys have shown that people in the least religious countries in the world, such as Scandinavia, showed less fear of death than people in more religious countries.

Every night our consciousness shuts down as we sleep, except for some mad file sorting within dream sequences. The only additional factor in death is that the body operating systems shuts down as well; however in deep sleep we would hardly notice that. So the factors that give cause for genuine fear are physical pain and leaving our loved ones. Pain which is chemical can in the main be managed with chemicals; bidding farewell to loved ones is mitigated by sharing the loss with others whom we love, ensuring the worth of our intellectual legacy and knowing we have lived life to the full. But it would be fallacious in the extreme to pretend that death and parting are not a difficult time for us emotional beings.

'For freedom' is the cry of a thousand revolutions and a thousand despots. It is probably the most misused word in any language. To the person incarcerated in a dark dungeon, the definition is easy and very clear - get me out of here. To the starving family freedom is food, even if distributed within the confines of a compound. To the investor expanding assets with the purchase of labour or the manipulation of financial instruments, freedom means the ability to move capital anywhere in the world without taxes. It means the freedom of the market and not having the encumbrance of minimum wages or safety regulations. The freedom of Milton Friedman and the Washington Consensus means that where capital roams, the law and its enforcement agencies of police and military will maintain that 'free' world, at any price. Freedom means the right and ability to worship, to practice and defend religion and to ridicule reason. It also means the right to respect and defend reason and ridicule religion. Both options - religion ridiculing reason or the reverse - are perfectly acceptable as they are focused on ideas, on philosophy, but human dignity demands that the individual or group - holding these points of view - are not ridiculed.

Freedom, on an emotional level, is inimical to our humanity. It is comparable to well-being but it is not some immutable word or concept. Its definition is relative, for none of us are in fact free in any total sense. We are all controlled by thousands of internal and external stipulations as to how we live our lives. We are never free from the struggle for survival, our needs for food, fighting disease or postponing death. Our instincts for replication ensure we are never free from constantly courting, building and maintaining our status and nests. We are never free from the demands and the myriads of rules and regulations of the social order but what freedom we have gained within the intellectual and practical space available - such as political democracy - must be vociferously guarded or it will slip away. Too often we fall to timidity and flee the responsibilities of freedom. Hiding our intellect in the face of an irrational consensus is perhaps what we do most often, a safe but ultimately craven choice. Bertrand Russell once said 'man would rather undergo privation, starvation, and torture than think!' We must discard the crutches and diversions that society can provide or the comfort of a philosophy without questions for that is what makes us essentially human and free.

I believe in joining the dots of life's myriad branches to make as much sense of it as possible. I believe in enjoying the ride on board this beautiful spinning sphere as it flies through the cosmos. I travel with my genes and evolving ideas in the company of humankind and all our related species. If I can carry my intellectual cargo safely to the next harbour, enrich it as I go, and can contribute in some positive fashion to all I encounter along the way then I will not have lived in vain. When challenged along the voyage by the chant of *'you believe in nothing'*, I am left to respond with my credo.

- I believe in the book of evidence, an evolving university of knowledge accumulating from the creative and rational mind of humankind, all open to challenge and change.
- I believe we live on a beautiful spinning sphere packed with wonder and it behoves us to engage with it in every way and attempt to understand its every facet.
- I believe I am responsible for the dignity of my own intellectual and physical life, for if I am not true to myself, love myself, then, I will have little to be true to, and be unable to love others.
- I believe that a positive involvement with fellow beings and a contribution to their individual and collective well-being gives the greatest satisfaction and happiness. A belief that has led to writing this book.
- I believe that a morality based on natural human empathy and responsibilities to humanity is better founded and more secure than any based on fear and rewards for service to the gods.
- I believe we have at present an acute poverty of philosophy leading to catastrophic failures in morality and lack of

direction for society. To build a secure morality based on human empathy and the well-being of humanity is a priority.

● I believe that training children in supplication is grossly destructive to their dignity and confidence. It conditions them for a life of petitioning landlords, bankers, bondsmen and corporate capital.

● I believe our species has the imagination and capacity to negate the divisions of class, race, gender, religion and nationalism and devise economic and political systems that enhance the well-being and dignity of all human kind.

● I believe in an egalitarian, transparent social order achieved through the power of democracy extending over capital.

● I believe in the international and collective nature of production and that greed and competition cannot be the basis for a rational economic order.

● I believe that the exponential growth of our species and its consumption of finite resources are of grave concern, the resulting threat to our survival may be the catalyst to the unity of humanity.

● I believe in respecting every creature and organism on Earth with whom I share a common ancestry. While I consent with the killing and consumption of living creatures, their care and slaughter must be to the highest humane standards.

● I believe in the treasures of human endeavor and in the great riches our hearts and minds can gain from the exquisite art, architecture, literature and music that we have created.

● I believe that the love between humans can transcend the bare instincts of replication and intensify to enrich our lives.

● I believe we owe our children, a child-centered, unified secular education with critical thinking, free from the burden of unexamined traditions.

● I believe that understanding the problems and the possible solutions affecting humanity is insufficient, it is change that matters.

I believe our most precious possession to be an open mind, bereft of certainty. All beliefs must be open to change by new evidence; to be comfortable with uncertainty is the essence of a free mind.

Chapter 7   Sex, Death and Dignity

On the edge of the philosophical debate between idealism and materialism is one that concerns the nature of humanity. Are we intrinsically evil, mean, aggressive and generally nasty to one another and to nature? If so, perhaps we do require a church and state to calm the savage beast with carrot and stick, rewards of heavens or threats of hell. However, we are neither intrinsically good nor evil, we are but an organism, a species struggling to survive and reproduce. The terms, good and evil are subjective and usually occur when one individual or group thrives at the expense of another. What is good for one might be bad for another. If for example, one group of people with a technology, such as a net, was successful at gathering fish, they would consider that good. Another group who then found all the fish gone would consider that bad. If the first group had taken all the fish deliberately, knowing the other group would now starve, that could be termed evil. In most cases the instincts for survival are to gather as much as possible, without planned malice or thought to the future. That, to some extent, is how the competitive market operates. At another level it becomes a tragedy when the most efficient group successfully catch all the fish, ruining not just its competitors, but the fish stock and threatening the future of the group, a scenario neither good nor bad, but just plain stupid. The forum for dealing with this, the so called 'tragedy of the commons' is dealt with later. Here we will look at how such relationships, individual and collective, affect status and dignity.

Dignity is determined by how individuals regards themselves, which in turn depends on how they perceive themselves to be regarded by society. If they feel respected by their fellows, dwell in a living space of quality, have a productive life that is rewarded then they live with well-being and dignity. Underpaid employment or none, poor accommodation and social spaces, will all conspire to disfigure dignity. How humans inter-relate as either exploiters or enduring exploitation, to a large extent, determines their status. Ownership of little or nothing in a society where such ownership is deemed to be the essence of status is fundamental. The majority without ownership of property are repressed by the social ethos of its ownership, leading to a disconnection from society, a loss of dignity and depression. Even in relatively well-paid work, when the worker has no ownership or control of what is produced, alienation arises between the worker and the product and a phenomenon of general alienation arises. This situation pertains to the majority of workers and one which grows with the concentration of capital, for whoever owns the wealth and controls the economy moulds the culture and concepts of the state. One pernicious notion is that with hard work anyone and everyone can rise to the top of the competitive economic pile. While it can occur in exceptional cases, it is akin to the 1 in an 11,000,000 chance of winning the lottery. As being materially rich is the primary way to gain status and prestige in current society, it creates a frustrating, competitive dog-eat-dog situation.

The sight of a sharp-suited man circling share prices in a financial paper or that of a drab-dressed woman standing outside a local shop scratching a tacky-coloured card, the sound of a radio calling lottery numbers even when there has been no winner, men going from public bar to bookie shop, indicates a sad dysfunctional society. The majority are trapped in their station, with economic and social mobility growing more difficult and material advancement remaining as the measure of success, frustration grows. The hope of achieving instant riches becomes an obsession, a panacea to solve all problems and provide a quick path to material success, status and dignity. However, such status and dignity, if ever thus achieved, is already tarnished, as it is at the expense of others. A social structure that basis much of its economic life on gambling in the international markets and provides hope to its alienated citizens by the encouragement of public gambling diverts large sections of its populace from the possibilities of real progress to fragile expectations. A community, robbed of an ability to fashion and control its own life, reflects this alienation in the estates, streets and districts of litter and graffiti where the dispossessed exist rather than live. Some of the more enterprising youth of these areas, deprived of alternatives, seek to emulate the prevailing economic culture by the route to wealth and status open to them - drug dealing and theft. Money can be made and the economic system of the sharp-suited banker is there to be imitated by running the street with a similar ruthless efficiency.

Mind altering substances, such as alcohol, drugs, tobacco and multifarious other combinations of pharmaceutical uppers and downers, have been with us since records began and perhaps before. The reasons we indulge are complex and varied. The sheer fun and laughter associated with getting high, escaping from the reality of poverty and mortality, overcoming shyness, physical pain or grief is a reality for all. This is not to say that in a more rational society such use and abuse would not take place, mortality, shyness and pain would still be with us. However, there are grounds to believe that the control and responsibility associated with social ownership would reduce abuse caused by alienation. The 'Rat Park' experiments by Bruce Alexander indicated that isolation and environmental conditions proved to be the main contributors to drug addiction. Rats are social animals. Isolated without stimuli in cages, they were observed to descend into depression and self-administer stupor-giving drugs with abandon. When placed in a much bigger 'rat park' in the company of others of their kind, where they had adequate food and places to build nests, breed and play, they generally avoided the drugs and got on with their lives. While people in all walks of life self-destruct on addictions, statistically it is those socially deprived with little dignity that are most at risk.

The national and international war on drugs has been, like prohibition in the United States, a failure. It has resulted in a massive expenditure on enforcement and the criminalisation of millions. While there is evidence of drug damage, it is unpredictable and in quantitive terms less damaging than smoking tobacco and appears no worse than alcohol. When a large body of people continue to use drugs, regardless of prohibitions, it gives rise to profitable cartels and criminal sub-culture. Where drugs have been allowed and issued in a clean and ordered way by society, criminal activity by both addicts and drug gangs has plummeted as has related deaths. The book, *Chasing the Scream* by Johann Hari is an intense polemic on the failure of the war on drugs and the alternatives. He argues that all addictions are mainly a flight from mental suffering. For society to achieve any substantial reduction in drug and other addictions, its focus should lie with an understanding and alleviation of that suffering. All human and animal feelings, from depression to euphoria, emanate from chemicals within the brain stimulated by external environmental factors. It has to be accepted that humans will always strive to feel good by the importation of feel-good chemicals, whether those arrive via alcohol, drugs, food, gambling, prescription uppers or buying consumer goods. All surveys and conclusions now suggest that if society wants to reduce the social problems of crime, drugs, obesity, teen pregnancy or whatever, its only course is to understand the importance of status and dignity and build a society that respects all people from the cradle to the grave. It requires the building of an egalitarian society.

Our instinct for reproduction is second only to that of survival. The forces related to reproduction and how we resolve them are a major contribution or otherwise to status and dignity. When sex and passion rear their head, most rational thinking flies out the window, for otherwise perfectly normal people are prepared to risk marriage, status, reputation and money for the life-affirming adrenaline of sex. *The Selfish Gene* by Richard Dawkins gives a comprehensive assessment of why this is so. A brilliant description of the immortal gene passing from one generation to the next, using each individual human as a temporary survival machine, driving our brain and body to reproduce and pass the gene onto a new temporary home. Like instinctive breathing and the beating of the heart, sex does not have to be taught. The gene could not take such a risk and regardless of what barriers are ranged against it, it has evolved a thousand tricks to fulfil its destiny. The fact that we now have over seven billion people on the planet endangering our collective future and environment is a testimony to the pleasure of sex, the power of the gene and its lack of foresight.

Most religious viewpoints and the Catholic Church's in particular, have little understanding of just how powerful that sex drive is. The church is a main player in formal education and in its attempted control of sexual behaviour, it has brought misery to millions and itself almost to ruin. The attempt to repress sex with prayer and threats of damnation was a hopeless task. The legacy of oppression has made it a difficult subject to discuss even among enlightened people. We are unique as a species by mostly engaging in sexual activity in private, which has to some extent further contributed to perceptions of shame and inhibition. Another source of reticence is that humanity assumes itself to be a superior species, sophisticated and far removed from all other animals, it is a perpetual shock to our collective ego that our sexual features and methods of copulation are the same. However, unlike animals, over ninety nine per cent of human sex is not for reproduction but for fun, recreation and bonding. All in all we have developed a fraught and ambiguous relationship with reproduction.

Some taboos relating to our bodies are logical, many no longer relevant. The simple expedient of walking about naked would land one in jail in almost every culture. This was not the case in some early tribal cultures or in ancient Greece, where the original Olympic male competitors participated naked. Modern examples were East Germany where beach nakedness became acceptable and widespread, as it is now on thousands of beaches throughout the world. The origins of why we wear clothes are not that easy to discern but the most likely reasons were our evolving hairlessness, protection from the cold and abrasion. The association of nakedness with sexuality may have contributed to clothes wearing for desexualising socialising and pairing, and perhaps the concealment of male arousal. Over time being clothed then became a cultural norm, bolstered by religions and law. Clothes can themselves be statements of exaggeration, availability, arousal and status. Dress codes signal group identity, from the slum garb of baggy trousers and shiny track suits to the exposed braces and power dressing of the city. Some, such as high-heel shoes, tight skirts and fascinators of female dress have become an object lesson in style, worthy of anthropological investigation. If a raised heel and tight skirt were seen as emphasising a lengthening leg and sensual bottom and deemed to increase attraction, then every additional heightening of the heel and tightening of the skirt might perhaps be deemed even more so. Leading eventually to a situation where a woman is barely able to walk in astonishingly high shoes and hobbled by a skirt, altering the image from a sensual elegance to submissive helplessness. Perhaps this is a parody on the foot binding of an older China or a form of submissive bondage at a time of falling feminine confidence and the phenomenon of 'Fifty Shades of Grey'.

Clothes are a statement of status and rank. Claimants of royal blood turn out festooned with gold braid, plumes, gilded swords and rows of tacky self-awarded medals. We see similar displays of status on bishops and popes, but as doctrinal embarrassments intensify, a greater association with the common follower is sought, thus previous ostentatious displays are diminishing. Amongst the elite of capitalism, displays of status are mainly through artefacts of high-end production; the mansion, helicopter, Lamborghini and super-yacht. All such status statements are associated to some extent with replication and the power of that infernal gene.

Difficulties in discussing sexuality have various implications such as the definition of pornography. To some a naked human is pornographic as are descriptions of sex acts. To others these may be but erotic stimulation. A more rational definition of pornography might be any sex act that portrays or requires coercion, violence or involves minors. The reduction of sexuality in conversations to crudities is a further symptom of that distortion. This is where embarrassment is covered by bombast, manifesting itself in verbiage, saturated in crude, four-letter words for organs, orientation and sex activities. Even here, the coquettish sensitivities of the author prevent such a listing.

The elements involved in sexuality are the gene pushing for constant sex with multiple progeny, the church countenancing sex but within strict parameters and only in the context of reproduction and pontificating against sexual pleasure. The advancing knowledge of science brought the worst nightmare to church and gene - contraception. For the first time people could have pleasure without pain as in the unplanned burden of pregnancy, in one stroke both the strategy of the selfish gene and that of the church were thwarted. As far as the gene is concerned a woman should never have periods, the associated pain is some form of biological punishment for not being sexually active and constantly pregnant and as far as the church is concerned the pain is for being sexually active and using contraceptives. The church and conservative elements of the state battled furiously against the availability of such knowledge outlawing anything connected with contraception. But with all the power of the gene, church and state, the pleasure principle won out. It took mass campaigns and action to slowly change the law to allow people follow their own conscience. Except for the occasional disconcerting outburst from Rome, contraception is now off the agenda.

Many live with the uncomfortable paradox, knowing their existence to be conditional on their parents having had sex, a realisation that is buried in a deep recess of the mind. Nevertheless copulation with another is at the forefront of the same mind, perhaps such contradictions are at the root of much human neurosis. The term 'protecting the innocence of children' endorses a principle that sex somehow is not innocent. This points to why gods that became man arrived via a virgin birth, so they could arrive 'pure' without any link to that 'awful sex stuff'. Thus we have to protect the innocence of the gods as well as that of the children. It was only a generation ago that the Catholic Church stopped the 'churching' of women after giving birth, considering that childbirth made a woman unholy as it resulted from sexual activity, this allowed the 'unclean' woman to re-enter the church in a 'state of grace'. Veneration of females occurs generally in the context of their virginity thereby imparting a permanent guilt on all normal women. Such distortions of sexuality have had a negative impact on the dignity of females, the repercussions of this continue to surface in revelations, from the foundation of the state to the present.

The RC Church sought a celibate clergy to maintain its property, undivided by offspring. The unfortunate men who were inducted into the priesthood as boys were supposed to maintain their celibacy by the power of prayer and perceptions of a malevolent sexuality. This pernicious poisoning of the clerical mind spread through the church with frightful results. Amongst the clergy themselves, the suppression failed, for prayer is no match for the selfish gene. It burst like boils through the suppression with disastrous results of sex scandals perpetrated against the most vulnerable. The damaged priests were responsible for arguably the gravest and most systemic human-rights violations in the history of this state. While it is important that the perpetrators are brought to justice, it is more important that the philosophical foundations, from which these distortions sprang, be brought to trial. We owe it to those who experienced rape and abuse to demonstrate that the entire moral edifice was based on false foundations.

Suppression of sex in the general population has led to widespread ignorance and unhappiness. In situations where passion exceeds reason or drink has diminished inhibitions, unprotected, irrational or forced sex takes place with the result that approximately one in every 10 pregnancies is unwanted, leading to large numbers of pregnant women travelling abroad for an abortion - a traumatic situation for everyone concerned. These numbers would be substantially reduced with a rational sex education that should address sexual fulfilment with non-penetrative sex, masturbation, contraception methods and an emphasis on the fun, sharing and joy of sex. The encouragement of open dialogue between sexually active people and throughout society would substantially reduce the incidence of unwanted pregnancies, an approach that has been proven in the more liberal societies of Scandinavia.

The arrival of a planned child is a transforming joy in life. How quickly, as parents well know, strong gender traits emerge. The child grows up, matures and in turn becomes immersed in instincts for reproduction. From puberty onwards, vast quantities of, time, energy and expense will be expended in preparing to court the opposite sex, much of which will be done unaware. Millions of clothes shops, glossy magazines, beauty salons and gyms attest to our willingness to look well and be in fashion. In music, almost every three minute jingle is about the quest for love, the implications of its loss, jealousy and love again. This complex but rather delightful instinct for sex companionship and reproduction is part of an evolutionary programme wired into the brain. There is delight in comprehending why and how it all works and enjoying this wonderful experience that we call life. The level of dignity we carry through life is greatly influenced by how we deal and exist with our fellow humans on a sexual level. While this powerful force, like most others, is neutral in neither being good or evil, it can thankfully, in the majority of cases, enhance life and well-being. However, it can also lead to oppression and fear through rape and abuse.

Science has been unable to pinpoint why an individual develops his or her sexual orientation, be it heterosexual, gay, bisexual or lesbian. Genetic, hormonal, social and cultural influences have been examined without any provable conclusions. Nature and nurture are thought to play complex roles. Generally gays do not experience having or making a choice about their sexual orientation. In a society where a historical ignorance and lack of confidence predominate on sex, individuals who do not comply with the dominant heterosexual ethos are given a hard time. Some desperately insecure Islamic countries look for the death penalty for people expressing their love of one another in a way not in accordance with some diktat. In Ireland an ignorant approach to sexuality, and particularly to preferences which lie outside the perceived norms, has led to a spate of suicides amongst teenagers. Research would suggest that up to 30% of suicides by boys are linked to their having been bullied due to sexual orientation. It highlights appalling deficiencies in our ethos and educational system, it is also our individual responsibility that in conversation, a polite but comprehensive defence is made where homophobic, racist or sectarian opinions are raised.

A unifying factor of humanity is that we are all on death row, we are just not sure of the dates. While accepting its inevitability we want to get on with our lives and push such thoughts into the background. Nevertheless it remains as a nagging inevitability. The fear of our personal death and that of loved ones has been the mainstay of most belief systems. The promise of meeting deceased parents or children in heavenly happiness are at the core of religious power. For a rationalist, the dignity with which death is approached and the manner in which the rites are conducted can be a part of one's influence and legacy. Most people, even those who believe in the wonders of heaven in an afterlife, show doubt by being in no hurry to get there, wishing instead to live into old age. However, the implications of extreme old age might be loneliness and perhaps incapacity, with one's dignity slipping away. But, like most things in life, once the issue is confronted, its fears decrease. The question is often raised 'where do you think you will go when you die?' The answer 'the same place one was for all the years before birth' might sound trite, but each one of us has experienced the reality of non-existence.

Generally we avoid referring to death face on, we use phrases like 'he passed on', 'she went to the other side', 'he went to his eternal rest', etc. All are fully understandable for the loss of a loved one can be as devastating to well-being and happiness as to be alive and in love can be euphoric. Death is the price we pay for reproduction by sex rather than division. A few billion years ago our ancestors were bacteria. They maintained that form through a vast timescale in the oceans and later on land. As an aside; when space-exploration scientists say they are looking for life on other planets, what they seek would be similar to our microbial ancestors, akin to bread mould without the bread. These primitive life forms were asexual and expanded their numbers by division. They were held back by having to constantly carry strains of retarding bacteria down through the ages. But evolution devised a system, sex, where life could start afresh each time without this historical burden. After billions of years it became the dominant form allowing the emergence of all the complex and larger life forms we now know.

This change from reproduction by division to sexual came by chance, through billions of mutations and blind alleys over as many years. It brought a system which could build new life forms by only transferring the copying instructions, the plans and specifications of DNA, through sex. This modified the problematic transfer of bacterial baggage; the new organism inherited the still necessary package of bacteria from the female side only. When a healthy AIDS-free male ejaculates into a female, the fertilising sperm and carrier fluid are bacteria-free allowing the new organism time to build resistance and become symbiotic with the strains of bacteria carried forward by the female. In our species for every unprotected sexual encounter there is a hundred to one chance a sperm will join with and fertilise a female egg in conception. The chances for any one sperm succeeding are many billions to one and to decrease the chances further, 99% of all human sex is recreational. There is, as yet, inconclusive evidence to show that during each ejaculation only 1% of sperm is for possible fertilisation while 99% is designed for killing and blocking that of other males, which if true says something very interesting about our sexual proclivities a few million years ago. During a man's life time he is likely to produce 36 billion of that 1% of potential fertilisation sperm. This is enough to father the Earth's population many times over, yet after all the possibilities, on a mean average, he is likely to father but 2.3 children. However, despite the stress of such proliferate sperm production; few would doubt that the male got the better side of replication.

It is a jolt to our self-righteous dignity when we realise that our bodies are not the single whole creature we assumed. We are host to billions of bacterial colonies living and replicating at ferocious speed within us. In fact bacterial cells outnumber human ones by ten to one. With the majority of these inhabitants we have a mutually beneficial relationship as they carry out many essential functions. We need them and they need us. But, within these internal clusters of life, total harmony does not prevail. Prey and predators exist, as in all observed life. Likewise with all that cell replacement, DNA copying, repair and replication occurring in multifarious forms, mistakes and mutations happen, resulting in bacterial and virus-related attacks from both inside and outside. All life forms have a permanent relationship with bacteria, some of which are essential to the existence of the organism. Some co-exist but others are hostile or at least parasitical enough to retard the development of that organism and a few are lethal. Generally it is not in the interests of the parasite to kill the host for that would deprive it of its own living quarters defeating its own purpose. The gene of a lethal bacterium would have found other ways of transmission, jumping rapidly from one to another of its unfortunate victims. Such might be Ebola, Spanish flu or bubonic plague, transmitted by touch, insect or air, usually assisted by coughing and multifarious other ingenious ways the gene has evolved for cross infection. Between being bullied by genes and infested with bacteria, we are truly busy bodies, organised to grow, survive, replicate, wilt and die.

The maintenance of youth and the postponement of wrinkles, aging and death is an obsession for many and is the mainstay of the cosmetic and the pharmaceutical industry. Advancing years also bring a declining ability to resist infections, such as pneumonia which, a generation ago would have resulted in death. Now, at least in wealthier countries, advances in medicine have ensured that such infections are not much more than an inconvenience. An analogy between how the biological structures operate within our human bodies and motorcars might be as follows: for a few years after a shiny new car is bought, it is polished and all the regular servicing is carried out with oil and tyre changes. For a few more years there may be slight mechanical breakdowns and parts are repaired and replaced. The rough and tumble of the roads cause dents and scratches. These are filled and sprayed to perfection in a body repair shop. Over time the mechanical parts that require replacing get larger and more expensive. Eventually when the overall, scruffy appearance of the vehicle no longer justifies repairing the dents and scratches, the ever-increasing costs for repairs and parts are no longer justifiable. The car is scrapped and a new shiny model appears.

Likewise the internal biology of our body repairs most defects, bone breaks, bumps and scratches and keeps our machine fit until reproduction and the rearing of offspring is over. After which the body repairs decline, all the parts go slowly down together - sight, fitness, muscle strength and heart. It becomes less energy-effective for the body to engage in repairs, if one critical part goes into dramatic decline, it can and will shut down the entire operation. Interventions, like a heart replacement, combined with therapy can prolong life, we have the expertise, if the patent has the cash. But no matter how good the support and interventions, once the gene's survival machine has passed its 'best by' gene transfer date, it will eventually shut down, and die. To add insult to injury, the body - that magnificent survival machine - will immediately start to be consumed by its own now unregulated bacteria and enzymes.

There is no point in a female carrying eggs, or a male - as a potential fertiliser plant - without a mechanism to bring them together. Thus evolved the complex stimulations of attraction, passion and lust. The relationships formed can, if one is lucky, become a love that lasts a lifetime, or for some, a lifetime of one night stands. The former is the preferred choice of the gene, with occasional bouts of the latter. The resulting interactions of love, jealousy and hate are the foundation of almost every song, TV soap and novel. Attraction and beauty are rooted in the hard realities of reproduction, coloured by the prevailing culture. The males belief that he is free to choose, is true only to an extent for that is not how the gene, sees it. The male's attention is directed to the younger female, as she is likely to be healthier and live longer to raise progeny. She is slim wasted, indicating she is not pregnant, with generally the skin colour and face structure of the male's mother, it worked before so it will work again. Facial and body features will be symmetrical to imply general health and will be average for that specific culture, for perfect average is perfect beauty. In the Pigmy society of Africa or Inuit of the Arctic, different survival criteria apply, and therefore, different features will be deemed attractive. Exceptions to regional or ethnic attraction are now more frequent due to global media and travel. The female responds to a male who is fit and active and will look for status in clothes, car, education and wealth as indicators of support and security for herself and her children. The age of the male is of less importance and an approaching menopause by the female may introduce a more pragmatic approach.

The industry of attraction and beauty is omnipresent; hairdressing salons, beauty parlours, and clothes boutiques abound. Promise is everywhere, spend and you will be beautiful, your life will be brighter and happier. Glossy magazines are cluttered with impossibly beautiful, air-brushed models of all sexes selling a promise of status with perfect smiles and teeth. Bodies, formed by life's' realities and junk food spend copiously to be beautiful, but often, sad frustrations spring from false promises. Fashion has existed since we were cave dwellers and will exist in the most advanced future societies, one hopes it will survive in a less exploitative mode.

A recent manifestation of sexuality is internet pornography. Exploitative of our drive for replication, it is a relatively shy industry and statistics are unreliable. About 40,000 of the top million web sites would be classed as porn and 13% of web searches would appear to be for erotic content. A recent study in the United States could not find a single college male not frequenting porn sites. Looking at porn releases dopamine, a pleasure drug enhanced by novelty, causing addiction to novel experiences. If a male rat is dropped into a cage with a receptive female rat there is a frenzy of copulation. Progressively, the male tires of that female. Replaced with a new mate, however, the male immediately revives to fertilise her. This, he will repeat with fresh females until exhausted. The web is a place where a male can see more receptive females in 10 minutes than his ancestors could in multiple lifetimes. This can become an addiction, making it more difficult to maintain normal sexual function with a stable partner. It is perhaps, too early to ascertain its long term effects. The access to internet pornography by children, who may develop a virtual perception of sex could alter the whole debate in the near future, whether to negative or positive effect, remains to be seen.

Most of us has a circle of people we know, a life partner, siblings, children, neighbours, acquaintances and friends. Along the path of life children and grand-children arrive and we make and lose friends. When we lose a friend to death, it can be an inevitable passing, a glimpse of sadness or a crushing psychological blow from which we may never truly recover. Each friend enriches our lives; each death dims it. Suicide once resulted in a sanction on the deceased and a barring from church grounds. New levels of tolerance and understanding mark a more nuanced approach by society to the darkness of depression and the complexities of life. On-going battles rage about the right to die of gravely ill, pain-ridden patients. Our growing maturity as a society and tolerance of choice will no doubt contribute to a more reasonable debate and situation.

Death is marked by a funeral, a meeting, as friends assemble to celebrate the life of the deceased and mourn. We have always had rituals to mark life's main events, such as births, marriages and death which would have been bound up in evolving belief systems. As religions centralised, so too did the structure of the ritual, the format of which emerged when Latin was the sole language. The rituals would have sounded exactly the same in every land where the Roman church held sway. This imparted a universal feeling and was of particular importance when Catholicism was threatened by heresy and schism. With the expansion of self-confidence many realise that church rituals do not seem to engage with or reflect the real lives of the people. In funerals, the ceremony is irrelevant to the beauty and complexity of the deceased's life, being swamped with disconnected readings and desert stories. The relatives of the deceased now try to make the ritual more relevant by attempting to tell the story of the life and times of the deceased to celebrate a real past life in preference to the doubtfulness of the next. In many instances these interventions are blocked by church authorities. A growing number of free thinkers now step away from the church altogether, organising their own, child-naming ceremonies, secular marriages and funerals, but there is often a difficulty in organising such events in a suitable setting. The only social and architectural spaces are general churches, for this is where humankind has concentrated resources, architecture and art over the millennia, they were designed and built for ritual. Whether religious or secular, the social being that is the human will still require to celebrate the rituals of life. As the outlook of religion evolves and a spirit of diversity grows, perhaps these spaces could become more flexible in their use and become a shared space.

The day to day interaction of humans is for the most part cordial and polite. Observation would suggest that as privation, either mental or physical, intensifies it become less so. It has also been observed that as wealth soars above a mean average, the holders of such become less empathic and more arrogant. Furthermore each of us responds to dialogue as we receive it. Arrogance and rudeness beget arrogance and rudeness; warmth and kindness beget warmth and kindness. This simple approach improves the immediate well-being of persons we interact with. Likewise the governance can improve general well-being by how it communicates. Every sign erected, should never be threatening, they should be a greeting, an explanation and an apology for any penalties. Public engineering works such as bridges, piers, public spaces etc. usually and pompously proclaim the politician who opened it and nothing more. Such signs should state, in a small and well-designed plaque, who funded the project - usually the tax payer - and name the workers involved in the construction. Inclusivity, pride and simple good manners enhance the dignity of all concerned. It would furthermore contribute a perception of ownership and pride to a project, which will enhance its security and lower its maintenance.

Likewise, every letter from a government department should be as between equals, cordial and polite, containing the obligations and duties of both but without hint of intimidation. There have been improvements in such relationships between the civil service and the general population, but as in every step to higher levels of civilisation, vigilance and enhancements must ever be sought. There are many ways where the quality of life can be improved by a thousand minor steps, leading to larger philosophical transformations. What is sought is the elevation of all to a universal personal dignity, in a society with a collective social dignity. As one gets distressed with inequality, unfairness and sheer cruelty to a degree where action is required, solutions may seem impossible. However, by contact with people of the same mind through social media, groups or political parties, one can act and make a difference. The first and most critical step is the development of a free, analytical mind and the courage to walk that road as part of humanity, even with small steps.

CHAPTER 8   Architecture of Divisions

Architecture, whether the complex and carefully designed structure of buildings or the social order, never lies; it reflects the economic, political and philosophical status of its creation. Oppression, contradictions or progress within a society are written in the fabric of its art and architecture. The elite of slave and feudal societies had total control and exercised suppression over the wealth-producing majority; their social structures were stable over long periods. But when change comes- and dialectics will ensure that change always comes - it can be violent and often ends badly for the rulers. Such was the case in the French and Bolshevik revolutions. When democratic societies emerged with the advent of capitalism, the majority had the perception they could change the state by elective procedures and achieve control over all facets of their lives. In theory, this would mean democracy could be extended over economics to serve the collective interest of the majority. On the occasions when it happened the status quo quickly replaced the ballot box with the army. Modern social democracies have evolved well-structured layers of protection to their economic core to avoid the need for such interventions.

When humans were hunting and gathering in a primitive communism, with the tribe balanced on the edge of survival, a cultural identity such as language and a divine belief system contributed to its unity. The remains of such societies reflect their existence as they followed seasons and hunting grounds. Their temporary and mobile modes of shelter were organic and melted back into nature with little trace. The most enduring architecture of such societies are caves where drawings and carvings of the previous inhabitants have been found, the evidence of their food gathering and hunting was uncovered by meticulous explorations of archaeologists and anthropologists.

When later agricultural societies developed a food surplus, they were no longer on the edge of extinction, the conditions for possession of wealth had arrived. Survival then took on a different meaning, the survival of the ruling elite and their hold on power. In Egyptian slave society the social glue that provided cohesion was fear of a priesthood invested with unlimited authority and a pharaoh perceived as an actual deity. This political and religious union was expressed physically by the dark temples of the period such as the Great Temple of Ammon at Karnak with its foreboding forest of massive columns. The culture of death and the afterlife was underlined by the colossal tombs of the Great Pyramid of Cheops in contrast to the flimsy dwellings of the toilers. This combination of power and fear was so successful at overriding dissent it ensured a stable society for many thousands of years. The architectural legacy written in crumbling desert stone remains an accurate reflection of every facet of that society, it beautifully describes the endeavours of humankind and the transient nature of all structures, social and physical.

Greek civilisation with its lighter and more elegant temples and squares gave a hint of a broader democracy amongst the elite. Its magnificent development of sculpture giving homage to the human body reflects a humanist perspective. The power of imperial Rome is clear by the complexity of the city, its sewerage system, baths, the coliseums for mass entertainment, the forum representing the limited democracy. Its culture of many gods is attested by the myriad of temples, fractious deities that may not have provided the social glue of a single god. The adoption of a new monotheistic religion by Emperor Constantine of Rome may have been too late to save the over-stretched empire, but was the turning point for Christianity; it had won the ultimate corporate endorsement. The empire with its avenues of power and communications stretching across Europe ensured the rapid spread of the new religion. When the empire fell, the Roman Catholic Church became entrenched adapting the power structures of the rising feudal order, its power waxing and waning with the passage of time. A feature of Roman imperial terror, the cross of crucifixions, became an icon of Christianity and in turn became etched in the fabric of our architectural legacy, standing on even the most remote Irish church.

As the slave empire declined, feudal lords and kings became dominant throughout Europe, their seats of power expressed by strategic castles around which the towns developed. Wealth came from the extensive lands worked by serfs, town markets and turnpikes. The authority of the supportive belief system was reflected in the construction of magnificent Gothic cathedrals, soaring aspirations, which defied gravity and were drenched in exquisite craftsmanship and art. These buildings were not just repositories for the divine, but for the elevation of earthbound power with pomp, the investiture of princes and the crowning of kings. Church and state were unified and one religion covered a whole continent. The monotheism and immense power of the popes provided a unity which swamped the cry of the toilers.

This unity collapsed in 1517 with the reformation and schism. It reduced social cohesion and wars spread throughout Europe. However, the pressure for reformation came as much from the growing power of a city-based merchant class as from any theological divisions. One might crudely argue that the new protestant reformation represented the economic power of merchant traders against the old Catholic feudal aristocracy whose wealth was based on land. When the wealth of the towns expanded to exceed that of the surrounding land based power, a conflict of interests arose. The feudal princes controlled the roads through their lands and the trading markets with levies and taxes. The new order could not tolerate restrictions on their freedom to trade, hence the outbreak of revolutions throughout Europe as economic supremacy shifted from the land to the cities. Feudalism was a pyramidal top-down, power structure, the Catholic Church, adopted its mirror image. The new politics of the towns reflected the individual and innovative interests of a new class, who adopted a limited democracy, one which was also reflected in its religious structures. As it could not accept domination by a feudal structure, it could no longer accept a feudal pope. The Bible henceforth was to be individually interpreted and not directed by central power such as Rome, a freer personal religion was more in keeping with the economic ethos. The highly ornate places of worship and clothes of feudalism, as adapted by Catholicism, gave way to simpler more puritanical codes of dress and architecture. The victory of the towns sowed the seeds of democracy, initially confined to the wealthy male traders, but slowly leaking out into wider society.

These economic, political and religious innovations introduced a whole new dynamic within Northern Europe. The rise of trade and commerce instigated a concentration of capital, which brought a new vigorous period of exploration and innovation. The advent of steam power harnessed the ex-tenant farmers who owned nothing and had nothing to sell but their labour power. Huge steam powered iron and linen mills and cheap labour came together, production soared. The railway infrastructure with its amazing steel bridges and stations brought fast mass transport for travellers and troops. Large industrial enterprises were, by their nature, stationary as were the workers who were necessary to keep them going. Over time, labour organised and wages grew. Capitalism realised it needed to be less permanent, more flexible, expansionist and morphed into imperialism. International trade and troop movements by steam ships launched colonial adventures in a search for new markets, cheaper labour and materials. Over time the dark mills of production crumbled in Europe and were replaced by service industries, headquarters of banks, insurance and finance companies and multinational corporations. New service 'industries' that make their billions by shuffling capital to and from all corners of the globe at internet speed.

The soaring headquarters of the multi-national corporations are designed by celebrity architects as iconic brands, arrogant shapes competing for attention and status. They dwarf the previous centres of power, cathedrals, castles, big houses and production mills and cast a long shadow over public squares, houses of the legislature and the peoples' dwellings. The lesser towers that surround the corporate house are the lairs of accountancy and legal firms who are well paid to protect the accumulations. They employ the brightest of honour graduates, trained at great cost by the taxpayer, to ensure that any tax the corporations might be liable for is mitigated or avoided. The best legal minds wait to litigate on any criticism, infringement of patent or non-payment of some nefarious service. Where previously the slave trembled before the dark Egyptian temple, now humanity trembles before these giants of corporate power who control their existence. The gilded chariots of the pharaohs have been replaced with limos. Where the high priests of Egypt whispered advice into the ears of the pharaoh, now the high priests of accountancy and law whisper to the corporate boards. Cameras on every corner of their glass towers are monitored by a private army of the dark-suited who are on standby around the clock; layers of protection surround the accumulations.

The relationship between art and prevailing belief systems is coherently demonstrated by wandering the Louvre in Paris. Having left the dour but fascinating Egyptian section, the sculpture galleries of classical Greece pay homage to the naked beauty of humanity at hunt, play and love. What can surpass the image of Diane the huntress, beautiful, armed and dangerous, perhaps the perfect icon for women's liberation? The galleries on Rome again take up the theme and one's spirit soars amongst the sublime liberating art and sculpture, they work their way into your very essence. Then as one moves into the period of consolidating Christianity, gallery after gallery shows humans being tortured, demons, hellfire and damnation. The only portrayals of bodies are those being crucified, bound martyrs perforated with arrows, children being slaughtered, submissive women and sexless virgins weeping. One and a half thousand years of the dark ages crush the spirit. Dragging oneself through these galleries there is finally a hint of light, Michelangelo's David emerges from a solid block of marble. With the renaissance one can almost breathe again, but it is not until the peasant scenes of Bruegel is there hope, some fun and the belief that life might be worth living.

The built environment is a major contributor to our well-being. Most of our lives are spent in spaces enclosed by walls, solid and transparent. We keep the elements at bay, controlling air movement and our body temperature within a comfortable norm, we extend the day with lighting. To work, eat, love and relax within these spaces, it is imperative that they function efficiently. They are machines for living, but it is important that the spaces we inhabit, should enhance our lives, a union of function and art. Our lives are short, there must be no time spent in anything but beautiful spaces, how this is reflected in the reality of our existence is a measure of society. The quality of life is reflected and to an extent determined by the spaces in which people live and work. The physical manifestation of the city reflects its wealth sources, its social aspects and origins. The elite gathered and lived in the most desirable parts of the city with the best aspects and facilities. The slums housed the unemployed and workers, while the middle class occupied the various suburban areas, each street, reflecting rank and status. As the power of trade unions and their political parties increased, suburbia and social housing spread, accompanied by a rise in the quality of food, goods, entertainment and transport. The economic forces that formed the cities still exist, although there has been a dramatic change from industrial to service industries.

As formal education and human empathy expand, we see an increasing potential for a stable social society. Most European and Irish citizens are now less likely to litter or cause wanton damage to property. Bicycle hire schemes are a strong indicator of the growing maturity of a people showing they have become more caring and responsible. The order and ease by which supermarket shopping is carried out, even to the extent of people checking out their own goods, has favourable implications for the operation of a more rational society. Presently there is an enforceable element attached to this social behaviour, every move on streets or shops is recorded on CCTV, credit card transactions are timed to the second and every phone or electronic communication is monitored and stored. Never before has a society existed with such a level of surveillance, the comprehensive nature of which supersedes any previous police state, with it, future dissent will be far easier to control. Like the state itself one can envisage its withering with the rise of a rational egalitarian society. At present the authorities imply that such blanket surveillance gives protection from the evil-doer, however, if the direction of society fails to change, perhaps we are blindly walking into a dystopian nightmare of total corporate-state control.

The market square which was the centre of every town and city, is now the ubiquitous mall, surrounded by a vast car-park, car showrooms, service depots and car care emporiums. Nowhere is the unifying strength of global capitalism more obvious. It matters not in which country or city the mall lies, the car-park layout, the cars, the shops, brands, food, coffee, and clothes are similar. The assumption that competition would provide diversity has not been fulfilled, for the brands are in so many cases, but branches of the same corporation. The malls, unlike the more time-layered texture of an organic city centre, seldom provide any seating or rest areas, to sit one has to dine on the delights of the fast-food emporium. Everywhere are televisions gyrating to endless three minute jingles, the lights, the garish colours, nothing is left to chance, are all carefully designed to keep the customer moving, to every mall, every store, an architecture to make them shop, till they drop.

The majority of our species of seven billion now live in cities. This built environment constitutes a major influence on existence and well-being. Where the social nature of production within industry previously provided a unity of purpose to form combinations for resistance, so too might the mass of people within a city. While the disparate forces acting within a city would not have the more obvious class bond of the industrial floor, nevertheless the problems of mass housing, the flight of capital and speculative development, can conflict with the interests of the inhabitants and possess the possibility of a radical unity. The architecture of unity is as possible as the architecture of division.

Nowhere is the architecture of divisions more blatantly demonstrated than in Northern Ireland. The drums of the 'Protestant boys', can bind together the most exploited, poverty-stricken Protestant with the wealthiest of the unionist ascendancy, all waving the Union Jack and singing 'God Save the

Queen'. It reflects a hopeless division between catholic and protestant working people and the destruction, at least in the near future, of any progressive movement. The leadership on both sides repeatedly talk of reducing conflict by statements such as 'bringing our people together', at the same time vigorously maintaining denominational education. Sectarian residential areas are the default position, separated by bleak, concrete partitions, topped with barbed wire, covered in sectarian graffiti and called 'a peace wall'. The objective interest of the status quo is well served.

Exploitation is eased by division; of all the divisions in humankind, gender is one of the most intractable. Historically, only in societies which did not have a food surplus or private property is there evidence of female equality for in such society males had nothing to commandeer and bequeath, thus little to gain from the control and oppression of females. The progress of any society can be measured by the position and role of women, there will be no egalitarian society until legislation, politics and economics are gender balanced. That will require the demise of philosophical sexism, difficult, if not impossible, when the prevailing philosophy is a Christian theology with endemic sexism. Steady progress was made in the sixties and seventies in fertility control, education and the intellectual position of women in society, but reversals have become apparent. The fragmentation of the women's movement occurred at the same time as the collapse of the international feminist working-class. Thus the market has become empowered to use the female body to sell every product, turning the female body itself into a commodity, a sale of sexualised beauty within a culture still cowed by the biology of the feeding breast.

Feminism will regain its momentum when it coalesces in a struggle to construct a non-exploitative society. At present, it is diverted and timid due to its separation from the fight for structural change, equal pay and rights. The movement has been subverted by an agenda, pursuing superficial cultural changes in male views and values. Such demands are valid but idealist in character and isolationist, some even perpetuate the myth of fragile women. Previously feminists fought a political cause, demanding representation and full equal rights, gains were made and the movement was accepted as mainstream for it implied that feminism had accepted the structures of the status quo and was no longer a threat. The movement crept away from the international community and now sees the deprivation of millions of women as a separate economic issue. It could ignore the mass genital mutilation of young girls as cultural relativity and the isolation of Ayaan Hirsi Ali, but nothing stays the same. Capital concentrates, climate wags a carbon finger, the graphs of population and resources cross. These forces will conspire against lethargy and inertia. Feminism will regain the courage and passion of the suffragette movement and participate in the international struggle for equality in gender, race and economics.

The sponsor of female inequality has been private property and that of equality has been revolution, war, industrialisation, independent income, education, organisation and a diminution of religious belief - elements which now form an opportunity for transition. While universal suffrage is not in itself a panacea for equality it is an indicator of progress. New Zealand was the first to achieve it but it took revolutions in two of the biggest countries in the world for the concepts to forge ahead. After the success of the Russian Revolution in 1917, universal suffrage and full equal rights were introduced. Likewise in China, where women were extremely oppressed, full equal rights were instigated in 1930, including a prohibition on the barbarous culture of foot binding, on a girls fifth birthday their toes were bent under the soles of the feet and tightly bound. This physical suffering turned the young girl into a fetish, an object of love. Essential for marriage, the bound foot gains respect as it is an undeniable proof of the women's capacity to suffer and obey, an analogy that can be used in many instances. While other countries had granted rights earlier under similar pressures, none provided such a dramatic and immediate improvement to so many.

The instinct for survival, either that of an individual or nation state is supreme. An external threat to a nation provides a unifying pressure, forcing the state to allow the co-operation of divided sectors of society to fulfil the higher needs of king and country. Such was the case in the Second World War when tens of thousands of women partook in the production of ordnance, fighter aircraft, tanks and war materials in Germany and England. The participation of women within the labour force became accepted as it became essential, it provided a liberation from the claustrophobia of the private home. In the USSR, 800,000 women participated in frontline fighting, with a separate dive bomber and fighter squadron. They had their own night bomber command, termed 'the night witches' by the German forces, as they attacked with their engines shut down. The only sound was the swish of gliding aircraft through the black night before the bombs hit. Thousands of women were engaged as snipers, being regarded as more patient and deadly then men, none more so than Lyudmila Pavlichenko. However, with the consolidation of autocratic power and the end of war came the reversal or at least slowing of female liberation.

The correlation between religious belief, political power and female oppression has been obvious throughout history. The female's biological role as an attractor is an imperative for reproduction, her ability to mate with whom she decides has given her a power which has been universally feared as much as ill-understood. With the advent of surplus and private property, the ownership and control of women became necessary to ensure the inheritance of that property by the descendants of the male owner. Many thousands of years were to pass before a society of free, unexploited men and women could be envisaged. That could only emerge when a vast number of people without property grasped the concept of a society where economics was subjugated to democracy. It would be impossible to conceive of such a society while any subjugation of women exists. The oppression of one is the oppression of all.

An architectural expression of the treatment of women in Ireland have been the high stone walls of punitive mother and baby homes and the higher and equally cold walls of the accompanying social and cultural isolation. These expressions were of a time when the philosophical and spiritual poverty of a nation was so overwhelming, it swamped the closest family ties. It endorsed the isolation of daughters from parents, friends and lovers as they were cast to hell, into the pitiless care of those women or men whose human empathy had been destroyed by the same forces. As with the Inquisition there existed an absurd twist of spiritual logic, if god's forgiveness could be gained through suffering in this life, it would mitigate damnation in the next. The nuns and the inquisitors were thus convinced that their cruel behaviour was saving the victim's soul and helping them to everlasting happiness. As the inquisitors said "he screams and cracking of bones on the breaking wheel were but the sweet sound of heaven's gate, opening", nevertheless despite our slow recovery from such horrors the architecture of female subjection still abounds in our schools and behind the manicured walls of many a private house.

The icons and rituals of religion are of great significance. Over thousands of years humans devoted millions of work hours constructing immense temples, cathedrals and vast numbers of statues, because it believed that they were a vital part of inculcating belief. Likewise, the modern brand and advertising agencies would not exist without a proven benefit. Hence all schools are saturated with images of supplication. Girls' schools have icons of submission with countless statues and pictures of virgins, stripped of all vestiges of female sexual attraction, without the hips, buttocks, and breasts that make a girl a woman. An iconic vessel of celestial replication, testifying to an architectural and philosophical confusion, a young girl becoming pregnant by an angel, yet remaining a virgin, married to another. A constant message of submission in schools with a role that can never be really discussed without a great deal of intellectual embarrassment. Being educated in the midst of such barren philosophies is the antithesis of a *Republic of Reason*.

Communication and information technologies are developing faster than our imagination. We are locked into a new architecture of the pod, phone and web - a gateway to instant personal communication and search engines that can prowl the information of humankind, at the speed of light. We have petite boxes delivering music, sports, pornography and a thousand apps of infinite information, fact or fiction. Like any tool it can serve any cause, many believe that the internet is a true international people's media. A place where dissent and free expression can be unleashed. However, it is already being swamped with advertising and Vast amounts of money are being invested in legal and political lobbying to gain control of the network.

On the positive side, if the sum of overall human empathy exceeds that of indifference then such a transnational web of information and communication must contribute positively to human well-being. It allows instant campaigns on specific issues to spring up, negative as well as positive, time will tell how the balance will work out. If mass mobilisations of workers were in the past able to change economic and political structures, it may be possible that web users, acting collectively, could, with determination and dexterity, exert pressure for progress. It provides opportunities for the instant participation of citizens in existing and more inclusive future democracies. Either way, the architecture of this technology will have a large bearing on the future.

Chapter 9   Our Fragile Species

Each of us looks at the world in a self-centred way, we depend on interaction with it and our fellow humans for survival. We relate to people in a series of expanding circles of dependency, family, extended family, tribe, nation and out to all humans of the world, with the strongest ties at the centre and weakest at the periphery. Our perceptions of time are also self-centred. We live in the here and now, our history and memories stretch back only a few generations, looking forward as far as our grandchildren. Likewise we depend on exploitation of the planet for our survival, we relate to it, in what and how we take from it. Programmed as we are for immediate existence, we do not engage with the long-term prospect. The attempt to secure a sustainable future for ourselves and fellow species depends on our intellectual ability to break this mould, to learn lessons from the effects of our existence on the planet and to imagine our existence into the future. Biologists examining the life cycles of various species frequently observe that exponential expansion is often followed by extinction.

The Earth's population is now over seven billion and allowing for deaths is growing at more than 200,000 every day, the equivalent of a city with a million people every five days, all of whom need to be fed, housed and supplied with manufactured goods. The frightening reality of this growth is evident at the website Worldometers.info. Each new person requires an acre of cultivated land to provide the food for survival, an area that increases as living standards rise, the numbers of cattle, sheep, pigs and poultry escalate in unison. The space under grain, corn, wheat and rice is expanding and so are yields, but the limits of expansion in both land and yields are being reached. At the same time there are accumulative problems with water, fertiliser and carbon fossil fuels, all essential for food production. Basically we have an infinitely expanding population and demands for economic growth in contradiction with finite resources. Previously wild and species-rich environments are shrinking as the area under cultivation expands. *Scientific America* claims we are destroying over 80,000 acres of tropical rainforest, and losing 135 species every day.

Some contend that the Earth is capable of supporting just two billion people on a sustainable basis. Others argue that advancing technology and slowing population growth may turn the tide. Population expansion occurs on two fronts - the actual growth in numbers and increasing longevity. The impact of expansion is not just in the numbers, but in the growth of consumption as living standards rise, this will have a particular impact in the high-population countries of India, China and others as they seek parity of wealth with the first world. For example, private motor car ownership in China is 50 vehicles for every thousand people, while the world average is 120 and in the United States it is 740. If China were to achieve the same number of cars per head as the United States, the country would have to pave an area equal to the land it now plants in rice and would need 99 million barrels of oil a day. The entire world currently produces 89 million barrels per day and may never produce much more.

Reproduction, our second most powerful instinct, is regarded as a world apart from economics or the environment, an untouchable facet of our being. Chapter 1, outlined our evolutionary path and how instincts for survival and reproduction are driven through the gene's view of the world. But the gene is blind; it has a selfish, laissez-faire attitude, its only slogan is "the more survival machines (humans) the merrier". It does not see or care where it is going. The only reason for production and economics is to supply the necessary food and energy for the survival of these human replicators. The present competitive market mechanisms of industrial production are the same as that of the gene. Both are driven by inherent and similar blind forces, their motivation is growth, neither recognise the limitations of expansion and the finite resources of our planet. Only by the application of science and a philosophical approach to controlling the instincts of the gene can humans exert control over their fertility. Likewise, it is only through science and a philosophy of sustainability can humans exert control over production and economics. Thankfully, some of the gene's more rational survival machines, are attempting to do just that. The inherent blindness of reproduction and present day economics are capable of being rolled back by logic and advancing technology. Politically this requires groups of people that can agree on a clear agenda for survival, who can influence and change the political and economic structures. We will return to this in the final chapter.

While natural selection still applies in the wild, it does not apply in domestic species and plants. These are refashioned to be more useful to us through selective breeding and genetic engineering. Evolution, as it once applied to humans at the raw level of prey verses predator, whilst still proceeding under the rules of sexual selection, has also been generally usurped by science and medicine. Humanity and its domestic dependants have become a distinct group, separate from the wider wild world. The agricultural-food sector is a world-wide industry using science to increase productivity and efficiency, without which the world population would not be sustainable. However, this expansion of productivity is believed to be reaching its limit and if the human race cannot control its own numerical expansion by intellectual means, then more brutal methods of demand exceeding supply will apply - population control by starvation and thirst. United Nations statistics inform that for millions of those born to deprived families in poor countries, the situation is not some future theoretical threat, it is now. Globally, over 800 million go hungry and 20,000 children under five die every day. The children who die are far removed from the scrutiny of the media and the conscience of the world, they are invisible. Being meek and weak, these children become even more invisible in death. As the situation deteriorates in parts of Africa it directly affects us, as thousands flee to the European mainland or Ireland. We are seen as a lifeboat of wealthy nations for a sinking section of humanity.

Human control over nature, while essential for our survival, is often expressed as some lordly conquest. For many, the natural world is considered as something only for exploitation, even if manifestations of arrogance, such as photographs of the great white hunter, proudly posing with a dead tiger, are now, less acceptable. We cannot stand outside the natural world as though it is of some separate identity, we are body and blood, part and parcel of that world. Our dependency on the bountiful Earth obliges us - as the only cognisant creatures - to have a moral responsibility for the maintenance of its wonderful biodiversity on land, sea and air. What a huge loss humanity will suffer if, through our persistent ignorance and greed, we destroy something like the Amazon rainforest with its thousands of diverse species and only preserve disjointed bits in zoos and arboretums.

Only recently have we begun to understand the complexity of life and the relationship between all species and ourselves - for example; the role played by plants in the production of oxygen, insects in the pollination of plants and crops, bacteria in the breakdown of wastes. We have much to learn from our fellow species, let us not eradicate them. Leaf-cutter ants were farming many millions of years before humans. They cut through leaves with a scissors-like jaw and carry a section of leaf back to the colony where it is chewed down to a mulch, fertilised with nitrogen-producing bacteria, planted with mushrooms and sprayed with their own pesticides. On a similar vein, a species of termite herds and milks aphid, akin to humans with cows. To whittle away at the complex eco-systems of the Earth is to whittle away the foundations of our fragile existence. If we succeed, the Earth will need a billion years for life to recover the biodiversity it once had. The planet will get on just fine without us but, sad to say, with no one to perceive it; unless of course a new cognisant species should evolve.

Non-governmental conservation organisations try to regulate interference and preserve the natural world. However, the real responsibility for care rests with private ownership, ranging from small holdings to corporate interests and that does not auger well, for their natural imperative is the profit motive with a drive to exploit and expand all owned and controlled areas of the Earth. The original story of the 'tragedy of the commons' was used to redirect common ownership of land into what was thought to be 'safer' private hands, it is worth repeating: An area of ground is held in common by farmers whose cattle graze it, in the beginning there was no problem as the numbers were small, but as the years passed, each farmer added more stock, the numbers grew but the land did not. A time arrived when the cattle no longer prospered as the grass was being consumed faster than it grew, but who was going to be first to move? If one farmer decided to reduce stock someone else would increase theirs, so no one did and all the cattle starved, famine stalked the land. The solution was to divide the common land into individual private plots, so each farmer was responsible for that area of land and thus in their own long-term interest, would keep stock at a sustainable level.

However, nothing remains constant, farmers as well as cattle bred and the land was divided amongst their heirs. The population continued to grow, plots got smaller and were eventually unable to sustain livestock. In the Irish context, the adjoining imperial power that was England seized the land and granted titled estates to various 'lords' who used the best land for cattle and grain and rented the marginal land in small holdings. Between 1700 and the 1845 famine, Ireland's population increased rapidly, crowding the land and many were forced to rent plots of poor land on the Atlantic coast. A new miracle crop, the potato had arrived from South America many years previously and with seaweed fertiliser it thrived to become the base crop of the poor, just able to support the renting family in a barely tenable situation.

Then came, *Phytophthora infestans*, - blight. The crop failed for three years in succession causing the deaths of a million people and the emigration of a million more. At the same time, enough grain to feed all the people was exported, its use to alleviate starvation and death was blocked as that would have interfered with free market forces. It took agri-agitation ('terrorism'), political will, and human empathy to establish the first land commission, with farmers allowed to buy small-holdings of land on which they had worked. Revisions to increase farm sizes came after 1923 as holdings were still deemed too small to provide a decent living. Similar histories of land tenure occurred worldwide, although in many places, such as Scotland and England, the land clearances were more direct with the tenants forcibly shipped overseas to the colonies never to return.

Farming in Ireland is now supported by substantial subsidies, these can be up to 80% on beef farms, where in many cases the subsidy exceeds the income. The Irish State and the European Community maintain these subsidies for social, political and strategic reasons that stretch back to food shortages during the war. It ensures a steady supply of cheap food and provides the authorities with some leverage to encourage sustainable land use, water quality and habitat management. It is interesting that while the farming community at present might be regarded or regard themselves as a bastion of conservative social values, they are in fact involved in a vast taxpayer-funded social enterprise to maintain a life-style with some environmental considerations.

There is growing pressure to remove all such supports allowing the amalgamation of farms to a more viable size through commercial pressure. A move that would also encourage deregulation and a more laissez-faire approach to the environment. Either way, inexorable pressure will continue to expand the size of farms, for thousands of cattle in conveyor-fed rows, supplied by mile-long fodder fields, without ditch or hedge are more viable under one-dimensional accounting. The individual farmer would be replaced by industrial farming. As these enterprises become commercially profitable, their character changes as they morph into an ownership by disconnected shareholders, worked by alienated poorly paid operatives. The farms become a business corporation, open to speculation, bought and sold by remote traders, their CEOs obliged by law to maximise profits to the shareholders over any environmental considerations. Environmental regulations will come under pressure for negation as capital concentrates and ownership passes to shareholders far from the farms. The community of ownership and lack of responsibility will have come full circle. The 'tragedy of the commons' will have returned in a different form.

Agrarian transformation will emerge from the relationship between subsidy and production. It will also be influenced by the low rate of return on the capital value of the farm combined with the low return on agricultural labour. When the invested capital value of the farm provides a greater return than working the farm, then market pressure will be to sell. This will allow farms to combine. Such commercial realities will encourage those who inherit farms to sell, rather than work their inheritance. Despite fluctuations, the demand for beef and dairy produce will increase, as will production costs. As competition increases so too does specialisation. The mixed labour intensive farm of fifty years ago is gone and mechanisation has increased. Massive oil-dependent machines can cut enough winter-fodder silage for a herd in a few days. The concentration of stock makes the herd more susceptible to disease transmission requiring an intensification of monitoring and antibiotic inoculations which creep into the food chain. Their waste, both on pasture or in wintering sheds, can result in severe problems with ground water. The world's 1.5 billion cattle are responsible for up to 18 per cent of the greenhouse gases that contribute to climate change, more than cars, planes and all other forms of transport. Their stomach gasses and manure emit more than one third of emissions of methane gas, which has an affect 20 times more potent than carbon dioxide.

Biologically one cannot extract nutrition from grassland at present intensities without equally intensive fertilisation which depends on the finite resources of chemicals and oil. Despite these problems and the fact that we are stretching the limits of production, the world continues to produce enough food to feed its people for many years. However, the gap between food production and consumption by its seven billion consumers is becoming smaller and more fragile. While we can produce the quantity required, we do not have any equality of distribution, for as with the potato famine in Ireland, many countries whose people suffer from hunger and malnutrition, export food. Food and nutrition are not perceived as a right, but as a free-market commodity.

The commons, is now the entire Earth to be exploited with all its resources of land, forests, hunting and fishing grounds. All that matters objectively to a farmer is crop, stock and fodder. All else is pest - whether it be bird, plant or parasite - to be controlled by gun, machine or pesticide and this intensifies as we move from small holding to industrial farming. Conservationists act to hold back the relentless tide of arable land expansion and preserve wilderness, a position difficult to defend coherently while poverty and hunger are sold as alternatives. How can one attempt to stop desperate farmers from burning rainforest and creating arable land, which is precisely what we the inhabitants of Western Europe and Ireland did? Only a coordinated international response, offering paid guardianship of the forests to the farmers would work, but in a world of competition and corporate interests, co-ordinated international responses are not easy to come by.

Similar criteria apply to the world's finite, mineral resources of coal, oil, gas and phosphates. Here too environmental considerations are damaging to business. Competition between states for capital investment has forced legislative support for private and corporate power whose imperative is to maximise profit. This economic structure is in the ascendency, developing pressure to extend the imperialism of our species over the entire planet, leaving no wilderness unowned, untouched and unexploited. Such forces have the objective philosophy that if any sea, land, landscape, wilderness or species is not owned and exploited, then it is of no value. This self-destructive cocktail of poor farmers with small holdings, desperate for more land in order to survive and large corporations, expanding plantations, mining and logging, constantly gnaw away at the world's remaining forests and jungles.

Looking at humans dispassionately, one sees groups of people unfit and overweight. Many barely able to walk, not to mind run, abusing drink and drugs, uppers and downers, smoking and coughing. It is hard to believe they are members of the most dangerous and powerful species that has ever roamed the Earth. They are faster than the cheetah, more powerful than the lion or tyrannosaurus rex, not because of any individual trait, but due to their social and cooperative and inventive nature. Over the last hundred years the triumph of science in food production and over bacteria has resulted in phenomenal population growth. Humanity is becoming aware of the problem and some are realising that the solutions require collective action and consensus.

A large-scale intervention came with the regulation of family size in China, when couples were encouraged by cash, housing incentives and penalties to comply with the 'one family - one child' policy. Its implementation had anomalies, it did not apply in Tibet or to some ethnic minorities, in rural areas it allowed another child if the first was female. Despite its many problems over 75% of people in China support the policy. Its contribution to population reduction to-date is in the order of 350 million, which is more than the population of the United States. With the policy in operation, the population still grew over the period, doubling from circa .65 to 1.38 billion. This was due to the increase in average lifespan which had risen from 44 to 75 years since the revolution. The policy had unintended consequences such as a preponderance of 120 males to 100 females, for despite being illegal, there is a higher abortion rate on girls, a tendency that may self-correct, for a daughter has now a higher chance of finding a partner and is a better bet for ensuring the continuation of the family genes. Another consequence of the policy is that parents with one child concentrate their resources into his or her education and many of these children go on to third level. When these children in turn form a family, they are allowed two children and having been high achievers themselves, will insist on similar for their own children, leading to accelerated educational gains throughout the state.

The policy is being relaxed, as the increased level of wealth and education, particularly of women, is now the main element that regulates family size. A paradox is that as income and educational growth are determining factors in slowing the population growth, they will be the same factors that increase consumption. For example, the dwelling space for each inhabitant in China has grown almost three fold over the period. Looking at the problem through climatic rather than humanist eyes, it is a win some, lose some situation. If the vast populations of the north Pacific Rim reach the standards of education required to reduce population growth, they will seek a standard of living familiar in the west and prolong their longevity, thus increasing the demands on resources and climate. This is the first time such numbers will combine the dual pressures of population and economic growth. Humanity is caught in 'the red queen effect'- the faster we run, the faster we need to run, just to stand still. In many African states the provision of basic facilities, such as water, food, education and health, cannot keep pace with this dual population and economic growth. The developed countries of Europe and the United States, where conspicuous consumerism is rampant, are in no position to lecture against other people attempting to achieve similar standards of living. One way or another by the end of this century ten billion people are expected to live on the planet.

Such growth is possible due to the so-called green revolution, new forms of grain, rice, pesticides and fertiliser allowed a huge expansion of production with little increase in cultivated ground area. Clean water, better sewerage and waste disposal, coupled with gains in social health and medicine, such as inoculations, keep more children alive and allow people to live longer. Every one of these gains is of immediate benefit to those concerned even if the numbers themselves are a potential threat to overall human sustainability. Long term sustainability demands that the same human intellectual power and scientific reasoning that resulted in these material gains must be applied to counterbalancing gains in the philosophical, economic and political sphere. Lessons from history need to be learned and relearned.

These lessons may be found where the remnants of once-magnificent civilisations and cities crumble back into the dust. The poet Shelley in his *Ozymandias* tells of a once proud and splendid settlement fit for a "king of kings", who proclaimed his great and everlasting works: "Look on my works, ye Mighty, and despair". But now, "nothing beside remains: round the decay of that colossal wreck, boundless and bare, the lone and level sands stretch far away". Who, we might ask, in their right minds would have built a city here? What could possibly have brought people to settle on such a desert location? But imagine a time of a green and bountiful forest, populated by game and fowl and watered by bubbling spring and brook - a paradise, perfect for settlement. A clearance is made and the timber is used for construction and fuel. The game is hunted and the bountiful land is cleared for farming, life is good. The city, its people and its rulers grow in power and stature. Every day however, the trek to get timber from the forest increases; every day the game gets a little scarcer; every day the tilled soil gets a little more depleted. The rains, which were held in the sponge that was the forest and shielded from evaporation by the dense vegetation, now evaporate quickly in the thin soil which starts to blow away.

As prosperity crumbles, the once powerful army, fed on a plentiful surplus, now succumbs to poverty and like the city, capitulates before any predatory force. The once bountiful and fragile land blows into desert dunes, awaiting the return of a wetter cooler climate to re-establish a delicate foothold. This scenario is repeated hundreds of times with variations in the causes, best captured in Jared Diamond's book *Collapse*. The book describes various civilisations, such as the Fertile Crescent formerly Mesopotamia now part of Iraq, a foundation of civilisation, once a paradise of wooded valleys, abundant water, game, grazing and with sufficient resources to build a great civilisation. But relentlessly the forests were cut down, the land over grazed and the waters squandered. Some environmentalists would argue that the militarised states of the Greek and Roman civilisations required huge timber, agricultural, water and fishing resources to maintain their cities and were destroyed, not just by the fortunes of war and ambitious over-stretched armies, but by depleted land and ravaged forest.

There is a contention that a hive of bees is a life form, an organism in itself of which the individual bee is but a fragment. One can look at the modern city- a human cluster- as such an organism. Its sustenance runs within its veins, food and goods are trucked into the city on a web of highways, electricity and water runs to every dwelling and office, sewers carry off the waste, power lines energise street lighting, rail and road transport cut through the fabric of the city in all directions and levels. The brains of its inhabitants fuse as a collective and, riding a billion electronic paths, scatter through the city at the speed of light. The organism pulsates with scurrying workers, dashing between office-cells. It is an amalgam of workers and consumers operating through a caste system of hierarchies. The majority of people sell their time and labour to consume and survive and spend a life producing surplus capital for remote masters.

The city population lose knowledge of food production realities, their perception of the world outside the packaged supermarket fades, goods and food just arrive. This results in a diminished responsibility for any damaging interaction between food production and the natural world. There are no famines in this world of plenty, cost is the only criteria with copious consumption driven by blanket marketing. The cities, united by logos and brands become indistinguishable, blending together into a super global organism. There are no divisions in the world of consumption, no nationalism, no sectarianism, no racism, no sexism. This is a dichotomy, for while philosophical agenda of capital does everything to maintain power with divisions and diversions, its commercial agenda wishes only for the united consumer. But like the ancient residents of abandoned desert cities, the slow encroachment of disaster was not realised until flight to a more abundant land became essential. The modern dweller within the gigantic urban conurbations has alas, nowhere to flee.

Despite humanity's record on the environment, we can be intelligent social mammals with the potential to negate our impact. A need for regulation might be boosted by a growing realisation that there may not be any choice. There has been a fairly stable climate since the last ice age 12,000 years ago, but now there is mounting evidence that human activity is playing a large part in climate change. Most of the scientific community links this with population and industrial expansion. The problem is global and solutions can only be effective when organised on an international global basis. The solutions will infringe on international capital and humanity has as of yet, no effective worldwide organisation to regulate such a powerful force.

Every living thing depends on external energy sources. Energy streams down from our personal nuclear furnace, the Sun, in the form of light and heat. It is captured by the natural, green, solar panels of our planet - every blade of grass, leaf, vegetable, and grain crop. The plants use the sunlight to synthesize nutrients from carbon dioxide and water to grow and replicate. The herbivores of the world, including ourselves, are parasites on these plants, consuming them and accumulating their energy. Over millions of years carbon was absorbed by living organisms and as they died was stored in their tombs as coal, crude oil, and gas. Only in the last few hundred years have we started to dig up and use these carbon deposits. The vast majority of electrical power generation is dependent on coal, gas and oil, and almost all transport is oil dependant. Most countries, cities, and towns plan their entire infrastructure around the motor car on the assumption that the energy to power them will always be available. The advent of the electric car, while very welcome as a reduction of city pollution, is seen as solving an energy problem. The point is often missed that the energy required for the production of the vehicle is the equivalent to that of a conventional car and their electrical motive energy still requires to be generated, at least in the short term, by carbon consumption.

We now throw vast quantities of carbon dioxide, previously buried, back into the atmosphere at speeds faster than can be absorbed by nature, a major contributor to global climate change. If any industrial power agreed to reduce use of this energy, it would give a trading advantage to its rivals.

Governments trying to mitigate carbon use, by the introduction of carbon taxes, face a hostile reception from an electorate whose standard of living would fall, they would be voted out of office by parties promising the abolition of such taxes and lower fuel prices. The media which is instrumental in any electoral process is owned and controlled by the very forces that require to be contained. The issue will be clouded with obscuring data and many will encourage that 'the party should go on'. Selling of short term gains for political advantage is a major impediment to progress on that front. Perhaps a more dictatorial approach issuing top-down decrees might achieve more, but historically such regimes have always aligned on the side of capital, with the top echelons benefiting from even greater levels of exploitation. International attempts to get agreements are constantly thwarted by corporate lobbying or avoidance. Once a regulation is in place, be it a tax or environmental law, the first incentive of the corporate board, its legal and economic advisors, is how to mitigate or circumvent that law. This will continue until catastrophic climate events or an army of angry environmentalists bang so loudly on the door that they can no longer be ignored. Another factor which has a bearing on the debate is the finite nature of energy supplies. Many analysts say that we are already past peak oil production and the gap between what is produced and consumed is getting tighter, the vast reserves remaining are becoming more difficult and expensive to exploit. Dwindling energy reserves, will of course, be commandeered by those with the financial and military power.

Green energy solutions offer many false dawns. Images of giant wind turbines on a beautiful mountain landscape promising a clean bright future can be deceitful. While all alternative energy sources must be fully explored, it should be ensured that any cost benefit analysis includes: capital and carbon cost of manufacture; transport and erection; reduction of visual and habitat amenity; taxpayers grant aid; down time for maintenance; percentage time of windless conditions; back-up power plant during non-productive phases; life and replacement time of the installation; removal of all plant, recycling, and reinstatement of the site. It is essential that any government authority ensures that the operator is bonded to cover the removal of installations and the reinstatement of the site in the case of liquidation. Most cases of alternative energy looked at to-date fail on many of these counts.

While events at Chernobyl and the fear of external affects such as earthquake or tsunamis on other plants do not engender any great affection, nuclear power is still an option. France, with over 90% of its electricity emanating from nuclear or hydropower, claims that it is energy independent. It has almost the lowest cost electricity in Europe with an extremely low level of CO2 emissions per capita. The message is that, as yet, there are no miracle, alternative energy systems. Energy optimists predict a major technological break-through in power generation and they may be right. Cautious scepticism as encouraged here, may be a default position, but one is aware of the following statements of W. Thompson, first Lord Kelvin, an eminent man of letters and science who declared the following facts to be true:, "the world is far too young to have allowed for evolution, radio has no future, x-rays are a hoax and heavier than air flying machines will never be possible". Perhaps new technologies of nuclear fission and hydrogen-fuelled engines are around the corner and that humanity's ingenuity will triumph and discover everlasting clean energy. While such a scenario would radically change our perception of the future of energy, it would not remove the necessity for its democratic control, time will tell.

Energy saving is an easier route to travel and good progress is being made. Engines of all kinds have become far more efficient and insulating buildings against heat loss has improved dramatically. We might even overcome our fear of the dark and our need to light every street and motorway which pollute the night sky, but we are again at the 'red queen effect'. The faster innovation and efficiency rises, the more population and economic growth negates our efforts. Perhaps one can be overly pessimistic, but the growth of consumption and the concentration of wealth can lead to startling conclusions. The top ten percent who own and control the vast bulk of wealth have the most power and influence. They are the forces directing and gaining the most from production, consumption and expansion, but will suffer the least from environmental degradation and peak oil. The rich and poor will not suffer equally, for the wealthy have the resources to relocate where the impact is least and will continue to afford the benefits of energy long after it becomes unaffordable by the majority.

The intellectual space that should be occupied by philosophical debate on our interaction with each other and the natural world is presently occupied by abstract deliberations of theology and religion. However, the religious are not a unified camp, many adherents realise the plight of our fragile species and are coming to see corporate interests as the problem. In any case, the controlling forces of economics and philosophy presently represented by capitalism and the conservative church have no objective interest in a change of direction. Thus remedial action will not come from the top down, it will require to be driven from the bottom up, by the democratic will of a motivated and well-organised people, they will not act without a threatening and thus unifying cause.

Social entities, such as a state, uses strategies to stimulate unity, loyalty and co-operation, be it by a royal family, nationalism or religion, a unity that can be intensified by an external threat, real or imagined. To tackle global problems, a global unity is required. Science-fiction writers were correct when they implied that mankind would unite against an external threat such as an invasion of aliens from space. But the enemy is already here, knocking loudly on the door and so far the sound is being drowned by the clamour of individual, national and corporate self-interest and hymns of delusion. The enemy at the door is a troika of population growth, resource depletion and climate change. Scientists are screaming from the rooftops that climate change isn't just a bit of warming and some storms. They claim we are a fragile species, dependant on a biosphere which can crumble like a row of dominos. As the Earth warms, the Arctic ice melts and as it reduces, less sunlight is reflected which means more heat is absorbed. This is an accelerating cycle that leads to global, large-scale changes, like ocean acidification and rising sea levels. Worst case possibilities could bring irreversible changes, such as a rapid release of methane and carbon dioxide from a warming permafrost.

As the mechanisation of industrial and agricultural production dramatically increased efficiency, so also the mechanisation of weapons increased that of killing. Swords, cavalry charges, pistols and canon caused a great deal more carnage than the longbows and lances of previous eras. The advent of the First World War brought the machine gun, shell, mortar and gas and 10 million dead. By the time of the Second World War, long-range bombing, fast armour, submarines, gas chambers and a grand finale of the atomic bomb had enhanced our efficiency at killing, with over 60 million dead and Europe and the Soviet Union in ruins. After the war the ingenuity of humanity was applied to develop intercontinental ballistic missiles with multiple war heads. One could argue that the presence of such weapons actually brought a period of peace as the Cold War brought a stand-off between the two superpowers, on the principle of mutually assured destruction. There are over 17,000 nuclear warheads currently available for deployment. The international armaments industry still drives humanity into this dangerous but profitable competition. The military adventures of the United States, the rise of the religious fundamentalism in Israel and Pakistan, the breakup of the Soviet Union and the emergence of Islamic fascism, all contribute to international instability. Nuclear power falling into the hands of those more committed to the next life than the here and now, could well determine our survival? Suicide bombers and the 9/11 pilots were men of deep faith. Picture them with such weapons acting like those who, also with god on their side, coldly planned the fate of Hiroshima and Nagasaki.

Over nine billion of us are expected to live on planet earth by 2050, if we have not amended our ways of growth and competition by then, our existence may well be in jeopardy. The situation is unlikely to change while profit-seeking systems are in control. Only a co-ordinated international response by the concerned, actively engaged in mass education and political action can make gains. Transformative change from neurotic consumerism driven by greed and competition to an egalitarian sustainable society together with a coherent philosophy, will be required to save our fragile species.

Chapter 10   Struggle & Defeat.

The Bolshevik revolution of 1917 brought hope and confidence to a vast international social movement. The benefits that accrued to the majority of people throughout Europe were enormous and have yet to be acknowledged. Its success contributed to improvements in education, health and living standards worldwide, with a transfer of wealth to the majority. The reverberation of the events in Russia, combined with the return of millions of men from the First World War, conversant in the use of arms, sent a chill through the ruling class of every country where capital was king. They realised what an organised people could achieve and the potential that existed for such actions to spread. Fear, that great advisor of survival, ensured that concessions were made on all fronts. Socialist ideas had led the great struggles of the twentieth century; the emancipation of women, the fight against fascism and racism, they gave hope to the disposed worldwide. The anti-colonial wars of many peoples, from Southeast Asia to the Americas, were supported by socialist states. The collapse of the Soviet Union brought a decline of confidence to the socialist movement and instigated a roll-back of previous social gains which continues to this day. It gave buoyancy to unregulated capital and the concentration of wealth intensified as did every facet of the alienating order.

Innovations in science or business start with research, a hypothesis and chance. Similarly social revolutions require a concept or a plausible dream for the construction of a better future. In both cases, the conditions must be right but even then either may experience the risk of dead-ends and failures. Social history is generally perceived as a series of unconnected events - an almost circular movement of humanity, the coming and going of monarchs and their various battles and conquests. It ill serves an establishment to show any pattern of progress in history, for interpolations might lead to unwelcome conclusions. An emotive issue is the role of class contradictions in the formation of every economic system and state. It is the relationship between the owners of the means of production and those whose labour power is necessary for production, these forces determine the nature of an economic and social order. The ultimate resolution of class conflict is when the producers have the ability and responsibility to take ownership of the means of production.

The hundredth anniversary of the 1917 October Revolution in Russia, the formation of the USSR and its legacy will sharpen discussions on whether history can be progressive. The 80-year experiment with socialism in the Soviet Union will be used as an example of failure. Some argue, as they did at the time, that it is impossible to build socialism in one country and thus the experiment was doomed from the start. Many socialists agree that what happened in the USSR was a socialism which distorted under external aggression, isolation and internal paranoia. A related issue is the lack of understanding most people have of the aggression by the forces of capital against the Soviet Union, both at its formation and during the Second World War. A war which is often falsely seen as a battle between Germany and the UK on the one hand and Japan and the United States on the other. A more balanced history from pre-revolutionary Europe, through the events of 1917 to the collapse of the USSR, gives an understanding of the main players on the world stage and how they got there.

The oppressed have always yearned for a society in which their lot would improve. Slaves dreamed they might escape and return to an abundant hunting and gathering ground. Serfs in a feudal society wished freedom to farm their own plot of land and control their lives. Workers dreamed of a society without exploitation, where they would gain and share the fruits of their labour, to this end they organised socialist and communist political parties. But communists were not the only dreamers of the time. Fascists from Spain to Germany were the militant face of capital and the church, they realised that democracy and internationalism threatened the rule and riches of this elite, as was evident from the events in Russia. The main objective of fascism was the crushing of all working-class organisations and any democracy that might extend power over capital. They were the front line protagonists of their sponsors - the remnants of aristocracy and owners of industry. Their dream was the establishment of a permanent ruling class, bathed in the light of xenophobic nationalism which brooked no discussion or opposition. The German fascists or Nazis coupled such ideas with a notion of an Aryan master race and an empire that would dominate Europe for a thousand years. This explosion of dysfunctional capitalism resulted in the death of over sixty million people and left a huge section of Europe in ruins. It did unfortunately, to some extent succeed, for the unparalleled devastation that came in its wake sowed the seeds for the destruction of socialism and postponed any possibility of building a communist society.

The revolution of 1917 did not occur, as was predicted, in an advanced industrial state such as Germany or England, but in a relatively backward feudal one. The invasions that immediately followed the revolution were sponsored by international capital seeking to regain its wealth, weakened the state and contributed to internal paranoia and a diminution of democracy. An objective history of the rise and fall of the Soviet Union has not yet been written and may never be, as there are perhaps too many subjective agendas. The Soviet Union never progressed beyond commencing the building of a socialist state and certainly never came near being a communist society, as no state ever has, or independently can. We will never know if in different conditions it could have evolved into a truly communist, egalitarian society. But in any event the transparency, the checks and balances and constant democratic input from the bottom did not prevail. All of this and more would have been required to maintain the confidence and support of its people. While there might be the possibility of building a socialist state within a national boundary, such could not apply to the construction of a communist society, which by definition would require the withering away of state enforcement structures. That could only emerge if it were international and without internal or external threat.

Since the immortal opening lines of the Communist Manifesto written in 1848 - "A Spectre is haunting Europe - the spectre of Communism" - a certain unease has lurked deep in the minds of the holders of power and privilege. Their nightmare, that great hordes of the dispossessed, the people who sell their labour to exist, were thinking revolutionary thoughts and organising revolutionary parties to take power. In almost all cases the only reason organised workers become revolutionary was they were given no choice, their demands ignored and democratic movements suppressed. An early revolt of that nature was the Paris Commune of 1871 when municipal elections led to the formation of a commune government. It followed the French Revolutionary tradition with a programme that called for an end of support for religion and a limited number of social measures such as a 10-hour working day. It was short-lived, ending in suppression by the national armies of the elite. The French bourgeoisie took the challenge to their power and privilege very seriously and over 35,000 communards were slaughtered. The red flag, the workers flag, was raised in France for the first time about February 1848 and came to symbolise what was to be the recurring fate of those in the lower orders who dared seek equality. "For though their limbs grow stiff and cold, their hearts' blood dyed its every fold" *[song- The Red Flag- Jim Connell, Co. Meath].*

The century leading up to 1914 was relatively peaceful in Europe with a concentration on industrialisation, colonial expansion and the consolidation of nation states. The Industrial Revolution in Britain and beyond expanded the available consumer market and likewise the numbers of producers competing for those markets. It brought massive increases in productivity and great disparities of wealth, it brought the working class and class conflict. It stimulated alternative, socialist philosophies which questioned state and church power as never before. As an antidote to the growth of international socialism and to aid colonial expansion, nationalistic feelings were promoted within each country. Superiority over other nations was preached and the dangers they posed were embellished. European nations, especially France, Britain, and Germany, joined in the rush for overseas colonies. Industrialisation and superiority in arms allowed them seize land almost unopposed world-wide and build colonial empires. By the turn of the century most colonisation had taken place intensifying competition for the remaining areas.

The industrialised countries of Europe applied taxes on imported goods, prices increased, and trade declined. The masters of capital and politics sought scapegoats, blaming competing states which led to a spiral of tariffs, lower trade, rising unemployment and unrest. The unification of Italy and most especially that of Germany and its rapid rise as an economic and military power alarmed its neighbours. Nations reacted by building their respective military strength and forming alliances. France allied with Russia and England. Germany with Austria and Italy. Wealth, greed and competition became a toxic combination within and without the national borders of Europe. With the major powers in opposing camps, danger lay in any two members of opposing alliances coming into conflict, resulting in the possibility of a major war.

The awesome power of capitalism was being demonstrated by the creation of new technologies which, as trade and production of consumer goods declined, were diverted into the armaments industry. The mass production of weapons, such as the machine gun, long-range artillery, mortars, submarines, and battleships, triggered an arms race such as the world had never seen. This poisonous cocktail combined with the arrogance of national chauvinism plunged Europe into the First World War. Nationalism like religion has the power to overcome the common interests of humanity and gather it into opposing groups. In each country the national press demonised any internal opposition and blackened the people of opposing countries into vile caricatures. Most socialists were persuaded to abandon their internationalism and join the army where they trained to kill their fellow workers. Christian priests and pastors preached to both sides that god was with them. With much singing and flag-waving the armies marched off to war, all assured of their superiority and that victory would be theirs within a few months. Both sides were almost equal in armaments and the armies bogged down in trench warfare and unbelievable carnage. On the 1st of July 1916 at the Somme, with the aid of mine, mortar and machine gun 65,000 young men lay dead by the end of that single day. Most did not die clean, but screaming in disbelief and searing pain as they looked at their own scattered limbs or intestines. Millions of young men with common interests had been persuaded to support King or Kaiser and over four years slaughtered each other. By the end of the war, a war driven by competition and greed for markets and power between the giants of capital, 16 million were dead and 20 million injured.

On the eastern front, the autocratic rule of Tsar Nicolas II, the despair of Russian troops in a stalemated war, combined with radical movements at home to create a revolution. Russia was an unlikely place for this event, a land of approximately 170 million, where the majority of the population were peasants on a meagre existence with more than 60% illiterate. As Tsarist rule collapsed, many variants of politics briefly existed before the Bolsheviks took power. That organised workers and peasants were able to overthrow the Romanovs and extend democracy over economics brought hope to millions of the oppressed and fear to rulers worldwide. The rebellion took place in conditions of extreme scarcity for, in addition to the privation of Russia's people, the war had aggravated food shortages and disease. By October 1917 the country was under the control of councils of workers, farmers and soldiers. All productive property and land was brought under the ownership of the people. The Russian army, as promised, was withdrawn from the slaughter of the front.

The first phase of any new project has an exciting quality, a hypothesis that mankind could build a society without exploitation, with equality of gender and race, where the combined productive capacity of society could be harnessed to serve the common good. It was a watershed historical moment and an inspiration to millions as they witnessed economic power pass to its producers. But it was also a watershed moment for those who were losing their land, mines, railways and investments. It was a dangerous and threatening time for capital and the ruling elite worldwide who mobilised all the power and propaganda they could muster against this new state, for if this socialist revolution was not strangled at birth, it could spread. They were determined that it had not just to be contained, but reversed. Thus external capitalist powers invaded Russia trying to regain their investments and crush the revolution. Germany invaded from the west, American, British and French forces from the north, Japanese and American troops landed in the east. All these forces joined with the internal counter-revolutionaries forces as the old order of Russia fought to regain power and privilege. As many as 255,000 troops were involved from 14 different countries, capturing large sections of the country. It was November 1920 before the Red Army finally defeated all the invaders, subdued the internal opposition and secured the country. The invasions had brought devastation, economic ruin and famine. Those who had failed to bring down the revolution with direct military intervention now concentrated on blockades, propaganda and isolation.

The security of the revolution in Russia depended on its spread to advanced capitalist countries, in particular to Germany, where despite five years of revolutionary upheaval, the revolution failed. The new socialist state was left isolated, struggling internally with reaction and under attack from external forces. Consequently, instead of being able to concentrate on improving the well-being of the people, huge resources had to be squandered on defence. When the leader of the revolution, V.I. Lenin, was shot in 1918 this act further poisoned the atmosphere, substantiating the belief that there were enemies of the state everywhere and increasing the paranoia. Lenin's health deteriorated, he died in January 1924, but the struggle to build socialism went on. There is no greater school than a revolution and it is not surprising that some of the most innovative and successful literacy campaigns are those born when a mass of people fight for a better society. In such periods ideas matter as never before and the spread of literacy becomes a prime liberating endeavour. Education was massively overhauled with a tenfold increase in expenditure. Free and universal access was mandated for all children from the ages of three to sixteen years, the number of schools doubled within the first two years. Co-education was implemented to combat sex discrimination and for the first time schools were created for students with learning and other disabilities.

Revolutionary ideas in Europe were reflected by a surge of radical architecture and art, two centres of this movement emerged, the Bauhaus in Germany in 1919, a year later Lenin announced the establishment of the Higher Artistic and Technical Workshops - VKhuTEMAS. The aim was to use the visual arts in the training of technically, politically and scientifically educated architects and designers in all disciplines. It became a laboratory of modern architecture and art, in which diverse artistic ideas such as classicism, constructivism and futurism came together. The oppressive forms and pompous decoration of imperial grandeur were stripped away. During the ten years of its existence it was a leading light in the Russian and European avant-garde. The ethos of the school- which had close association with the Bauhaus- was to develop an architecture and art of socialised man and the machine age. It was a time of promise and endless possibilities, 'less is more' was the catch phrase. Both schools were to flourish for ten years and have a lasting international impact. However, in time the architecture and art of a growing autocracy in Russia could not escape its own reflection, nor could the free spirit of VKhuTEMAS and by 1930 the school was closed. During the same period, the Nazis saw the Bauhaus as un-German, degenerate and Marxist. Its links with VKhuTEMAS in Moscow did not go unnoticed, it was also closed.

Mass literacy was seen as crucial, for it is hard to propagate social ideas and develop an economy in the midst of illiteracy. Economic conditions did not help, they were described at the time: "Hungry children in rags would gather in winter around a small stove planted in the middle of the classroom, whose furniture often went for fuel to give some tiny relief from the freezing cold; they had one pencil between four of them and their schoolmistress was hungry." Over the next 16 years despite a diminution in democracy, progress was made in industrialisation, agriculture, science, education and social care. The emergence of the Soviet Union bolstered the confidence of trade unions and left-wing movements worldwide, allowing gains in living standards and social democracy. However, this was not happening unopposed. The enemies of socialism never sleep and fascism was emerging throughout Europe. In Spain a democracy emerged and subsequent elections established a republic but this was crushed by a right-wing army and ruling class revolt. This movement against democracy received support from reactionaries throughout Europe, including

Germany, and from some within the Republic of Ireland. Thankfully, for our historical dignity 275 Irish volunteers fought with the International Brigade and many died in the unsuccessful defence of the Spanish Republic.

In Germany, the rising Nazi party received its support from the ruling elite, not because Hitler was going to 'solve' the Jewish, gay or gypsy 'problems' but because he was going to destroy the organised workers, the trade unions, and communists. Fascism was the embodiment of competitive greed and 'might is right'. It gained support by opposing the reparation demands of WW1 and by fomenting a populist hatred against the Jews, a policy that led to a most appalling, organised genocide, the holocaust. It provided a diversion, a cry from a prophet Hitler, who was persuading his followers that if the Jewish, gypsy and gay 'problems' were solved, all would be well. But the main antagonists were at large, the spectre of communism was haunting Europe. The workers revolution had consolidated power in Russia and the great fear was that it could be repeated in Germany. The main aim of fascism was to thwart socialism in theory and practice. As early as August 1919, Hitler was lecturing returning German prisoners of war on the dangers of Communism and pacifism, as well as democracy and disobedience. He also delivered tirades against the Jews that were well received by the weary soldiers who were looking for someone to blame for all their misfortunes. The title of the fascist party, the National Socialist Party, while being a total corruption of everything socialism stood for, caused confusion. The promotion of xenophobic ideas, such as the superiority of the Aryan race and German nationalism, undermined international class unity, as had happened in the First World War. Thus the left in Germany was thwarted by the rise of the Nazi party who were supported by the ruling class terrified that they might suffer the fate of the Russian elite. Hitler was seen as a better option than another Lenin.

Historians and obscurants often equate fascism and communism as equal terrors of the time. The majority of leading intellectuals of the day and throughout most of the twentieth century were often criticised for their support of the Russian revolution while condemning fascism. This is not surprising for, as the fascists were scheming for nationalism, division, conquest, dominance and the negation of democracy, communists were dreaming of the international solidarity of humanity as well as negation of class divisions, equality, universal education and democratic control over economics. The call of the 'International' to unite all men and end the nightmare of war, was by far the most attractive governmental cause engaged in by our species to date. That the Russian revolution and the Soviet Union did not or perhaps could not reach fruition, is the major human philosophical, social and material tragedy of the last century.

When Germany invaded Poland in 1939, England and France stood by their allegiance and war was declared. The German army then swept west over-running everything in its path until it reached the English Channel. It was assumed the conquest of the United Kingdom would occur within a few months. However, air superiority was required to invade across the channel. The heroic air conflict 'The Battle of Britain' was a victory for the Royal Air Force and changed the tide of war on the western front. Those in Ireland of thoughtful mind and democratic bent breathed a sigh of relief, for had the Third Reich occupied England, Ireland would have quickly suffered the same fate. Even if the Nazis had not crossed the Irish Sea, they would have ensured that a government of their liking was established. Socialists, trade union leaders and Jews would have suffered the same fate in the UK and Ireland as their European counterparts.

If we thought English occupation was rough it would have been a picnic compared to the Third Reich. Resistance would have been dealt with the same brutality as that suffered by the village of Lidice outside Prague where a Nazi officer was assassinated and 173 men of the village were shot, any Aryan looking children were sent to 'good' German homes and the remaining children, together with 183 women, were sent to the death camps. The village itself was levelled. The Republic of Ireland has come under criticism for remaining neutral in the Second World War, but it was weary from the war of independence and a civil war. Besides it did not have an industrialised army to contribute and there still existed a sentiment amongst the population which was hostile to the UK. An ambiguity towards fascism had been strengthened by the support given by the Church and media for the crushing of the Spanish Republic. However, while Ireland remained officially neutral an estimated fifty thousand Irish men and women served with the Allied and UK forces. Furthermore, Allied airman downed over the Republic were returned to their bases within a few days while Germans who suffered the same fate were confined for the duration of the war.

In the east, Hitler and Stalin had signed a non-aggression pact which fooled no one, least of all the Soviets who immediately started to move their armament factories east of the Ural Mountains. It was to be a short-lived respite. 'Operation Barbarossa' - called after the Holy Roman Emperor who led a crusade in 1189 to free the 'Holy Land' from Islam - began in June 1941, a crusade to free the world from socialism. It was the biggest military operation of all time; a mainly German invasion of the Soviet Union with three million men and 3,500 tanks, this was more than two and a half times the number of German troops operating on the western front. This invasion was planned not to be a war of conquest but a war on annihilation, to form a space for the expansion of Germany. In the Deutsches Historisches Museum in Berlin, there is a plaque which reads:

> "On June 22 1941. Germany attacked the Soviet Union. The rapidly advancing tank forces helped the Wehrmacht to make massive territorial gains. At the end of 1941 the German army stood before Moscow, certain of victory. Yet the Red Army's counter-offensives in snow and frost halted the advance on the capital. In the summer of 1942 the Germans once more seized large areas of the southern section of the front, but were soon forced to retreat. The war in the East, unlike that on the West was carried out as a war of annihilation. The primary aims were to suppress Bolshevism, seize Lebensraum, living space, exploit the occupied areas and make use of the population as forced labour. The East was to provide the German Reich with food and to be colonised by Aryans. Hence the death of many millions of Soviet citizens was an integral part of the plan. Captured Red Army soldiers were deliberately left to die of hunger. Mobile killing units operating behind the front lines - the Einsatzgruppen - systematically killed the Jewish population along with Roma and Sinti as well as communist functionaries. The entire Soviet civilian population suffered from the terror of the occupation, which led them to retaliate with bitter guerrilla warfare. By 1945 the Soviet Union had more than 25 million dead to mourn."

Hell had travelled east and every village, town and city taken by the German forces was destroyed. By August 1942 they were at the gates of Stalingrad. Initially the Luftwaffe reduced much of the city to rubble with a massive bombing campaign. Then German armour and infantry fought street by street driving the Red Army defenders back in constant close combat. In November with the deepening of winter and in freezing conditions the Red Army counter-attacked and surrounded 265,000 Axis troops, mainly German but also Hungarian, Romanian, Italian and

Croatian, who had been forbidden to surrender by Hitler. All were eventually overrun and the entire course of the war turned. Stalingrad is now recognised as the most decisive battle of the war; it lasted just under six months. At the end of the fighting there were almost two million casualities on both sides. It had been the biggest and bloodiest single battle of not just the Second World War, but ever in human history.

The Red Army, having broken the back of the Wehrmacht, started its push west and by May 1945 reached Berlin and the war was over. The Soviet Union paid a very high price with 25 million of its people dead, 70,000 villages and 1,710 towns, together with thousands of factories, power plants, libraries, schools and hospitals destroyed. To place the scale of the Allied losses in context, the United States lost 420,000, mainly military personnel, in the Pacific and European conflicts and suffered no damage to its industrial base. The UK lost a total of 450,000 military and civilians. Total German losses were over 7,000,000 and the country was in ruins. In the countries where the Red Army pushed back fascism, socialist governments were established. At the Yalta conference, the Soviet delegation demanded a sphere of political and military influence in Eastern and Central Europe making the point that this bulwark of allied states was an essential aspect of its national security. This effectively partitioned Europe between the western capitalist economies and the eastern socialist ones. The power and wealth of US capitalism was then directed to rebuilding the economies of Western Europe in a mode to suit the free reign of capital. Huge amounts of aid under the Marshal Plan were poured into rebuilding West Germany. The decimated USSR was not in any position to match that reconstruction in the east. In the world of free capital everything was done to promote anti-socialist thinking and contain the influence of socialist ideas. By 1950 the red scare and McCarthyism were in full swing in the United States, the part played by the Red Army in WW2 was being written out of history. An intellectual iron curtain was drawn down on socialism and the physical border between the two systems in Europe became another. The cold war developed.

Towards the end of the war with Japan, the United States had demonstrated how two nuclear bombs could immolate a city and 130,000 people in a flash. This forced Japan to surrender but it also forced a now very nervous USSR to divert a vast amount of its resources from badly needed reconstruction and social projects to nuclear deterrence and defence. The United States was bolstered by a flourishing arms race. This forced the Soviet Union with its much damaged economy to do the same, thus seriously impairing the building of socialism. The fear of external attack forged its strategic thinking regarding the states that lay between it and the perceived threat from the west. While Soviet Russia had rendered anti-imperialist support to many countries worldwide and respected their self-determination, it would and did intervene to ensure that states adjacent to its border remained under its sphere of influence within the Warsaw Pact. This paranoia of external attack effectively prevented socialism from flourishing in the Soviet Union and any chance of building a communist society was doomed. To this day the fear of external aggression dominates Russian military thinking, it will go to great lengths to maintain influence on its neighbours to ensure they remain allies or at least non-aligned.

By way of comparison, on September 11th 2001 after the destruction of the World Trade Centre and the death of 3,000 by hi-jacked airliners, the United States was gripped by paranoia. The war on terror commenced and countries that were completely innocent were invaded and destroyed. Suspects were collected worldwide and flown to Guantanamo Bay to be held without charge and tortured. Imagine the reaction of the United States if an actual ground force invasion had occurred and 25 million Americans had been killed, 70,000 villages, 1,710 towns, thousands of factories, power plants, libraries, schools, hospitals had been destroyed.

Up to 1991, the USSR made erratic progress in production, health, education and living standards. However, the investment in armaments was to prove evermore crippling. That such a relatively backward state could, after so much destruction, match the United States in nuclear firepower, achieving a capability of mutually assured destruction, speaks volumes for the organisational ability of a people under pressure. Unfortunately the building of socialism and securing the well-being and happiness of a people requires a very different environment, a problem that highlights the difficulty, if not the impossibility, of building socialism in a single country, particularly a threatened one. Deep governance problems arose, a lack of balances and transparency within the system allowed power to move away from the worker councils and fall excessively into the hands of the Communist Party and leadership, finally concentrating in Stalin. Inherited characteristics of supplication from the legacy of Czarism and religious orthodoxy re-emerged, a cult of leadership flourished with a leader who was both feared and adored. Nothing could be further from the foundations required to build socialism from the bottom up. Huge mistakes were made in the economy. Corruption, bureaucracy and inefficiencies grew. Finally in 1991 the contradictions of external pressure and internal betrayal brought about a coup by President Yeltsin. When it became obvious that he would lose the next election and knowing he had support from the IMF and with billions in aid promised from the US congress he abolished the constitution and dissolved parliament. Having doubled military salaries he surrounded the parliament building with troops and ordered an attack. About five hundred were killed and a thousand wounded, democracy was effectively crushed and the socialist state was replaced by a corporatist one. Naomi Klein says in her book *The Shock Doctrine*, "former communist party apparatchiks and a handful of western fund managers ....teamed up with Yeltsin's Chicago boys and stripped the country of nearly everything of value, moving profits abroad at the rate of $2 billion a month". Never have so many lost so much over such a short period, the pillage required terror and oppression and the country that strove for egalitarianism now languishes with an elite of billionaires and bulging poverty.

The collapse and the break-up of the USSR was grotesquely celebrated by the western media and the elite worldwide, they were relieved when a fistful of men grabbed the wealth of the USSR and became multi-millionaires overnight. The spectre of communism was at least temporarily over, the world could now perhaps be free - free for the dictatorship of capital. With the collapse of this intrepid peoples experiment, went the confidence and influence of left-wing movements worldwide. Capital regained its confidence and accelerated deregulation and further accumulation at the expense of the majority, its global range and power increasing in inverse proportion to the diminishing power of national democracies. Workers international solidarity diminished with the growth of divisions through nationalism and religion. Most movements against oppression which had previously been led by secular left-wing forces had been subverted and splintered into divisive religious fundamentalism, toxic to reason, but ultimately of no threat to global capital. Nonetheless the innate desire of humans to build a just egalitarian society, a co-operative internationalist community will not go away.

Chapter 11   Education

Children are not owned by their parents, state or church, they are inalienable and individual beings, who never asked to be born. Our responsibility as parents and that of society is to prepare them, to the best of our ability, for whatever joy or terror their lives might hold. We owe children love, care and protection and must nurture them with food, shelter and knowledge. They are born with basic survival and replicating instincts wired in but not much else. Compared to the speed at which other species of vertebrates begin to walk and forage, humans are exceedingly slow. The complexity of the brain, our main tool for survival, requires a long time to gather the knowledge for that task and master language and co-operation.

> NOTE to CHILDREN: "You are in the process of being indoctrinated.... We are sorry, but it is the best we can do. What you are being taught here is an amalgam of current prejudice and the choices of this particular culture. ....
> You are being taught by people who have been able to accommodate themselves to a regime of thought laid down by their predecessors. It is a self-perpetuating system. Those of you who are more robust and individual than others will be encouraged to leave and find ways of educating yourself....those that stay must remember, always, that they are being moulded and patterned to fit into the narrow and particular needs of this particular society."
>
> Abridged from: Doris Lessing. The Golden Notebook

Preparing a child to survive on its own takes well over twenty years. The specialisations required to engage in production call for an inordinate amount of time in formal education, before exiting the nest. The earliest period of learning, their most formative years, is when children absorb information at the highest rate, at which stage they have open minds and are chock-full of questions. This is when their emotional security and self-confidence are built. This is also the period where they first discern the limits of the intellectual space in which they will be constrained to operate. Society has always felt it necessary to contain the learning process, it does not want challenges to its beliefs, economic or political structures. Although the mechanics of education appear like some vast conspiracy, that is only partly so, for control springs mainly from the objective survival interest of the power structure. It is the unambiguous agenda of this book to expose the reasons for that control, to argue against the intellectual limits placed on children and to highlight the essentialness of critical thinking.

The young child has an inquisitive nature and would naturally develop an analytical mind. However, that is also the time when the tendency can most readily be quashed. Education is structured to form quiet, compliant children, who will absorb unexamined ideas and accept the direction of authority without question, one-dimensional students who will work diligently throughout their formal schooling, learning and reproducing the curriculum. The objective is that they will emerge from the highest levels of academia as well qualified, polite, compliant operatives and consumers, trained to work in any sector of production or service diligently selling their expertise while generating wealth for small elites of corporate business. It is intended that they support the institutions of state and church without question. In the past, those who were similarly conditioned poured out of trenches with fixed bayonets and slaughtered their fellows by the millions and were in turn themselves slaughtered - actions which hardly served the interests of themselves or the majority. Now compliant children on becoming obedient and conditioned adults, will vote for unexamined parties and wallow in unexamined belief systems. They will believe and behave as did the family and society from which they emerged, little will change and for the majority it will not be to their benefit.

Despite increasing demands for science and innovation, state and church do not objectively want any real change in education. Many employers say they seek innovative graduates with higher levels in the sciences and maths to function in an advanced technical and business world. What they really seek is that their operatives innovate and think scientifically within the confines of the companies agenda, such as in consumer gadgets, 'apps', business models, financial instruments, all geared to boost the company's competitive money making. What is not sought is innovative thinking in relation to the social order or the development of a morality applicable to social or environmental responsibility.

Achievement by students is judged almost solely by grading, it focuses on individualism and is a conditioning to serve an individual or company. Such structuring separates the student from responsibility to the broader society. The qualified solicitor with the highest grades and a master's degree, will serve the best law firms and spend their lives defending the interests of corporations against the interests of society. The finest brains in accountancy will be well paid to invent financial instruments to defend and protect fast moving capital from taxation. They will be clean in conscience, feeling no level of responsibility for the grinding levels of exploitation and the poverty of those who might suffer from their actions or the millions whose deprivation increases in proportion to the concentration of capital. They will live comfortably protected by distance, layers of law and a consciousness and philosophy structured to negate social responsibility.

The educational training needed is one which would engender a moral responsibility for the well-being of an entire society, which in turn needs a large section of pupils not just learning and reproducing science, but thinking scientifically with a social conscience. Whether such students become self-employed or work for a company or the state, they should be sufficiently aware to question the project in which they are involved and be sufficiently conscious to ascertain how their work benefits all of society or otherwise. They should also have sufficient moral courage to intervene in compliance with their convictions. It is imperative that we envision a time when the socially educated scientist will harness the power of his or her rational thinking for the benefit of the broad social order.

Parents and teachers who govern that critical early period of learning, effectively build the ethos of society. Both are statistically likely to be culturally religious rather than possess any strong convictions and both are subject to the ongoing drift to more a humanist outlook. The majority of parents are engaged only in a vague way with the details of religious teaching within the schools. If they were truly aware of how their children's critical faculties were negated and the long-term implications of that they would be profoundly shocked. The case for teaching, based solely on evidence, would soon gain the upper hand. Teachers themselves are likely to be the most conservative element in education as the route to primary teaching is through established training colleges, religious institutions which require a student to suppress secular tendencies or personal dissent. It is difficult for a progressive teacher who wants to engender critical thought and encourage their students to range through the intellectual cosmos. However, they are caught in a dilemma, for within the religious schools they are required to teach children complex illusions as facts and reward them when these are accepted. Of course there are and have been dedicated teachers who encourage children to find a way through these contradictions.

An additional way in which critical thinking is effectively disallowed is that teachers are inculcated with a responsibility to teach within the confines of the curriculum and are given very little time in which to range outside it. A busy curriculum overloaded to match the time available and an exam-focused system safeguard that objective. Such a situation mitigates against enlightened teachers encouraging their pupils along more challenging intellectual paths. Exams have become the determinant of a student's future life, forcing the teacher into an onerous position of responsibility to the student and parents, obliging them to focus strictly on the curriculum and exams. An open, passionate teacher with a sceptical mind would prove disastrous in terms of the existing ethos and if detected would be surely asked to move on. To progress a moral, ethical and intellectual society, these institutions require a root and branch reformation.

Female genital mutilation [FGM] is usually carried out on girls between five and ten years of age within some highly misogynist cultures mainly African Muslims and immigrant communities closer to home. It affects millions of girls and women worldwide. It involves removal of all or part of the clitoris and clitoral hood, carried out with the consent of parents, family and friends. These organs give the female pleasure and sexual climax in adulthood - a natural life-affirming experience. There are strong analogies between the oppression of a free sexual libido and the oppression of a free critical mind, both of which are practiced with social approbation. The mutilation of young girls is so obviously immediate and hideous that it triggers social empathy, whereas the suppression of a child's critical faculties, occurring over a protracted period, appears more readily acceptable. While this practice of mental mutilation might be equated with FGM, at least in many countries throughout the world the latter is becoming illegal.

Rule 68 applying to National Schools states: "Of all the parts of a school curriculum Religious Instruction is by far the most important, as its subject-matter, God's honour and service..... Religious Instruction is, therefore, a fundamental part of the school course, and a religious spirit should inform and vivify the whole work of the school." The *Alive-O4* teacher's book - a modern day catechism is an example of how bad things are. The first rather telling item, is the book marker, a cartoon of silly sheep in a line. Perhaps someone in the printers had a humorous or an anarchist streak! The *Alive-O* programme is a series of instruction books for faith formation, covering five days a week for the entire school year. It encourages great reverence for the Bible describing how it should be moved across the classroom with ritual, a procession accompanied by flowers and incense. It explains how despite being the word of god, humans wrote it for adults in a different period and one must take great care with its intended meanings - perhaps an admission that the Bible is the Achilles' heel of Christianity. The programme states that both hell and mortal sin are off the agenda and not to be mentioned. Overall there is a shift towards humanism away from the 'God of Wrath' catechism of old. However, the pervading message of the *Alive-O* programme is that the teachers have to pretend to know something they cannot know and persuade the children to pretend to know what they also cannot know. This is the essence of every depressing page.

The teachers are encouraged to stimulate the children's sense of awe with religious pictures, statues, candles, incense and the sprinkling of holy water, to evoke attitudes of prayer. A whole week is dedicated to the study of sheep, which would be perfectly acceptable if they were taught about the evolution of that species, how they were adopted by humans and how the different breeds are achieved. They could also be taught the reason shepherds mind sheep in the first place −for their slaughter and consumption, there are hundreds of worthwhile lessons that could emanate from a discussion on sheep. Instead, the children devote five days looking for lost sheep, naming the sheep and equating themselves to being a lost sheep, a ghastly distortion and exploitation of the child's natural empathy. On page 230 of *Alive-O4*, the children are told: "Close your eyes, still your body, feel your breath as it flows in and out of your lungs..." When they have adopted this trance-like situation, they are asked to: "Imagine, Jesus the good shepherd is standing in front of you, he is holding a little lamb... lambs frolicking with other lambs .... Jesus is holding you... feel the strong arms protecting you..." Twenty-seven lines of carefully structured indoctrination slowly washes over their brains, then they are told to "open your eyes... stretch... relax". The teacher then reads a prayer, concluding with "and I, a sheep of your flock" with the children in unison repeating every line. Similar sessions are enacted, day after day, week after week, while the young, bright, questioning minds of the children are slowly subdued and they too are turned into sheep. This tragic crucifixion of the intellect is being celebrated in over 3,000 schools every teaching day, funded by the taxpayer.

The Catholic Schools Partnership says of these institutions: "Children have a safe place to learn, play and pray; adolescents grow into a deeper intellectual, emotional and moral world. Teachers use their personal and professional abilities to nurture and challenge new generations. The leaders of tomorrow are in the classrooms of today. Fostering a commitment to critical thinking and creativity is the heartbeat of any living tradition and Catholic schooling is an expression of just such a living tradition. The hope is that by 17-18 years of age a young adult who is free, rational and capable of mature relationships will be able to cross the threshold into higher education or the world of work." To equate this ongoing tragedy with fostering critical thinking is beyond comprehension, this is an ethos which has permeated schooling since the foundation of the state. The Partnership proudly proclaims that these schools have been and they quote: "the heartbeat of our living tradition and Catholic schooling". Yet, it is these very schools that have laid the foundations for the repeated collapse of morality in the religious, political and economic institutions of our society. Building the moral values of our people and society on illusory foundations does not work; it is a proven failure. Imagine what could be achieved, if instead of *Alive-O*, every teacher had in hand, books like *The Magic of Reality*. Such would encourage the formation of a morality based on the realities of human evolution, empathy and environmental responsibility. Such a profound change would mean that the divisive concept of Catholic, Protestant, Jewish and Muslim schools would become an anathema. Formal school education would be evidence-based and secular. Faith teaching would become the responsibility of the parents and the various religious denominations. Such a move, in addition to liberating the schools, would provide a focus to the various religions, strengthening the participation of their congregation and expanding the raison d'être of the church itself.

We formerly allowed children to be sexually abused when through ignorance they were denied the information to protect themselves. This ignorance sprang from an endemic shame connected with the story of original sin, shame of the body, shame of sex, shame of reproduction, shame that we are a species whose organs for reproduction are similar to that of animals. The only time they were exposed to images of near nudity were in the icons of the crucifixion. They couldn't even name the body parts associated with producing children, vagina, penis and even feeding organs of the breasts were taboo. This was done to preserve the innocence of children, which implied that reproduction was somehow less than innocent. By having no knowledge of the mechanisms of sex organs and the powerful forces that drive them, children had no way of understanding or communicating what was happening to them, they were ripe for abuse.

When abuse finally came to light, the church contended the abuse to be the fault of a few evil individual priests and nuns. A similar approach was taken by the many sex abuse investigations, to expose and punish the culprits. Such methodology ignored the foundations of ignorance, an ignorance which had both formed these dysfunctional abusers and deprived the victims of defence. Ignorance, piety and prohibition had little hope of dealing with the reproductive instincts of those unfortunate celibate priests and nuns, all their flaws burst like boils to the surface. This constant sexual tension within the clergy was suppressed and hidden as were the resulting crimes when the church had the supremacy to do so. With the diminution of church power and consequent rise in confidence of the abused, the truth slowly emerged. This was devastating for the church as it controlled almost all the institutions in which these abuses flourished. Even after all the horrors of the past, the social order still allows the religious, that control.

Parents were complicit in the repression of sexual knowledge, not for any malign reason, for they too lacked the skills to question their unexamined inheritance. They concurred with the protection of innocence approach and did not envisage that would expose their children to such abuse. Parents are still complicit in the repression of critical thinking, again, not for any malign reason, but because they have not analysed the consequences, they do not envisage the limitations being placed on their children by such unexamined belief systems. The rights of the child are not subservient to the rights of the parents or school patron. The rights of the child must be paramount - a right to have access to all available information to enable him or her to make choices, develop judicial thinking and choose his or her own course through life. Education is far too important to be left to a simple case of bullying, that might is right. No one should be permitted to force, restrain or slap a child to act or learn in any way because it is bigger and stronger. Likewise no ideology should be permitted to stifle a child's thinking just because it is old, large and thinks it has all the answers. Such an approach is well past its sell-by date.

When a 15-year-old child, Anne Lovett, lonely beyond comprehension, terrified and in agonising pain died giving birth to her still-born baby under the vacant stare of an unmoved plaster virgin, we collectively knew, that by closing the gates of knowledge, we had opened the gates of hell. After dozens of further ghastly tales from orphanages, laundries and borstals we had portfolios of public enquiries, reports and public apologies from our leaders and promises that such could never happen again. Anguished parents say "if only we had known". To some extent this has now been accepted in the corridors of power with sex education and protections slowly being put in place.

The connection between the deprivation of sexual knowledge then and the continuing deprivation of critical ability should be obvious. The policy that sees children deprived of a rational education is critical for the future of the children and society. While the Catholic Schools Partnership might believe the young adults they educate are free and rational, this is certainly not the case. They have been taught to absorb information regardless of its content, they have been conditioned for supplication. Once trained in begging favours from celestial royalty they are likewise conditioned to beg favour from terrestrial bankers and bondsmen, to live by soliciting from corporations and to traipse around the globe at the whim of capital and its fluctuations. They are grossly ill-equipped to provide for themselves or deal with the levels of work and wages in the fast changing world. At what time in the future will we witness further statements in Dáil Éireann apologising for how we have let our children down, yet again, with poor education?

When this happens, parents and politicians will yet again plead ignorance, crying, we did not know. Will huge claims for damages be made against the state for negligence, resulting from a purposeful annulment of critical faculties where the child, now an adult, is incapable of innovation, of creating their own work and income in a situation of no alternatives? Could punitive damages be awarded for compliance in brainwashing or causing direct damage to a child, under child protection legislation? Using *Alive-O* as evidence, it could well be possible. If such a case was won, it is likely that the church would wash its hands and walk, while our supplicating governments would ensure the taxpayer picked up the tab.

Most parents start out with the intention of feeding their children wholesome, nourishing food. But with busy lives, fatty, sugary and fat-fried food slips in through a combination of child-centred demands and convenience. A natural desire to keep children happy, combined with relentless advertising encourages desires for instant gratification. The discipline of delayed gratification, a vital tool in health and education, slips away. Fatty sugary food used to be a joke, accompanied by comments like 'Ah sure he/she loves it - it's only puppy fat', but much of the humour has disappeared since obesity has become a major concern. Likewise, there is little humour now attached to a teacher chain smoking in the classroom. Arguments for massive taxes on cigarettes have been sustained on health and safety grounds, are we coming to a time when similar taxes can be placed on the foods of Colonel Saunders and Ronald McDonald? Might it then be possible to place similar discouraging taxes on those feeding, mental junk to defenceless minds or organise warrants for the theft of children's critical faculties? At the end of the day it is a well-educated public and parents that are vital for education, all must assume responsibility for both food and knowledge intake. When the body dies, the mind dies and when the mind becomes intellectually flabby so too, does the body and society.

It is a delight to watch children learn to walk, run, swim, cycle, and play team sports. Outdoor pursuits such as climbing, sailing, horse-riding, surfing and many more should be encouraged with children who are not comfortable in teams, for them to discover their forte in a physical and intellectual capacity is of great help throughout their lives. All children should have equality of access to such pursuits. Similarly children throughout the state must have access to such basic tools as telescopes and microscopes which are extensions of their vision, allowing curiosity to expand beyond their immediate environment. These, combined with free thinking and the right tuition, can bring children face to face with their origins and take them on an exploration of the cosmos and their future.

A recent problem of physical activity is that of health and safety and how quickly a parent can go to court seeking compensation for injuries. While such accidents are rare, they have been exaggerated and have preyed on fear to become detrimental to any even slightly risky activities. Because the damage from inaction by children is incident free and is spread over many years, it is not easily assessed and therefore inaction becomes favoured. This is a challenge to be solved jointly by government, the legal profession and judiciary, they have a responsibility to ensure legislation is balanced between the necessity of risk and requirements of safety. Risk-taking and its benefits must be a priority over the fear of potential consequences. The management of fear, both mental and physical is a vital part of our analytical and survival armoury.

It is difficult, if not impossible, for an education system to have an ethos loftier than its supporting society. It cannot be some abstraction producing brilliant, socially thinking philosophers onto an employment market seeking well-trained operatives who think only within narrow parameters. It would be idealist and naïve to assume that one could revolutionise learning, separate from the social order, or that a revolution in education would alone lead to a revolution in society. But that does not mean inaction, for without a questioning and critical student there will not be a questioning and critical electorate and without that, there is no chance of a progressive shift in the structure of the social order.

For society to progress, it requires to coalesce, to overcome the divisions of class, gender, nationalism and religion. Opponents of progress contend that such divisions are natural and lend colour and diversity and that an egalitarian society would result in a sterile social order. That, however, is the vision becoming a reality under the global corporate order. For as the majority are drained of their critical abilities they conform to the idea that the corporate world order, is the only order. The divisions of humanity provide a background weakness and 'colour' to help maintain that order. But within any structure the complexity of the mind with its inherent diversity ensures that children of the same parents and extended families, going to the same school in the same environment, religion and influences, do not turn out as such. Amongst the myriad of life choices there is always some inconsistency, proving the point that even at these superficial levels, humans don't lack variety. Such observations also thankfully demonstrate that within a dystopian oppression some mutations shall exceed the superficial and voices of dissent will arise.

There are no challenges against the basic subjects within education, it is the division of subjects into unconnected streams, and streams divided into unconnected events that is a problem, also the subjects' disconnection from the existing social order, a distance that fosters alienation from education itself. How the exciting, bloody march of history can be relegated to a list of disjointed events is a case in point. History can be told with sound and fury in the blood and mire of greed-fuelled wars - its enslavements, its exploited armies of the innocent, who for the glory of some king or country, die in despair with shattered limbs. It is not the events and dates that matter it is the how and the why- the causes. It can be a story illuminated by the music, architecture, literature and belief systems of its time, with tales of rebellion bursting through repression, of courage and exploration. Students could and should be held in thrall by the very smell of its relevance, for only when they feel themselves to be players in the fields of human endeavour and see how they can influence its future, will they become committed.

The obsession of students with the web and social media can be harnessed. It will become more challenging for teachers to compete with the fast-moving presentations on everything from YouTube to TED talks and maintain interaction with the diminishing attention spans of their students. A greater integration of education with the digital world - provided that world can be kept out of the clutches of the global corporations - may herald a new era in education.

Evolution is a science that can dramatically relate to the existence of the individual students. If they can understand the fascinating tale of how their species arrived through natural selection and how evolutionary thinking can be applied to almost every facet of life they would be well on their way, to analytical thinking. If they had a grasp of the amazing arms race between the species to achieve the diversity and beauty we are immersed in, they might comprehend how our own success as a species, could be a threat to human existence. Such species based concepts would supersede all petty divisions of creed, race and nation. Unfortunately, such worthy objectives are not the purpose of the current educational system, its agenda is compliant learning to prepare for a students' compliant participation in the workplace and society. Such learning for competitive regurgitation does more than prepare the compliant student to serve, it unfortunately diminishes the various subjects in the students' mind, which as soon as exams are complete, are dumped and forgotten. Education has always been structured to serve the interests of its sponsors and is thus limited, its full potential can only be realised when the interests of the system, students and society are working with common purpose.

The perception of beauty needs to play a major part within education. Every moment lived in the built environment requires to be elevated by the quality of its architecture. It should be a prerequisite that the design and quality of every item of clothing and piece of furniture enhances existence, design appreciation and its role in the quality of our lives needs to be intrinsic to schooling. On such subjects, schools would benefit by the introduction of external speakers. The school could become a forum, organised by the teachers, a place where working architects, fashion and furniture designers, artists and musicians, farmers and fishermen, union organisers, builders and business people, indeed people from every walk of life, regularly engage. Such interaction with the community would greatly enhance the student perceptions of the real world and their responsibility to it, it would also be a beneficial experience for the external teachers. Illustrated talks on an exciting subject, delivered with passion, has a profound impact on students, it is much easier for a visiting lecturer to convey that passion over an hour or two than for a permanent teacher who must take a longer more dispassionate daily view.

Tax funded schools should not be a place for faith formation, as faith formation by its nature is divisive and without evidence. Religion, however, has had a profound influence in all aspects of life, it stands as a testimony to human imagination and needs to be part of a curriculum. Within a secular school, religions should be taught by the comparative method, set in a context of their origins, world cultures and history. It is a fascinating story of sun gods, gods of Egypt, Greece, Rome and the emergence of the monotheistic religions of Judaism, Christianity and Islam with their multifarious offshoots. Learning how to discuss belief systems, their origins and aspects in a critical manner without insulting adherents would be a difficult but relevant skill.

A denial of knowledge based on evidence to children on any basis, is an abuse that cannot be excused regardless of the parents' traditions, fears or deficiencies. Parental rights are limited, they do not own children. Parents have no right to abuse, no right of negligence, no right to remove their children from school. They have no right to insist that their children be thought of a flat Earth or how it was created in six days. Society, while rightfully recognising the primary role of parents, has set limits to those rights and has deemed the rights of the child to be greater. If a society attempts to build a morality for the well-being of all, it will depend on the moral ethos of its children. It is self-evident that the more input a child has in its own moral formation and the more reason and logic they discern in that formation, the more secure those moral foundations will be.

The United Nations Convention on the Rights of the Child is the most accepted standard on children's rights in the world. Ireland committed to promote children's rights when it signed up to the Convention. The four general principles that underpin all childrens' rights are bullet marked below:

- **Non-discrimination:** This means that all children have the same right to develop their potential in all situations and at all times. For example, every child should have equal access to education regardless of the child's gender, race, ethnicity, nationality, religion, disability, parentage, sexual orientation or other status.

We do not provide equal access to education for all children, wealth provides far higher levels of access to all branches of education. To lift the children in the most deprived areas of the cities to an 'equal-access' status would require positive discrimination. Children are deliberately divided in education by religion. Female children are discriminated against philosophically at every level in religious schools by a deep-set misogyny.

- **The best interests of the child:** This must be 'a primary consideration' in all actions and decisions concerning a child and must be used to resolve conflicts between different rights.

The best interests of the child are not being served by deprivation of the child's right to make choices on moral formation. Likewise, they are not being served by deprivation of critical education and scientific thinking.

- **The right to survival and development:** This underscores the vital importance of ensuring access to basic services and to equality of opportunity for children to achieve their full development.

The child is being denied its full potential for survival and development by the deliberate suppression of its critical thought process and its choices.

- **The views of the child:** The voice of the child must be heard and respected in all matters concerning his or her rights. For example, those in power should consult children before making decisions that will affect them.

Decisions on moral formation and philosophy which will burden or enlighten a child will greatly affect that child's life. Children are not consulted and their voices are not heard, education must be child centred and evidence based.

As the educational system improves, it is essential that it expands the horizons of its students. For example, it is a tragedy that children of the city seldom, if ever, see the night sky as a brilliant star field. Living in a world of perpetual light, they miss out on a visual treat and philosophical stimulus. They may never see the source of their foods, the milking of cows, chicken farms, wheat fields and slaughter houses. They need to physically spend time in such an environment. Likewise the children of the countryside need to spend time in the museums, art galleries and concert halls of the city. Understanding the reality of life's beauty and brutality brings us to the core of our spiritual and contemplative existence. Generally children now have less opportunity to break free; to run and hide in truly wild places, plunge naked into dark pools, climb trees, make contact with parts of our ancestral formation, camp rough and light fires to cook simple fare of smoky taste, organise their own toilet, wipe and wash without products. These adventures are becoming more difficult as land is fenced and health and safety regulations are ever layered by fearful bureaucrats. It is the responsibility of every one-time, wild camping child, now turned adult, to turn the tide somewhat in these matters. Education is indeed hard work!

Third level education, once the prerogative of the rich, is now more accessible with over 40% of students opting for it. Some see it as a panacea for life, to emerge with a degree followed by well-paid employment, perhaps the only route to achieve personal status and prosperity. The original model of the university, was for the study of theology. Over time as they encompassed many other disciplines, it was perceived that academic interaction would in-itself enrich knowledge and serve society. However, the core function of the university remained to perpetuate social privilege and maintain the status quo. Universities provide the state with an intellectual buffer against demands from the majority for a greater share of wealth. Their law departments study and write copiously on the rights of private property. Their economic departments train the highest levels of financial wizards that they might enrich themselves, their masters and impoverish a populace. Economic responsibility to the collective society is not on the agenda. Academics may have been perceived as the brain for the protection of society, highlighting its problems and offering solutions. Instead they have overseen, with blank academic faces, every moral collapse, every economic and political scandal. They have remained aloof and watched with detached interest the intellectual repression of children's minds. It is only when some radical idea or political movement needs to be buried by a hostile media that some professor is dragged out to bamboozle and defend the system with philosophical smoke and mirrors.

Mary Gallagher in her book *Academic Armageddon* writes "higher education is now being reformatted along commercial rather than academic lines". The institutions are rated on league tables according to the number of students passing with higher grades and on the quantity of academic papers, global indices that are compiled by the CEOs of corporations, amongst others. Higher grades can be achieved by increasing pressure on students and dumbing down course standards, academics can be pushed for more papers to secure sponsorship and perhaps their own futures. Higher league tables mean more foreign students and bigger fees. Reflecting the economic imperatives of capital, third level education is being reduced to the profit motive. The race for universities to become commercial enterprises has gained precedence over academic values and certainly over their service to the community at large. Sponsorship brings pressure to research and establish patents, not for the university but for the sponsoring corporation. Likewise, much sought after philanthropic donations coming as they do from the wealthiest and most exploitative institutions in the world exert their own conformist pressure. The independence of the university wilts and they become a state-subsidised service to the corporate sector. As in most corporations the remuneration of the top echelons increases with bonuses while those of the lower orders diminish, and employment conditions deteriorate.

How did highly trained minds, the leading lights of the universities, the serried ranks of lecturers, deans and professors become so tired to allow this to happen? Once optimistic but too long plodding the dry deserts of scholasticism, did they lose their way through relativism and why did their scepticism denigrate to cynicism? The passion for learning might dim on the realisation that scholarship had never been for the service of society - but had some academic principle - but now, even that, is slipping away. The possibility that their students might excel and be of service to society has been damaged by an alienation from society itself and they realise their role in that estrangement. This melancholy of ethos has spread to the student population. Having had their critical faculties suppressed at primary level and been driven through secondary schools in a grades chase they are now conditioned to absorb and regurgitate even more information in the competitive pursuit of a degree. The hives of debate and protest that once were the universities, now echo to the eerie silence of the lambs.

Chapter 12   Economics & Commodities

The Washington Consensus of corporate capitalism and its ethos now objectively aspires to occupy every moment of our existence and niche of our being. It bestows great financial benefits on a minority, like a vampire squid, it envelops whole countries, bringing them to paralysis as it drains their labour, intellect and empathy, conveying the capital produced by the work of millions to an elite. It contrives to leave its victims, individuals and whole societies struggling in perpetual debt. This dictatorship of debt and casino economics casts a dystopian shadow over our lives and alternative ways of organising the social order. But nothing stays the same, internal contradictions, growing alienation and climate problems have set an opposition in motion. The present financial crisis and series of bank and market crashes have shown deregulation to have been a calamity, making capitalism more unstable. The blind growth of capital combining with the blind growth of replication are leading to unsustainable concentrations and are incompatible with restraint in the face of climate change and resource depletion.

During the 1800s and into the beginning of the twentieth century, massive inequalities of wealth existed. This was the era of the great houses, with large retinues in livery, which were the hub of vast landed estates. Many of the owners were also investors in industry and most were rentiers, living lives of indolence on the produce of their tenants. All was to utterly change, for the First World War and the Bolshevik revolution brought about a new era and a shock to capital. The period signalled a socialist trend in politics and began a transfer of capital from private control into the public infrastructure and services. Trade unions and the political climate slowed the re-emergence of powerful private capital until the 1970s.

In the 1950s the economist Simon Kuznets projected that social inequality within capitalist countries would fall naturally as industrialisation progressed and this would be reflected within the underdeveloped countries emerging from colonialism. Such an optimistic theory was important during the cold war, helping to retain these countries within the 'free' world, part of the theory was that 'a rising tide will lift all boats' or wealth at the top will trickle down, these concepts are still believed by many. Throughout that period the ideas of John Mayard Keynes dominated economics in the west, which was regulated capitalism with the state providing infrastructural support and general social welfare. Combined with strong trade unions and social democracy this type of economics brought prosperity to the middle classes. However, since the late 1970s the economic policies of Milton Friedman and his ultra conservative University of Chicago have held sway and have spread like a cancer. In Latin America it was the ideology adopted by the military juntas of Argentina, Uruguay and Chile, where with the support of the US, democracy was overthrown and tens of thousands of socialists and human rights activists were imprisoned, tortured and murdered. The elite within each country became extremely rich while millions were plunged into poverty, this doctrine has now established itself almost worldwide.

Gross inequalities have emerged with the top one percent owning and controlling almost half of the world's wealth. The bottom half of the world's population owns the same as the richest 85 people in the world. In the US, where the rich have got vastly richer and withdrawn into gated communities, the wealthiest one percent gained 95% of growth since 2009, while the bottom 90 percent became poorer. The majority have advanced materially over the period, however the system is dysfunctional in its wealth disparities, its economic philosophy is based on competitive greed. For about 250 years, versions of this model have been operating in the world's leading capitalist country the US, it has demonstrated its ability to only provide a violent, divided, dysfunctional society. It is well to understand the model, for without correction this is where Ireland and Europe are going.

James B. Glattfelder, investigating ownership of the major international corporations, found that 737 of the top shareholding conglomerates, or about 0.1 % of the total, control 80% of corporations. These are primarily financial institutions, based in the US and the UK, and at their core there are only 146 tightly intertwined companies. He found that of the top 49 companies in the world - all except one - were purely financial institutions creating nothing but profit as they shuffled the wealth created by others. These are the companies that can and do operate outside the law or lobby politicians to create laws to suit them. They are deemed too big to fail and secure the co-operation of politicians to protect their interests worldwide, their sole responsibility being to serve their shareholders and CEOs. The World Bank is portrayed as the human face of international capital helping to lift countries out of poverty. The list of previous CEOs would not instil confidence; Robert McNamara, who oversaw the horrors of bombing and chemical warfare that killed about 3 million Vietnamese people; Robert Zoellick of Goldman Sachs otherwise known as the 'The Great Vampire Squid' and Paul Wolfowitz who organised the destruction of Iraq, resulting in well over 100,000 deaths. The World Bank is not subject to any democratic control, its executives are appointed by powerbrokers, such as the US. Its economists are of the 'Friedman' Chicago School, who ensure that within every country of operations, they can veto any action contrary to the banks interests and for any action they cannot be held legally accountable. The bank's mission is linked to the neoliberal ideology, demanding the suppression of wages and the privatisation of the public sector, in return for loans. The benefits of such aid have been limited and 25 years after receiving it most countries were no better off. Thirty eight countries have amassed $71 billion in unpayable debts. Many leading African scholars want to stop all such incoming aid claiming it entrenches a corrupt elite. For many years the World Bank and the International Monetary Fund (IMF) have been pushing the Washington Consensus extending the range of free global capital, keeping a distance from, but using military juntas to suppress opposition. The letter of resignation of Davison L Budhoo (available on line) from his post at the IMF, exclaims how he must wash his hands of blood; the blood of millions, of the poor and starving and refers to the economic nonsense that has forced governments and people to kneel before them begging for a sliver of decency.

When the function of money passed from being a convenient exchange facility and concentrated to allow its use for lending, its nature changed to capital. Capital is then invested or lent for return with profit, which in the normal society is an essential ingredient for funding business start-up and mortgages for property. Deregulated capital, coalescing with modern financial institutions, has assumed a life of its own. It has moved from a mere service to commerce to its centre. It operates across the free world, leaping national or continental borders without passport or baggage check. The financial wizards create vehicle corporations, non-bank entities or shadow banks specialising in bypassing regulations and avoiding tax. They package and resell loans with hedge funds and aggressively managed asset pools and play in the debt markets. They produce nothing, living behind a palisade of smoke and mirrors, made flesh by corporate law firms and protected by legal structures. These institutions have learned, as would a parasite, to extract the maximum blood or in this case capital without killing the social order that produces it. Some just can't help themselves and driven by their own internal dynamic, step over the mark, bringing disaster to themselves and society. The level of wealth such institutions and CEOs harvest in Ireland is determined by the level of control they exert over the media, law, education and politics. Democratically elected governments may come and go but the structural dynamics of the system remain.

Financial institutions are the domain of the super manager with CEOs whose aggressive commitment to competition and risk-taking match an ego reflecting the success and status of the company, a status given by the only value that is respected - money. Apologists for the competitive market state that everybody earns the value of their social use, so if a worker earns €25,000 per annum and a chief executive officer in a financial institution, €5 million, it's because the CEO, they argue, has contributed that much more to society. While society needs to encourage innovators and entrepreneurs with a level of reward, that remuneration needs to be expressed relatively and reflect the social context. For example, with a median (average) income of €35,000 a decent incentive for innovation or gaining higher skills might be an income of €100,000 two or three times higher than the median. Society has to democratically determine how many multiples of the median have to be paid to an executive before it turns from creative encouragement to an addiction that becomes destructive? The argument in favour of unrestrained income fails, when very high remuneration combines with share options allowing the recipient to save and invest large reserves. The inequalities of return on large capital then flow to the entrepreneur who thereafter is perpetually enriched by money managers. Thus, the entrepreneur changes from a working contributor into an indolent rentier. The pay gap between managers in the UK and the workforce is widening with CEOs of the top 100 listed companies earning a multiple of more than 120 times that of the average employee, their chief executives average total earnings is given at €4.4 million by the Incomes Data Service. Barclays Bank was adjudged to have been fraudulent and was fined $420 million by regulatory bodies, the bank still paid $61 million to its executives, including $27 million to its investment head. But as heads of the institutions, the recipients are the determinants of their own pay and interest rates.

Thomas Piketty's book, *Capital in the Twenty-first Century* refers to Liliane Bettencourt who, never worked a day in her life, inherited the fortune of L'Oréal. Between 1990 and 2010 her money increased from €2 billion to €25 billion growing at over 13% per annum, well above the rate of any smaller investors. With such a fortune, relatively little has to be extracted to live and the best of advice and protections can be bought. As nearly all of the return on the investment can be retained in the portfolio it allows, theoretically, infinite accumulations of wealth, all without merit or work by the owner, this is the basis of the rentier society. Top proprietors would have thousands of buildings to let, they would own or part-own enterprises and have portfolios of stocks and shares. Each wealthy owner is cossetted by teams of accountants and legal experts and live off the work of their tenants or operatives. Without international taxation of capital the concentration of capital will continue. It remains to be seen what levels of persuasion or repression will be required to stem the inevitable reaction to this contradiction.

The more astute apologists for capital are looking for ways to mitigate this concentration. They recognise the predictions of Marx and others that enterprises of all sorts organically combine into monopolies. Anti-monopoly commissions, anti-cartel institutions and credit regulations were not introduced for the protection of consumers but for the perpetuation of the system. However, in the 1970s, the neo-liberal face of capital combined with the rising politics of the right, rolled back much of these restraining laws. They formed financial instruments, bonds, shares, options and futures, hedge-funds, subprime mortgages, which are complex and justified by finance-speak gibberish. This Mad Hatter's tea party of capital brought crashes, ruin and hardship to millions but great riches to a few. It put the system on an unsustainable road, its exorbitant displays of wealth and distain for the majority is developing a more challenging political climate.

With highly paid expertise and access to international advice, together with the lessons of previous crashes, one might assume caution and a degree of responsibility by the banks. But the corrosive inducements of competition and bonus structure drives them every so often, over the brink. The apologists for these institutions proclaim they are essential to an economy, some even having the nerve to proclaim their motivation is for the well-being of the population at large. Time and again, not alone did they not add to national wealth but through greed or ignorance and sometimes knowingly, crashed such institutions, losing peoples savings and pensions. Society and the taxpayer had then to pay the price with austerity to support these failed entities. Rational economics would see public and private capital finance as an essential part of providing money to fund and support enterprises or facilitate mortgages, but when the money, the capital itself and the greed it can engender becomes the actual core, it corrodes society and those who manage it. There is no rational argument to justify any banking institution to be in private ownership. In addition, to save capital from itself, economists like Piketty, propose the progressive taxation of not just income, but all forms of profit and directly on capital itself, he also proposes expanding death duties. While the prolongation of an exploitative system is not the objective of this book, such measures would in the short term benefit the well-being of the majority.

Richard Wilkinson's and Kate Pickett's book, *The Spirit Level*, highlighted how social ills are linked more to income inequality within a country than the income per head of population as measured against other countries. Measuring disparities within selected societies, they compare the wealth of the top 20% against the bottom 20%, one of the most unequal in the world is the US. In Europe, Portugal has the highest inequality, Finland is the most equal. They demonstrate how inequality relates to a wide range of health and social problems, such as life expectancy, literacy, the percentage of people in prison and how they are treated, obesity and teenage births. The higher the level of inequality in a society the worse all these social problems are, they also show how the reverse holds true.

Social and economic mobility - a belief that anyone can rise from humble origins to riches - was the bedrock of the American dream and part of popular culture. However, in recent years several studies have found that vertical financial mobility is now lower in the US than in most other countries. As Richard Wilkinson quipped, "If you want the American dream, move to Denmark".

The intellectual and productive capacity of humanity has created a Garden of Eden on Earth, a place of surplus. We have surpassed our need for daily hunting and gathering and with mechanisation, computerisation and robotics are on the edge of surpassing the need for physical work of any kind. The US economy in 2012 had 2% of the workforce engaged in agriculture, 18% in production, including construction, and 80% in the service sector. Ireland will inevitably follow, with soaring rates of productivity the numbers engaged in production will continue to fall. The genius and co-operation that encouraged these advances has an additional driving mechanism of greed which can lead to other problems. In many areas of our lives most of us know when we have enough. When healthy, we don't strive for extreme health. After a good meal, we don't consume another one just to augment our satisfaction. Studies show that the accumulation of wealth over what is required for comfortable survival, can become addictive, such addictions distorts human empathy and has negative effects throughout society.

After the political shift to the right in the late 1970s, the transfer of wealth from public to private hands began. These economic changes in the UK and US were to have a huge influence on events in Ireland. Thatcher and Regan had broken union power using the media and police and began the liberalisation of economics. Thatcher's political inspiration was a book by Friedrich Hayek, *The Road to Serfdom*, an argument for building an economy on the free market and a contention that any form of social involvement or democratic socialism would lead to communism or fascism, which Hayek claims are one and the same. Nonetheless, prior to this, social democratic parties had come and gone in many countries in Europe. They built social housing, hospitals and state schools, they had nationalised rail systems and coalfields, all without the sky falling in. During this period, a marginal transfer of wealth and power had shifted away from the elite to the producers, a situation that could not be tolerated by capital. As the unions crumbled and wages fell a problem arose within capitalism, for as the purchasing power of workers fell and so too, did profits. The answer was credit.

Vast amounts of credit were released. It was poured into property which soared in value and everyone who invested got rich almost overnight. Nobody could lose. All one had to do was borrow, borrow, borrow, get into property and watch one's wealth grow. Those who lent clouds of money gambled on vast interest returns, capitalism was triumphant. All and sundry were issued with credit cards, restrictions were lifted, regulators were bought off or ignored. Mortgages were easily available to all for first, second and third houses and 'buy to let'. Advertising for housing, apartments, cars, SUVs and consumer durables was everywhere, the media carried slogans such as 'take now, no repayments for six months'. Dim developers and their accountants who had no understanding of where wealth actually comes from, fell in with the pack. The few voices that called for caution were told not to spoil the party. Capitalism and the market were truly free, the possibilities were enormous.

But, someone, somewhere realised that there was an oversupply and one house fell back in price. The impossible had happened and on the steep slope that one little stone became an avalanche. The party was over, in no time, vast quantities of properties reverted to their real value, debt littered the ground. Sheep-like governments frightened and out of their depth were the guardians of the system rather than the people and guaranteed the return of the gambled money plunging the people into long-term austerity and emigration. They took control of the failing private banks and bailed them out ensuring the taxpayers would shoulder the losses and rebuild them over a generation. No doubt, when the banks become profitable, they will be returned to their 'rightful owners'.

The push for privatisation is comprehensive. Over the last 35 years a third of all homes in the UK which had been state owned are now in private hands. This was a bid to turn the country into a conservative, property owning society. Water services, sewers, power stations, the phone and postal system, the railways, air and sea ports, airlines were sold to private interests. While these decisions were explained through the compliant media as a struggle against bureaucracy and the power of the trade unions, it was more an ideological and class struggle. The privatisations had some unforeseen repercussions. As Brian Meek explained in his book, *Private Island*, during this period shares held by private individuals fell from 40% to 12% undermining the vision of a shareholding democracy. He argues that while the nationalised industries became more efficient when privatised, this could have been achieved by normal commercialisation, but no option, other than a sell off, was considered.

Privatisationfailed to demonstrate that such companies always do better than nationalised ones. It failed to demonstrate that greed, bonuses and just avoiding bankruptcy is the best way to realise universal prosperity. For over a third of a century, concepts of duty, service to the public and pride in work has been denigrated. When a section of British Rail was privatised as Railtrack in the 1990s, large numbers of its engineers, signalling and maintenance staff were sacked. It then experienced a series of rail crashes, the company went about infrastructural upgrades with new technology which failed and it then collapsed and had to be rescued by a return to public ownership. The water companies were privatised to conjure up competition - an impossibility in such a utility - and costs to the consumer soared. Electrical supply was fragmented and is now a chaos of producers and venders, much of it now owned by European companies, some of which are nationalised within their country of origin. During the Tory years, progressive taxes were cut and VAT jumped from 8% to 20%, a tax which has far greater effect on the less well off. However, the overall policy has worked for its instigators. It has transferred money into the hands of the few at a cost to the ill, the unemployed and those working in less secure jobs for less pay.

Much of what has happened in the UK occurred here and more will be attempted. The ESB has been forced to sell power to electrical companies which have no power stations, do not produce electricity, have no power lines and no expertise in running any such system. These popup fake companies now bombard the consumer with a plethora of complex packages and transitory special offers. These new companies do not need to invest in a new power station, turbine, a length of wire or even a solar panel, just a building, a billing, payments and customer management system. That is all it needs to skim profit from energy supply.

While many well-paid jobs have disappeared, they have been replaced by a few highly paid executives and a great number of ill-paid operatives with few rights. Income tax reductions, on the grounds that the state no longer has to support nationalised enterprises, result in an upward wealth transfer. Some nationalised enterprises had been supported by the state through progressive taxation, with the greatest burden falling on the rich. When the enterprises are privatised they become nominally, self-supporting, this at first glance appears to provide a service at a more competitive price with each use being fully paid for by the user. In the case of utilities such as water, gas, roads or power the user has no choice and so the burden of 'use tax' now fall on the poorer majority, wealth transfers upwards.

In both the UK and Ireland a system of turnpike roads operated from about 1729. When a traveller came to a road blocked by a spiked pole or pike, a toll was paid and the pike was turned to permit passage. The money went to the estate through which the road passed, who were responsible for its maintenance. This was at a time of huge wealth disparities and road toll or 'use tax' was one of the myriad ways to continue that situation. All such impediments to passage were abolished about 1854 with the roads becoming freeways maintained by county councils. The construction of the national motorway routes from the 1990s gave private enterprise its opportunity to resurrect the scam when they managed to persuade feeble-minded politicians to allow them build and toll these roads. The West Link system in Dublin cost in the region of €58 million. The National Toll Roads Company almost recouped the entire construction costs in 2007, when it took in €46m from motorists. It then did a deal to get €50 million compensation a year for ten years after it reverted to the state. According to the National Roads Authority, NTR's total earnings from the West Link, from 1990 to 2020, will be a staggering €1,155,786,122. In corruption terms, the paltry sum of €18,000 given in bribes to a few politicians, demonstrates how utterly out of their depth they were and, from the scale of the finance involved, how remote they were from any sense of the public good.

Divergence in wealth, often forced, exists between countries. This is particularly evident in Africa where during the colonial occupation mineral, timber and oil resources were seized at the point of a gun. Ownership of these property rights have been largely maintained by western companies into post-colonial times. It was on that condition that the countries in questions were to remain part of the trading world and receive aid in loans. Such residual ownership is now reframed as foreign investment. It basically takes the form of asset stripping with very little return to the local economy except wages. Corrupt governments who claim little if any taxation from the multinationals, but protect their interests, are the side beneficiaries of such deals. Their security forces quell strikes or protests against land encroachment and any political movement that might arise to protect peoples' rights. In the ten years leading to 1998 the US provided hundreds of millions of dollars' worth of weapons and training to African military forces and much of it went to governments that were linked to wars throughout the region. The US, France, Germany, Britain, Russia, China and Italy have all sold arms to states currently involved in conflict. Any notion of justification falls when one considers Saudi Arabia, illiberal, undemocratic and intolerant, governed by an autocratic royal family, where dissent of any kind, is heavily punished with hundreds of executions, floggings and amputations annually. This regime is a huge customer of Britain's arms industry. Moral arguments concerning human rights and individual freedoms fade in the face of the firm unity among those who believe in, and benefit from, the primacy of capital and oil.

When Nelson Mandela walked free from 27 years in jail in South Africa, apartheid was over, the world celebrated. However, it was soon realised that while political majority rule was being established, the existing ownership of land and wealth was being entrenched. Through cunning advice and conditions attached to aid from the IMF, the Washington Consensus had won the day. Everything in the 'Freedom Charter' the dream of ANC street fighters, had been betrayed. The redistribution of land was blocked by enshrined property rights, the creation of jobs through subsidised textile and auto plants was blocked by the World Trade Agreement, plans to raise the minimum wage were thwarted by IMF pressure for wage restraint, free AIDS drugs were blocked by intellectual property rights, the money for housing, electricity and water in the townships was diverted to service the massive debts of the apartheid regime. Any thought of reneging on the deals would be punished by traders in New York and London with capital flight, currency crashes and isolation. As Naomi Klein said in *The Shock Doctrine*, capitalism had been democracy proofed. Since the overthrow of apartheid, inequality has increased, half of the population live in poverty, it has the highest murder and rape rate in the world, the life expectancy of black South Africans has dropped by fourteen years since 'liberation'. The white exploitative regime has been displaced by a black one, the rich have got richer, all with the connivance of global capitalism.

For humans to survive, they have to produce. The way production is organised determines the social order which influences every aspect of society. The present social order buys and sells commodities and objectively turns all aspects of nature and society into commodities, its toxic touch affects sport, art and entertainment. Furthermore, it distorts these commodities into its own image. Sport is big business, with a global value in the region of €400 billion, mainly derived from television rights, advertising, merchandising brands and infrastructure. The industry is growing faster than the GDP of most countries. The Spanish club, Real Madrid is at present the most valuable football team. They generated €560 million in 2013 and are now valued at €3 billion. Their global brand signed a €45 million-a-year kit deal with Adidas and a €34 million-per-year shirt sponsorship with Emirates. Manchester United is valued at a mere €2.4 billion, but a €490 million seven-year shirt deal with Chevrolet helps. On top of the sponsorship is the merchandising and its magazine. The English Premier League 2015 TV deal for €6.9 billion or €150,000 a minute is a 70% increase in the value of its television rights for the 2016-19 seasons, leaving the rest of club football across the world far behind in terms of domestic television income and the lower 72 football league teams in the UK struggling for survival. Not only does the system turn everything into commodities, it too, like capital, concentrates. Only capitalism could turn a kick-about on a patch of grass between factory workers into such an industry. It provides entertainment to millions, the comradery of a club and the excitement of the terraces. The clubs are followed with a religious zeal but, like religion, are the mentor of an exploitative system and a further mechanism for the concentration of capital. It sends hopeful boys for intensive training, receiving a cursory education some are kept and bound under contract to be bought and sold at will. The top few do very well, turned into megastar, super-rich celebrities; the discarded find broken dreams and unemployment.

The whole ethos reinforces the trust of the market place. The immense pay and transfer fees of players and managers engenders the celebrity culture on which the system thrives. The media hums with obsessive repetition of the constant match and goal replays as one set of branded logos plays another. The intellectual side of the sport is represented by the interviews with managers, which is a study in itself. The same 'professionalism' is now pursued in every marketable sport - rugby, cricket, golf, boxing and many others, the pressure to succeed drives many athletes into taking illegal performance boosting drugs. A notable exception is Ireland's Gaelic Athletic Association (GAA) which, while tinkering with commercialism, has thus far avoided that road. Its highly committed, unpaid players are to its credit, together with its vast network of local voluntary clubs in every corner of the country.

In the world of gymnastics and figure skating, abuse of girls and distortion of image have become intertwined. Starvation diets, debilitating injuries and the tactics of tyrannical gymnastics masters were highlighted by Joan Ryan in her book, *Little Girls in Pretty Boxes*. It portrays the horrors endured at the hands of the coaches and sometimes their own families in the desperate race to get to the top- an exposé that helped reform Olympic sports. Some gymnasts objected to blaming coaches or parents for turning out bitter, broken-down athletes, claiming they were living their own dream. Is it normal that such an encompassing and life distorting ambition should emerge at 10 years of age? In fashion photography and modelling similar pressure arises to transform normal, young women into gaunt, emaciated models in keeping with the fashion of the day. The lure of money and fame can induce a sacrifice of the self, often with catastrophic physical and mental results. In the film *Fifty Shades of Grey*, the hero possesses extraordinary wealth, giving his character celebrity status. The beautiful female falls under the spell of smouldering sex, packaged as consummate consumerism, love from the hero can only be expressed through a relationship of control and the status of dominance. A possible liaison of equality surrenders to one of submission. The message is, that if we, the observers, are compliant, blindly submissive and agree to become a commodity under the perversity of capital, we might get to share its glitz and glamour.

Art too, has been commodified. The market and ethos of the day form what is acceptable, success is solely judged by a monetary value. Most children and young people are very creative but as they get older, their output lessens or ceases. Instead of producing art, they consume it, in all its various forms. Creativity withers, for the ethos of the system is that unless one is both professional and successful and the art has a monetary value, then it has no value. It is not likely to be pursued for its own sake, except perhaps at some curative, therapy class. It would require a renaissance in the character of society before sport and art could be liberated from the bondage of monetary value and reformed as concepts of play, fun and creativity. This commercialisation reflects the concentration of wealth and every investigation of its structure exposes its links to, and reflects the nature of corporate capital. Our relationship with sport, art and entertainment is constantly distorted by an epidemic of competition to be the fastest, the strongest, the celebrity, the winner and each and all of them reduced to a batch of money. Is that our only option, to reduce every facet of human endeavour to a monetary value - the only value we will know and cherish?

Will the world in 2050 be owned by those who at present control the mineral resources such as oil, or a company of traders or China? One way or another it is essential to understand distributional trends, for if concentrations of wealth and increasing levels of inequality continue, states will require astonishing levels of persuasion or repression to maintain the status quo. It is also likely that these agencies, the police and military will themselves be privatised, allowing a blurring of responsibilities. To maintain the semblance of democracy, the intelligentsia of the establishment understand the potential difficulties and would favour greater regulation. There are many others who want the party to continue, the politically powerful corporate and banking lobbies in both Europe and the United States.

Naive politicians, even conservative ones, seem surprised as to how little control they or the democratic system has over these forces. The concentration of capital is reflected in the concentration of political power in a small cohort of four or five ministers in a government. This suits capital, as the more remote the core of power is removed from democracy, the easier it is to influence - and corrupt. The dedicated elected socialist will be surrounded by a cluster of extremely polite, well trained economic advisers from the IMF who will give polished presentations on the Washington Consensus and how after privatisation and investment, a tide of wealth will trickle down and lift all people. They will be offered generous loans to increase their own pay and that of the army and police, which they will offer to upskill.

Evolution has taught how simple organisms have progressed by countless tiny improvements to complex ones, nature's great trick to achieve the seemingly impossible. Likewise, progress to higher levels of economics, defined as being in the objective interests of the majority, might be achieved, built on countless tiny economic, social and political improvements. These changes, accumulate in quantity to achieve a qualitative change, a new organism, a rational social society. But as in evolution, an organism can survive only in the conditions within which it has evolved and adapted to. Likewise, conditions must be suitable for the establishment and survival of socialism or communism, such complex social orders cannot survive in conditions of conflict, in a social climate of low morality or one in which there is a proclivity for supplication.

Since the middle of the last century each generation anticipated upward social movement, they expected to be somehow better off materially than their parents. There now appears to be a discernible change as qualification requirements for work eligibility have increased. Where once a Leaving Certificate sufficed to obtain work, the same position now requires a degree. The investment in time and money to achieve these higher levels of education have grown enormously and education itself has become a commodity. As wages fall and paid holidays diminish, internships and other stunts to get free labour increase. The concept of well-paid secure employment has almost disappeared, the challenges of living what might be termed a normal life, of securing accommodation and having a family at a young fertile age is becoming more remote. As relative socio-economic circumstances fall, it becomes more obvious that economic conditions at a child's birth are the biggest factors in the trajectory of its life. Despite all the hype concerning the most competent rising to the top, the concept of the level playing field is illusionary, the young are faced with the collapse of a meritocracy. Established wealth and power have never been more cosseted by the educational and legal system. The children of judges and accountants are most likely to be judges and accountants and children of the poor will most likely be poor. Children who inherit large enough reserves of capital will never have to work and comfortably live their lives on the labour of others. To the state and its beneficiaries, this is the correct social order, since whoever has economic power determines what the correct social order is.

Blind replication and the exponential expansion of a species can in certain circumstances lead to extinction. Likewise the only survival mode of capitalism is growth and expansion which may perhaps lead to its extinction, for it now operates within contradictions such as growing resistance from a more aware majority, in a world of finite resources and climate change. The system is the source of wars, boom and bust cycles, alienation and despair. Only alternative economic and political structures determined by an informed democracy can deal with these questions. Theoretically 'democracy' means popular government for everybody by the efforts of all. The people must be able to say what they want, to nominate the executors of their wishes, to monitor their performance and remove them when they see fit. This presumes that all are able to express an opinion and exercise their franchise. It implies that everyone is politically and economically independent and no-one would be obliged to submit to the will of others. Errico Malatesta said in his book *Neither Democrats, nor Dictators*, 1926: "If classes and individuals exist that are deprived of the means of production and are therefore dependent on others with a monopoly over those means, the democratic system is limited and only serves to deceive the mass of the people and keep them docile with an outward show of independence, while the rule of the privileged class is consolidated. Such are the limitations of our democracy"

Democracy as we know it, has its limitations, but it is the best system of political governance so far derived. Initially it was confined to the propertied classes. However, the wish to engender national unity in a time of war and pressure from trade unions and others slowly extended the democracy and with the suffragette movement the franchise became universal. But it did not extend over commerce, which remains protected behind constitutions and layers of law and the judiciary. The free market and the conflict between capital and labour still marks this phase of economic and social existence. The first move in extending democracy over capital, is transparency, to discover in each bank, country and safe haven its quantity, ownership and location. It's a vital first step and will be opposed by the brokers, bankers, and businessman who wish they could go about their daily lives without the encumbrance of inquisitive people. The claim that it is their private business, does not hold true for they did not produce the wealth, just because they have the skill of money management, access to the international money trough and the protection of the law and state, does not change the situation

The boom and crash cycles are gaining pace, the fabric of the system requires increasing taxpayer support. A stable sustainable economic model must be sought. We do not require to propose an alternative economic model solely on an ideological basis, but to critically seek what best serves the well-being of the majority. Society can determine that its function is not to serve an economy, it is not there to process, package and supply compliant operatives and consumers. Forums to pursue these simple questions have been eroded, economic philosophy needs to be refocused to service the well-being of all. Despite many hurdles, as the contradictions intensify the majority will have no option but to think and act collectively in its interests.

For parties of the left and their supporting electorate it is worth pursuing objectives such as intensifying regulations on capital, increasing wages, controlling prices and using taxation as tools to redistribute wealth. A problem arises as parameters are moved to form an egalitarian society, the owners of capital and production simply change location. Governments who propose to control the movement of capital will be threatened by the wrath of the global corporations. They are then reduced to outbidding others in offering tax incentives, labour training schemes, a servile labour force, buildings and infrastructure. As the frustration of the people surfaces, the true face of the state emerges when it has to provide violence through its police to enforce private contracts and crush civil protest. To mitigate such conflict, we require innovation to grow indigenous companies from the private, public and co-operative sectors. This can only be achieved by having the confidence to overcome the ideologically based restrictive practices of the Washington Consensus on a broad European theatre. This requires high levels of education by the electors and the elected, which returns the emphasis to the vital foundations for such a possibility - critical education.

We have a political system with curtailed economic power, an economic system that depends on greed, gambling and exploitation for wealth creation, with the hope that wealth may trickle down to the majority. These structures are patently not the best the ingenuity of humanity can devise. If we can accept democracy over political structures, we can accept democracy over economics? As economics is the most important element in our survival, we require national and international social-economic laboratories bigger and better funded than any centre dedicated to the investigation of particle physics, medical science, space or oceanic research work. These are activities central to a *Republic of Reason.*

Chapter 13   The Republic of Reason

The Republic of Reason, is a way of thinking as well as a conceivable society. If it were to be a society, it would be a democratic expression of such thinking. The raison d'être of such a society, a grouping of humanity, would be the well-being of its people, its sustainability and equality. It could only emerge from the will of a confident and well-informed democracy with economics as the servant of its social order. It would be a popular movement capable of inspiring people with a vision of how to form a coherent social grouping that would be a substantially better place to live. The foundation necessary to achieve that confident and intelligent democracy is in the critical education of our children. These children, who growing into fully fledged adults will believe that there is a reason to live, who can raise themselves out of ignorance, who can find themselves as creatures of intelligence, skill and excellence, who can learn what it is to be really free, who can soar, are our future.

As long as the exploited have existed they have dreamed of a better life. When migrating humans were crossing swollen rivers and deep valleys, struggling for survival, they dreamed of being like a bird, effortlessly crossing such obstacles. From their desire and imagination emerged the human figure with wings, spectres of angels and fairies. To dream was not enough, humans had to fly themselves and so, from the sketches of Leonardo de Vinci's helicopter to hundreds of failed attempts with flapping wings, they tried and tried again. In time the technology and the dream came together. In 1901 Gustav Whitehead told of harnessing a light combustion engine to an assembly of wings, wire and flaps and taking flight in a heavier than air machine. Every day since with tiny modifications, aircraft design has been polished and improved. Millions of people now traverse the skies in jet aircraft every day. Likewise many attempts have been made to construct societies that better serve the interests of the majority - from slave revolts to the Paris Commune. Most failed and the price paid was often death but the ideas persisted. In countries under imperialist domination, such as Ireland, time after time obstinate uprisings were put down but dreams of freedom persisted and progress was made.

The Republic of Reason & *The Poverty of Philosophy*

The foundation of the Republic of Ireland was a remarkable achievement, philosophically moving away from - and potentially beyond - the moribund semi-feudalism of the United Kingdom. While the modern state of the UK is a liberal one, it is never the less a kingdom with a hereditary aristocracy. Its monarch is also head of the Church of England and the people are subjects, thus class and sectarianism are endemic to the fabric of the state. In the Republic the people achieved citizenship and while the revolutionaries aspired to equality for all, whether Catholic, Protestant or dissenter, it was not to be. For, having achieved freedom from a foreign monarch, the new establishment felt the chill of naked liberation. It fell back on its knees in supplication. It sought a new monarch and oppression - the Church of Rome and an inward-looking nationalism. Since then, it has taken time, struggle and heartache to see the signs of a renaissance. The dark age of church power and reactionary nationalism is eroding before internal contradictions and emerging reason.

The proclamation of 1916 resolved to pursue the prosperity of the whole nation and cherish all its children equally, but it was a democracy of free capital. The notion of equality was superseded by one where inequality was acceptable, if it served the common good. The benefactors of the economic imbalances proved resilient and have assumed an international character. The local farmer and entrepreneur have been replaced as the main social driver by the more powerful and polished capital of international corporations. The educational system, originally termed by the revolutionaries of 1916 as 'a murder machine' crafted by British imperialism to induce supplication, has been inherited in its essence. It continues under new management to render the majority into compliant operatives and consumers. The state has made gains since independence but not to its potential and at great cost to the dignity and self-esteem of its people and the loss by emigration of so many children. The political system, an unexamined inheritance, is a limited democracy which, over a long period, offered a choice between Fianna Fáil and Fine Gael - two conservative parties of no discernible difference - with a Labour Party, compliant in keeping one or the other in power.

The *Republic of Reason* is as much a state of mind as a location, even then, one not confined by national borders. It is a determination that a society, dedicated to the well-being of its people, can be built, exist and thrive. It is a belief that individuals can work in harmony for the collective good and live with an economic model which would serve the collective interests of society. It is a belief that we have the possibility of achieving an iconic rational society which could influence the world. The recent passing of the marriage equality referendum is an example of how the expression of an idea can be an intellectual export, an idea of great human value which can be replicated a thousand times over. We are acquiring the human empathy needed and examples abound of our ability to co-operate in complex economic and political systems. From these examples, well-crafted and tested economic and social models can be built and exported. A non-imperialist history would help in challenging the Washington Consensus and influence change in the European social order. To strengthen this position we need to distance ourselves from US military positions. An enhanced neutral world position would help contributions we would make on climate change and the fragile state of our species. As human-centred honest brokers we could play an invaluable role in these questions and overseas conflicts. We could become a centre of excellence for egalitarian data on capital, ideas for alternative social structures and a refuge for courageous whistle-blowers.

If a qualitative change in our society is required to make such progress, and most surely it is, shall it be through revolution or reform? There is no appetite for revolution nor are there mass revolutionary parties here or in Europe. Lessons from twentieth century revolutions have not been good. They have brought rivers of blood, misery and even bloodier counter-revolutions and interventions. The alternative to revolution is reform or progress through social evolution. Natural evolution demonstrates how small mutations and adaptions in large enough quantities lead to qualitative change. While biological changes take place over great swathes of time, the exchange and evolution of ideas capable of influencing social development now happen at great speed. It might be assumed that this could be expressed through the democratic process, each election reflecting the interests of the majority and leading to a more progressive government. Unfortunately, it does not work like that, for a ruling order never willingly cedes power. A complex mechanism exists to ensure that the objective wishes of the majority are not easily expressed. The control of education is the first vital step for the production of citizens who accept the status quo and the limited parameters of debate. Ownership and control of TV, radio and print, ensure that debate and alternative ideas are kept within acceptable boundaries. The justice system with legal constraints of all kinds, is the final fortification against any real extensions of democracy over economics.

Acceptance and inertia are the default position for the majority of people for there are never demands expressed for change until there is no choice. Such demands for real change evolve as slowly as their necessity. Confidence in the state, church and economic institutions is whittled away in tiny bits with every scandal, scam and stroke. Despair is deepened by every lost job, falling wage, increased working hour and every son or daughter forced to emigrate. The opposing interests within society are the demands for a better life, wages, time off, health care etc. - from the majority on one side - and pressure from capital to extract more profit on the other side in a process formerly called class struggle. The centre line of this conflict is always in flux. Over the last forty years, the power of the majority has collapsed and the intellectual base of socialism has been in retreat. The advantage has moved in favour of capital which has been in the ascendency ever since, shedding restraints and regulation. However, the emasculation of the majority in the face of concentrating capital has its own contradictions. A growing number of people here and worldwide are questioning the concentration of wealth and formulating opposition. While reforms for a more logical and caring society will be opposed by the elite, every day there are more cracks and crevices opening up to gain footholds and surmount the barriers. It is worth remembering that while previous gains may be diminishing, they were all made in the first place by organisations engaged in economic and political struggle.

Despite fluctuations, the overall well-being of humanity increases over time, it is well to understand this historical progress as it provides the necessary optimism for struggle. Such progress can only be judged over long periods and it is relative, for what might be seen as social and economic progress to one group or class of people, could be a disaster to others. Eighteenth century slavery was a wonderful improvement to the lives and wealth of the traffickers and the plantation owners but, from a slave's point of view, it was unparalleled misery. Its abolition was not just a step forward for the slaves but a liberation for all of humanity. Present education does not encourage such a linear vision of human historical improvement. Whatever complaints we might have now, we are better off with capitalism than feudalism or the previous slave society. Viewed on a large historical scale, humanity is increasingly better off and has seldom been more at peace. Even the poor within western societies have achieved a higher standard of living with regard to life-span, health and nutrition and are materially better off than royal families of yesteryear. However, those who are now coping with the struggle of day to day living are not easily persuaded of this proposition.

At present this general improvement in living standards is retreating before the growing power of capital. An international dictatorship of capital has been established and alternative agendas are not tolerated, the natural opposition of the majority is weakened by divisions. However, people have overcome divisions many times in the face of a common enemy and they may do so now to tackle this dictatorship. Real change will come when people with sufficient knowledge and confidence in the possibility of an egalitarian society organise to achieve it. When they understand that capitalism is just another stage in economic relations and extend democracy over it, they will have achieved a revolution. The growing empathy of humans to one another and to the environment is the social glue that would ensure the sustainability of such change.

The computer has brought the world together in a way never thought possible and the internet gives us access to the knowledge of humanity. In this fast-moving world of information or disinformation, the requirement for analytical minds has never been greater. The internet can be a tool for advertising and promoting consumption or for disseminating rational ideas on a vast scale. It can forge links between nationalities, races, creeds and combat environmental damage. It can sow division and hatred; what we see on the net needs to be tempered by informed scepticism. How successful we are at that is determined by an early critical education, our vital building block on the road to liberation. Building a rational education requires the intellectual support of at least some sections of society. Likewise material support must be in step, for one hungry child, lacking shelter, or who perceives itself to be without love or a worthwhile future, will challenge the intellectual validity of any such plan. The concept of 'an injury to one is an injury to all' requires to be wired into our social consensus and a fundamental building block in every child's right to a rational education - an education laden with play, music, art and poetry as well as a path to critical thinking.

Critical thinking involves an engagement between opposing ideas, then following a logical series of deductions, the adoption of a position which one perceives as true. It requires an understanding of how the physical mind works and how decisions may be controlled by prior beliefs. It is the application of statistics and evidence to prove a theory from diverse sources. It is understanding that the method of thinking scientifically, is primary, for the method itself is more significant than any actual discovery. Such an approach then needs to switch from compartmentalised thinking to link across disciplines and comprehend all social and environmental implications. If that thinking can in turn be harnessed to serve the well-being of humanity, it forms the basis for a sound ethical and moral outlook.

The education system that builds such a process must be one that treats all children in the state as equals for they are the centre, they are the future, they must know it and grow into that responsibility. The building of courage and self-confidence by their parents provides the vital platform for the love and respect they might show for others. Divisions, such as separating schools and therefore children on a religious or any other basis, would be incomprehensible. The competitive nature of children would be focused to develop the skills of each individual within the context of the collective good. Declamatory statements such as these, a wish list for the future, cannot be explored or expanded in detail here. They require specialist thesis and on-going assessment. Such education would contradict the inherited system which has been carefully fabricated over the last hundred years and would not be achieved without opposition and struggle.

Educational transformation would ideally come from the demands of all its participating parties from students to the general population. It is a matter of attempting to deepen discussions already in train and turn them into practice. There are proposals to include philosophy in the curriculum. It will be challenging to ensure it promotes more than a remaking of theology. At present, schools bring in external speakers and that perhaps is where rational individuals or organisations can exert some influence. Requests for one per cent of time within schools to put forward alternative views on belief, politics and economics would be difficult to refuse. Stimulating viewpoints, if argued with polish and passion, may gain more traction than expected. The demands from employers, educationalists and parents that students should have more science and analytical thinking could be used as a springboard. Pressure can also be leveraged from the top through teachers' organisations and legal action could be considered in the reformation of the curriculum.

Interventions could be akin to some intergalactic detective solving a thousand crimes and asking pertinent questions. Why was there such a catastrophic collapse of morality, why are our ethics so weak, why are schools sectarian, why can't we build enough houses, why does society work so hard to transfer wealth upwards, who stole courage, who stole the analytical minds of children? Our responsibility is to allow children develop into adulthood with their own analytical minds and with a developed social conscience. If they see injustice, they will scream from the roof tops and ask, as all good detectives ask, *cui bono*, who benefits?

Critical and judicial thinking on their own are relative tools which can serve liberation or oppression. To promote human progress, such thinking requires to be combined with human empathy, social morality and courage. When this point is reached, the comfortable clothes of inherited belief begin to fall away. We then stand naked and feel the chill wind of reason and the warm wind of human empathy. It is only then, will we comprehend that we alone are responsible for our destinies and that we are the mortal gods. That realisation is frightening and challenging and the responsibilities are onerous, for then we can create social structures, no longer controlled by fear and exploitation, but patrolled by human empathy in just and sustainable societies.

A *Republic of Reason* cannot be imposed from the top down. It can only come from the bottom up by transparent, well informed mass movements. We have been witness to the usurping of many revolutions, when in the post-euphoric period the people revert to supplication and saviour seeking, opening the way back to pyramidal, exploitative structures. A new society can emerge and endure only when there is a sustainable material surplus, peace and a majority possessed of high levels of education, social confidence, courage and human empathy. Such confidence will be signalled when the mass of people lose the need to worship celebrity or seek saviours, either terrestrial or celestial. It requires imagination to envision a society where economics is an ordered tool serving the interests of society and where the well-being of individuals is a priority. It likewise requires imagination to have a society populated by individuals possessing a morality based on the well-being of that society.

The organisational structure of the society would render itself inept in war, oppressive policing and running prisons. Institutions or states can only be effective in oppression and war when possessed of top-down, military-type structures, from the rigid church hierarchies of the Middle Ages to Hitler's Third Reich. It would be a general truism to say that the more rigid the top-down power structure the better for war and oppression, with the opposite holding true for its alternative. To examine existing societies it can be observed that the most unequal societies with the highest proportion of their people in prison are the most likely to go to war. That holds true even if they have a veneer of political democracy.

Since universities emerged from their theological past, they assumed themselves to be bastions of independent learning. This was never the case. They were always the defenders and part of the mechanism of the establishment. Now, any pretence of independent learning has slipped further away as they become service centres of capitalism and as corporate identities themselves. While competition between students intensifies for grades, competition amongst the universities intensifies for international rankings, which in turn determines the amount of investment from corporate interests and international philanthropy. The investors then, to a large extent determine the type of research and patenting carried out on their behalf. If the universities were to begin to serve society, research would extend to social and economic projects in the direct public interest. Such might seem tame, but would be almost revolutionary. They would become the intellectual and ideological core of society, all society. This would be a satisfying existence for the universities with their intellectual capacity liberated from being a mere business, serving corporate interests. They would engage in the development of economic, political, social systems for an egalitarian culture. Many of the staff, who have invested their careers in a compartmentalised discipline, would find it difficult to abandon ideological positions and serve society, for challenging academic ideas can be akin to challenging religious ones. But change is the antonym of paralysis and universities in the real sense would thrive.

Society has all the expertise and resources to produce or trade for any service required by its people. It has capital, researchers, economists and all the skills of management and marketing. It has witnessed, and hopefully learned from, success and failure in public and private enterprise, both operate on similar mechanisms and both can succeed or fail. The argument that the state has to support ailing public enterprise is valid, but no more than for private enterprise, where the taxpayer has been picking up very big pieces from spectacular failures. Private and public enterprise can be motivated by similar incentive and management mechanisms. While profit motivation in business by its nature has an objective ethos in contradiction to the well-being of its workers, in many instances with regulation, it is a valid form of enterprise.

In some instances profit motivation is too divergent from the function of the business. Healthcare is a case in point where there is an objective conflict between profit and care. The argument that private care is run efficiently may look attractive, but once two-tier health exists, it will draw the best professionals away from public health care and the system loses its focus. The public hospitals are over populated by the uninsured and as staffing levels fall, queues grow, fear and a panic buying of insurance spreads even to those who cannot afford it and health becomes another commodity. A step towards efficient public health would be a prohibition on all those employed or in any way connected with it, including health ministers and their staff, from holding private health insurance. Such a simple incentive would focus minds on perfecting the service they themselves would have to use. Similar logic should apply to any private service where a profit interest contradicts the reason for the service, such as prisons or centres holding asylum seekers. The longer the inmates can be held, the more profit can be made.

In a comparison of business models, private enterprise will have an advantage as current culture rates companies by return on capital. National economies are ranked by similar criteria; on speed of growth, level of debt, consumption and capital accumulation. Wider social benefits or environmental considerations are objectively ignored and are not rated, neither is the care of workers, whose protection will only come through their own diligence, a union, minimum pay and safety regulations. In a public-sector enterprise the motivation is one of service to the community and the advantage to the operatives can be an increased level of involvement and responsibility. Such enterprises generally had remuneration levels to provide a decent standard of living and better working conditions. This was the case in the public enterprises, which transformed many European states including Ireland through the first half of the twentieth century. But these enterprises were a barrier to upward wealth transfer, hence the race for privatisation by the status quo.

The exponential growth of the World Wide Web and social networking could promote human progress, combining the collective brain of humankind. It is a perfect vehicle for the formation of new ideas, operating outside the constraints of nation, church, race or gender, it is in a position to surmount divisions. If it is true that human empathy is expanding, as all indications suggest, then it will be progressive. The fact that some corporations and states are trying to privatise and control the net means the threat is realised. The vast cyber spy databases, monitoring and storing information on billions of individuals demonstrates how the net can serve different interests. However, a generally young and skilled user-base might have the motivation and innovation to keep ahead. These cyber activists witness the pillage of the Earth's resources and the concentration of wealth. They can watch or act. The net is both the creation and creator of an age where humanity is chasing the 'elemental particle' to find the building blocks of life. This chase itself, becomes part of our life philosophy, the answers will engender further questions. It is from such, that the construction of twenty-first century morality and politics will evolve. Perhaps the net's influence on philosophy and social structure will be the message of the medium. Time will tell.

Governance in exploitative societies or institutions organises in a top-down pyramid. Feudalism had king, princes, landlords and peasants. Similarly, a church had god, pope, cardinals, bishops, priests and people. Companies have a CEO, executives, middle managers, floor foremen and operatives. Such arrangements efficiently serve the financial and power interests of the top centile. An egalitarian society would structure its governance in a horizontal net form. Each knot or hub would consist of anything from an individual to a department of knowledge. Some would be elected decision-making hubs. These concepts, and the tool that is the internet are tailor-made to reach out through the citizenry to form a horizontal, participatory, transparent democracy. The possibilities are already demonstrated by our interaction acquiring knowledge and engaging with the market. As alienation diminishes and a sense of belonging and responsibility increases, society would begin to run without coercion and enforcement. A correlation can already be seen in societies with greater levels of wealth equality and transparency.

Transformative governance is dependent on a broad social education where morality is rooted in collective awareness and responsibility. The degree of comfort in the relationship between governance and people depends on the degree of transparency. As a state changes to a society it loses its oppressive character. The pace at which that oppression diminishes is proportional to any threat to that society, be it ideological or criminal, and its demographic stability. In addition, there is the question, deliberated amongst anarchists for millennia, of who is going to lock up the psychopathically insane? The former points are perennial questions leading to the impossibility of building such a society without at least the adjoining states following a similar path. A *Republic of Reason*, with its high levels of social theory and organisation requires its philosophy to spread like ripples in a pool until it becomes universal.

The point has been made throughout this book that the foundations of a society of reason are its children, their ability to reason analytically, to achieve social awareness, morality and courage. Divisions of gender, race, religion and nationality do not emerge spontaneously from children, they come from inherited prejudice and unexamined beliefs. They have to be taught. Enlightened schools would understand the interdependency of humans worldwide and develop an international outlook. To recognise that our entire species emerged from a small area of east Africa before spreading across the planet would be unifying. The ethos of the schools would be to link human empathy and science internationally across diverse cultures. Likewise the pupils would be immersed in the advance of science and its relevance to them. They would have a basic understanding of economics and how our material goods are dependent on the co-operative work of millions of people worldwide. Everywhere, there are fields of worthwhile exploration.

When reason reaches into the economic sphere it has to tread carefully. The present international power of capital allows little possibility of forming an independent, self-sufficient state outside the existing global model. However, because of our small population and advantageous position on the edge of Europe with regard to food resources we have some leeway. To make progress initially, we can look at two existing models of capitalism - the United States and Europe. Both show the 'rentier' and the 'super-manager' society (explained in the previous chapter) to be in the ascendancy, so we are basically searching for the best in a poor choice. Both systems run in the interests of an elite with growing disparities of wealth. The worst example is the dystopian model of the United States, where Matt Taibbi in his book *Divide* describes the development of an outlook which grovels in terror before the rich who seek and receive lower levels of regulation and taxation. The culture displays a profound hatred of the losers, the poor. This manifests itself, by the US having the biggest prison population in the history of civilisation and these prisons are now a large privatised money-making enterprise. A clever crook from Wall Street can steel a billion dollars and never see a court room while a black teenager goes to jail for standing at a corner. In Europe things are a little better. Sections of it still have aspirations to move in a more egalitarian direction, with some Nordic countries providing the highest standards of governance and the fairest and most transparent capitalist societies.

The Nordic countries are not perfect but are worthy of study. In his book *Society without God*, Phil Zuckerman outlines how they have the lowest levels of income disparity between the top and bottom earners and have the highest levels of social equality and care. They also have the lowest level of religious belief - a relationship which he claims is intrinsic with the social quality of their lives. Another and very different model is Cuba. Unfortunately from its inception as a socialist state it has been embargoed and brutalised by the interests of its very powerful neighbour, the United States. Invasions and threats have forced Cuba to maintain a military strength well above that which might be required in normal circumstances. Despite this, it has made progress with health care, life expectancy and education, comparing favourably with developed western nations and well ahead of most Latin American countries. The collapse of its benefactor, the USSR, in 1991 was followed by a tightening of US sanctions. Cuba has many internal problems emanating from these pressures. However the resilience of the people has been a beacon of hope for those who believe that a society can exist outside the corporate, consumerist market of the Washington Consensus. It is a model whose position in history and economics is too far removed from the situation in Ireland to have any bearing, except perhaps to learn from its admirable obstinacy.

As an example of critical thinking and how it might apply to a social situation, an intriguing way to dramatically cut the numbers in jail and reduce crime is outlined by Johann Hari in his book, *Chasing the Scream*. He argues that the war on drugs is a pretence that is lost and that if legalised and taxed, the gangs and associated crime will diminish. As in the US when prohibition was abolished and alcohol was taxed, the gangs disappeared and the state made money. Such a change of direction when rationally applied, and assuredly it must, would have liberating consequences for society.

While learning from international examples, the objective would be to lead not follow. Economic and social models need to be appraised in a similar manner to a science-based project, theoretically conceived and practically tested. Other explorations would arise as society sought growth, moving from consumerism to intellectualism. This does not mean any brake on technological growth. On the contrary, innovation can reduce consumption. In the past, a message to America would have gone by sailing ship with a large crew and a month on passage, now any teenager can send and receive a complex message there in seconds. A light at night once required the killing of whales, extracting oil and burning it in a foul-smelling lamp for a dull result. Now a sensor and light-emitting diode gives a far brighter light for a fraction of the energy. The same applies to the rising efficiency of engines, farming and every productive arena. While such advances are worthwhile, unless humanity extends philosophy and responsibility over the growth of population and consumption these gains will be negated.

In design we could emulate the role played by the Bauhaus or VKhuTEMAS, schools founded in Germany and Russia in 1919 to reflect the industrial age and the rise of socialism, combining architecture, sculpture and painting into a single creative expression and bringing quality design to the masses. Similar art and craft-based curricula encouraging artisans and designers are needed to enhance an egalitarian society, bringing sustainable design and architecture to every classroom and home in the country. As a concept, think of IKEA, the Scandinavian design model, but with a focus of service to society rather than the shareholder. Such schools would interact with universities developing both commodities and knowledge-based systems, such as how to set up and run an enterprise, economic structures, education at all levels, medical and health care, police and military forces but specifically to serve an egalitarian world. The IDA, for example is well versed in attracting international enterprise, providing buildings, trained personnel, subsidies and massive tax breaks. With just one more step and a different emphasis they could set up a myriad of public industries. Where Ireland used to send missionaries abroad for the salvation of souls, a *Republic of Reason* would export knowledge for the salvation of human dignity. It would strive to become the moral leader of Europe.

The rebuilding of Europe after the Second World War was led by the Marshall Plan. So many were drawn to socialism that the US government opted to allow Germany split rather than risk it all, to the left. The Marshall Plan was to quickly build a market economy that would thrive and tolerate workers protection, public health and social welfare. This was not done for any reason of altruism but as the Soviet Union and its ideology was at the doorstep, the battle was for the soul of Germany and Europe and the objective was to drain socialism of its appeal. The later development of the European Union and its Euro was the first example of an international, stateless currency where capital, goods and people could move about freely. It was formed for the good reason of mitigating nationalism and war, but shaped in the interests of capital. While the states of the EU carefully record the movement of people, equal care is taken to obscure information on the movement or location of capital. Regulations within the EU fostered by the Washington Consensus force privatisation and obstruct public companies serving the public interest.

With cunning, the bastions of Europe can be infiltrated by reason, elected representatives pressurised, laws made transparent. This would be the role of a confident team of socially conscious accountants, lawyers and mass movements of people. Shrewd literature and visual arts with socially progressive content could remould development laws and achieve progressive taxation. There is much common ground within Europe to get support on these issues and find solutions to enslavement by national debt. Thomas Piketty, points out that debt and its repayment is a method of transferring wealth from the poor to the rich. Public wealth in Europe is virtually zero yet private wealth has never been so high. There is no debt problem but there is a distribution problem. He proposes progressive taxes on income, profit and capital and eloquently argues that such steps are necessary even in the terms of saving capitalism from itself. His book concludes with a plea to all social scientists, journalists and activists to investigate and follow the money and deal with numbers. To turn the tide against the dictatorship of capital, the left has to be more knowledgeable on the mechanisms of corporate capital than the capitalists themselves. It must infiltrate the ranks of capital with hundreds of ethical whistle-blowers and provide them with legal safety nets. Only such a disciplined and organised approach will turn the tide in the interests of the majority.

Any challenge to the ideology of the free market and taxing capital will be strongly opposed. It will be argued that taxation on capital will cause its flight. However, if financial centres worldwide are either transparent or isolated, capital would have nowhere to fly. Those leading such campaigns and whistle-blowers would have their personal lives trawled and attempts would be made to ridicule and embargo them, witness the treatment of WikiLeaks, Edward Snowdon and Chelsea Manning. If fear is the main weapon of reaction, then courage, humour and confidence would be the defence. The responsibilities would be international. Imports from third world countries would be monitored to ensure the welfare of the producers. If this were to increase costs, then so be it. Ethics comes at a price. Observations on foreign affairs would be robust with international comment and policies based on human empathy, human rights and the environment. Conflicts throughout the globe are driven by divisive ideologies. Further plunder by the forces of capital are countered by the insanities of Islamic caliphates, Zionism or Christian fundamentalists. Rational combat against such exploitation or ignorance requires an army of the intellect, armed with the most advanced weapons of mass instruction, powered by a polished media, dropping bombs of logic and firing shells of reason. It would occupy the high moral ground. However, as there are few things more prone to a fall than occupying the high moral ground, self-criticism and total transparency would be required to keep us on our toes. What a delight it would be, living where philosophy and economic responsibility would be our conversation.

Stable societies, even exploitative ones, with an abundance of food are a mecca for the less fortunate of the world. Despite the growing problems of casino capitalism, it appears as paradise to many in the third world. The population is exploding in parts of Africa, while food and water supplies diminish. Recent imperialist interventions have exacerbated the situation bringing devastation and fanning sectarian tribalism. Per capita income is twenty times lower than Europe and they are prepared to risk all in a bid for survival. The same pressure drives them to Europe as drove the destitute of Ireland in the 1800s in their millions to the US. Over 40,000 people are already moving towards Europe every year and thousands drown as they cross the Mediterranean. The receiving countries, Italy, Greece and Spain are insisting that all EU countries take a fair share of the migrants.

The reaction can be a gated Europe, with the migrants who have spent all on the perilous voyage being shipped back into worsening conditions. This would deeply wound European self-esteem, making it impossible to build an ethical society with any claim on morality. The migrations can continue, allowing ghettos of language, culture and religion to form in areas which become alienated from society, provoking a culture of despair. Perceptions of crime, stolen jobs and undercut wages will provoke divisive reaction by the politics of the right. The best alternative is to allow a controlled migration where people are assimilated into the society and culture, with their children attending a unified secular, educational system. They must be welcomed with an integration policy that emphasises the unity of our species before any divisive multicultural considerations. National minimum pay rates need to be increased and applied to ensure that no migrant can be exploited by working for lower pay rates. Such an approach, together with an understanding of the reasons for the migration and an involvement in the countries from which the migrants are fleeing, stabilising them and assisting development would be the path to follow.

The need to expose how western corporate involvement in Africa extracts more money from the continent and its people than is supplied in aid is paramount. This is done by the corporate ownership of resources and corrupt dictatorships that defend that ownership, both of whom lodge their wealth in the financial institutions of Europe, where it is protected by ranks of compliant accountants and lawyers. Capital never drowns in rickety boats crossing the Mediterranean. This capital, exposed and properly taxed by stable governments, would build societies which would mitigate migration.

In philosophical and practical terms the church is struggling to maintain its position as leader of the moral ethos. It is burdened by its attachment to biblical roots, historical misogyny and its role as mentor to exploitative systems. While debates between secular materialism and religious idealism are basically irreconcilable, a great number of clergy and believers would support the political and economic ideas espoused. They would oppose the unconscionable deaths world-wide of over 20,000 children every day from malnutrition and dirty water. They would oppose the suffering caused by vast disparities of wealth and a rampant market. In such causes the humanist and religious would be united by a common human empathy. Sections of the church in Latin America, had adopted 'liberation theology' in the 1970s. It would have been its saving. Unfortunately it was suppressed by the Vatican of the time. Many Catholic leaders, including the Pope, are again turning in that direction as they look at poverty and to the climate debate for new strategic foundations. The Pope's comments that 'the earth, our home, is beginning to look more and more like an immense pile of filth' and 'we have to hear both the cry of the Earth and the cry of the poor' are to be welcomed.

As religion loses relevance and practitioners, more of its buildings will fall into disuse - a pattern well established all over England and Europe. Some are converted into art galleries, music and social venues and many fall to ruin. But a case could be made for churches of reason, public forums for philosophy, places of wisdom rather than worship. Social spaces where local communities interact on social issues and celebrate the rites of life, births, marriages and death, shared with those who wish for secular ceremonies. This would provide a challenging and enlivening and more inclusive prospect of society than a moribund church. Imagine a church where half the time was dedicated to talks or lectures between theists and non-theists, a dialogue between idealism and materialism. That would indeed make for a lively Sunday morning and a large assembly. Freedom of religion and its expression would be maintained, but religion coming to terms with a fair society would be encouraged to remove all statements from their core documents of the Bible, Torah and Koran that instigate harm or division from any group or person on grounds of belief, race or sexual orientation. The swearing of oaths on these religious texts should be discontinued. It would be an indicator of the maturity of our society when this practice fades without acrimony.

With the move to service industry and computing technology one might think that the age of heavy industry is past, thus mitigating the twin problems of resources and climate. Gigantic industrial cities in China are choking in pollution while the west discusses green agendas. Heavy industry has just relocated to find cheaper labour, but it is still our production as they are the goods we consume. There is not a climate of the east and a climate of the west, for as we are one market, we are one climate. The future is innovation but not as an accelerant to production and consumption. The innovation sought is for a philosophy promoting human well-being, connected to reality and new ways of organising economies, society and the world. That elusive gap in the market is not in commodities, it is in the intellect. Humanity has to solve the problems inherent in the blind economics of capital and the gene. The gloomy predictions on the environment may become that powerful enemy, forcing humanity to coalesce.

We are programmed to survive and we are programmed to replicate. Human progress and well-being is dependent on how we focus our critical reason on both of these instincts to promote the well-being of people, social harmony and species sustainability. This delicate balance can be achieved through the application of a philosophy, enriched with a love of humanity and an understanding of our fragility. While the visions of society as proposed in the book are deliciously far-fetched, they should be humanity's greatest pursuit. It is a path that requires shrewd courage and it could be taken with cool pride and some fun. As stated at the beginning of this chapter; there is a reason to live. We can raise ourselves out of ignorance. We can find ourselves as creatures of intelligence, skill and excellence. We can learn what it is to be really free! As we spin through the cosmos on our little blue planet, let us dream and build our *Republic of Reason...*

Note to Bibliography

Since humanity learned to write, it has committed its stories and observations to parchment and paper, reflecting every disaster and triumph, oppression and liberation. Humanity's understanding of itself comes from millions of tiny insights, papered together over the epochs to form a comprehensive view, a form of philosophical evolution complete with mutations. Observations and conclusions built on the foundations of history and evolving viewpoints are coloured by the economic and social structure of the era. Thus, all writings striving for some truth are a modification of preceding ones, their authenticity or otherwise established by observation and analysis.

Thankfully ideas are not copyright, only their written format. This restriction stretches back only a few millennia and emerged to control sedition and heresy as much as to protect authors. This book does not claim copyright, believing it is difficult to assert any truly original work - a concept that is problematic in a philosophical sense - for the ideas expressed in all books are but an evolving part of mankind's collective knowledge. In addition, the labour of millions is required to provide the surplus of sustenance and time to enable authorship, consequently the weight of comprehensive citation would be onerous. The answer is to acknowledge all labour, language and literature for what it really is and accept that this author and book are just a tiny cog in humanity's vast endeavour of recorded knowledge. The work is a polemic and a series of hypotheses and if it engenders debate, that alone is a validation. It contains no dogmatic conclusions just possibilities and an effrontery to say why not! The work of observation, the formation of ideas and the struggle for human well-being are on-going and endless, at least while cognisant life survives.

Any transcribed author is acknowledged within the text and I acknowledge with thanks the influential authors and their work mentioned hereunder. Thanks also to all those who strive to make the world wide web a place of shared information and in particular those who made Wikipedia what it is, a valued first source of information. Any part of this work, may be used, in furtherance of the causes argued.

Bibliography

Ayaan Hirsi Ali	*Infidel*. 2008, Simon & Schustter UK ltd. London.
Ayaan Hirsi Ali	*Nomad. 2010, Harper Collins Publishers, Australia*
Azad Bahman	*Heroic Struggle Bitter Defeat*. 2000, International Pub, NY.
Boghossian Peter.	*A Manual for Creating Atheists*. 2013, Pitchstone Publishing.
Chomsky N.	*Hegemony or Survival*. 2004, Penguin Books London.
Clark R.W.	*The Life of Bertrand Russell*, 1975, London, Penguin
Collins C.	*99 to 1*. 2012. Berrett-Koehler Publishers Inc. California.
Darwin Charles.	*The Origin of Species*. 1859-1979 New York Random House.
Dawkins Richard.	*Unweaving the Rainbow*. 2006, London Penguin books Ltd.
Dawkins Richard.	*The Selfish Gene*. 2006, New York, Oxford University Press
Dawkins Richard.	*The Blind Watchmaker*. 1988, London Penguin Books Ltd.
Dawkins Richard.	*The God Delusion*. 2007, Transworld Publishers, London.
Dawkins Richard.	*The Ancestors Tale*. 2005, Orion Books Ltd. London.
Dawkins Richard.	*The Greatest Show on Earth*. 2009 Transworld, London.
Dawkins Richard.	*The Magic of Reality*. 2011 Random House Group Co. UK.
Dennett Daniel C.	*Breaking the Spell*. 2006, Penguin, Allen Lane, London.
Diamond Jared.	*Guns, Germs and Steel. 2005, Vintage, London.*
Diamond Jared.	*The Rise and Fall of the Third Chimpanzee*. 2002 Vintage London
Diamond Jared.	*Collapse*. 2006, Penguin Books Ltd. London.
Diamond Jared.	*Why is Sex Fun?* 1998, Orion Books Ltd, London.
Deutscher Isaac.	*The Unfinished Revolution*. 1967 Oxford Press London.
Eagleton Terry	*Why Marx Was Right*. 2011, Yale University Press. London.
Fishman Ted C.	*China Inc*. 2006, Simon & Schuster UK Ltd. London.
Fisk Robert.	*The Great War for Civilisation*. 2005, HarperCollins, London.
Fletcher Banister	*A History of Architecture*. 1928, B T Batsford ltd. London.
Gallagher Mary.	*Academic Armageddon*. The Liffey Press, Dublin.
Gardner Martin.	*Did Adam and Eve have Navels?* 2000, W.W Norton & Co. NY.
Grafen &Ridley	*Richard Dawkins*. 2006, Oxford University Press. London.
Goldacre B	*Bad Science*. 2009. Harper Perennial. London.
Harris Sam.	*Letter to a Christian Nation*. 2007London, Bantam Press.
Harris Sam.	*The End of Faith*. 2005. The Free Press. London,
Harris Sam.	*Lying*. 2013, Four Elephants Press, USA.
Harris Sam.	*Waking Up*. 2014 Simon & Schuster, New York.
Hari Johann.	*Chasing the Scream*. 2015, Bloomsbury, 50 Bedford Sq. London
Hitchens Christopher.	*God is Not Great*. 2007, Atlantic Books, London.
Kerrigan &Brennan	*This Great Little Nation*. 1999. Gill & Macmillan Ltd. Dublin.
Kolakowski Leszek.	*Marxism and Beyond*. 1968-1971. Paladin, London.
Kalnin Laurence.	*The God Fallacy*. 2010. Kalnin Corporation Ltd. Sydney, Aus.
Lamont Corliss.	*The Philosophy of Humanism*. 1982. F. Ungar Pub. Co. New York.
Lovelock James.	*The Vanishing Face of Gaia*. 2009, London, Allen Lane.
Marx K. Engels F.	*The Communist Manifesto*. 1850-2003. International Pub. USA
Naomi Klein.	*The Shock Doctrine*. 2007, Penguin Books Ltd. London.
Gormley .Hyland. Maloney.	*Alive-04*. 1999. Veritas Pub. 8 Lower Abbey St. Dublin.
Marshall George	*Carbon Detox*. 2007, Octopus Publishing Group Ltd. London.
Misc. Man/God.	*The Holy Bible*. 1966, Tyndale House publishers Inc. USA.
Misc. Man/God.	*The Koran*. Translation J.M. Rodwell, 2004, Bantam, NY.

Piketty Thomas.   *Capital in the 21st Century*. 2014. Harvard University, London.
Russell Bertrand.   *Why I am not a Christian*. 1957. Simon & Schuster, London,
Russell Bertrand.   *Education and the Social Order*. 1932-1967. Unwin, London.
Riddly Matt.   *The Red Queen, Sex and the Evolution -*. 1994, Penguin, London.
Taibbi Matt.   *The Divide*. 2014, Spiegel & Grau, Penguin, New York.
Wilkinson Philip.   *Religions*. 2008, Dorling Kindersley Ltd. London.
Wilkinson R. & Pickett K. *The Spirit Level*. 2010, Penguin Books Ltd. London.
Wolpert Lewis.   *Six Impossible Things before Breakfast*. 2006, Faber, London.
Zuckerman Phil   *Society without God*. New York University Press 2008.

Glossary of some relevant terms

An agreed meaning of words is essential for constructive debate.

Atheism- a knowledge that there are no gods; a non-theist.

Atom- the smallest particle of a chemical element; a defining structure of an element, typically consisting of a nucleus of protons and neutrons with orbiting electrons.

Anarchism - liberation from the dominion of religion, property and government; a social order based on the free grouping of individuals.

Capital- an accumulation of money obtained from the purchase of labour power and appropriating the surplus value created; money advanced in order to regain it with an increase.

Class- within a society, whereby people are divided into groups of common economic interests and objective antagonism between such groups; it is the workers interest to maximize wages and the capitalist's to maximize profit.

Communism- a social organization with productive property owned by the community; each person contributes and receives according to their ability and needs; characterised by the absence of social classes and high levels of ethics and responsibility.

Dialectics- resolving truth through contradictions emerging from constant change; intellectual investigation.

Dictatorship- rule by one person or small group with total power of an organisation or state.

Economic system- organisation for the production and exchange of goods and services and the allocation of resources within a society.

Evolution- the mechanism of natural selection through which all living organisms develop from earlier forms.

Existence- the fact or state of being; having a cognitive understanding of reality.

Freedom- the ability to think, speak and to determine ones political and economic life as one wants; not being imprisoned, enslaved or exploited.

Gene- a unit of genetic information in the DNA which is transferred from a parent to offspring and is held to determine some characteristic of the offspring.

Humanism- rationalist idea asserting the human to be the creator of all gods and the imagination; primacy of humanity's well-being over any other.

Idealism- the principle that the spirit or idea is prime, creating matter and energy; the story of creation; the elevation of the power of ideas.

Ideology- a system of philosophy, forming the basis of economic and political theory and activity; a religious belief.

Materialism- the principle that matter and energy are prime, that they alone give rise to ideas should a cognisant being evolve.

Morality- the distinction between right and wrong, relative to a viewpoint; a value of behaviour between humans, to other species or the environment.

Philosophy- the study of the fundamental nature of knowledge, reality, and existence; an individual or collective viewpoint.

Property- a source of wealth; possessions claimed or legally allocated.

Rationalism- the practice or principle of basing opinions and actions on reason and knowledge rather than on religious belief or emotional response.

Religion- the belief in and worship of a superhuman controlling power, a personal god or gods; a particular system of faith and worship.

Socialism- a political and economic social organization where the means of production, distribution, and exchange are democratically regulated by the community.

Society- the aggregate of people living together in a more or less ordered community.

Supplication- the action of worship, asking or earnestly begging for something of a terrestrial or supernatural ruler.

State- a territory with an organized economic and political community controlled by a government in the interests of a specific class.

Theology- the study of the nature of gods and supernatural belief; religious theory.

Washington Consensus- the ideology of world-wide freedom for unfettered corporate capitalism – proofed against democracy.

Index